Islam

Ruqaiyyah Waris Maqsood

Every effort has been made to trace and acknowledge ownership of copyright. The publishers will be glad to make suitable arrangements with any copyright holders whom it has not been possible to contact.

For UK order enquiries: please contact Bookpoint Ltd, 130 Milton Park, Abingdon, Oxon, OX14 4SB. Telephone: +44 (0) 1235 827720. Fax: +44 (0) 1235 400454. Lines are open 09.00–17.00, Monday to Saturday, with a 24-hour message answering service. Details about our titles and how to order are available at www.teachyourself.com

For USA order enquiries: please contact McGraw-Hill Customer Services, PO Box 545, Blacklick, OH 43004-0545, USA. Telephone: 1-800-722-4726. Fax: 1-614-755-5645.

For Canada order enquiries: please contact McGraw-Hill Ryerson Ltd, 300 Water St, Whitby, Ontario, L1N 9B6, Canada. Telephone: 905 430 5000. Fax: 905 430 5020.

Long renowned as the authoritative source for self-guided learning – with more than 50 million copies sold worldwide – the **Teach Yourself** series includes over 500 titles in the fields of languages, crafts, hobbies, business, computing and education.

British Library Cataloguing in Publication Data: a catalogue record for this title is available from the British Library.

Library of Congress Catalog Card Number: on file.

First published in UK 1994 by Hodder Education, 338 Euston Road, London, NW1 3BH.

First published in US 1994 by The McGraw-Hill Companies, Inc.

This edition published 2010.

The **Teach Yourself** name is a registered trade mark of Hodder Headline.

Copyright © 1994, 2003, 2006, 2010 Ruqaiyyah Waris Maqsood

Typeset by MPS Limited, A Macmillan Company.

Printed in Great Britain for Hodder Education, a division of Hodder Headline, 338 Euston Road, London, NW1 3BH, by CPI Group (UK) Ltd, Croydon, CR0 4YY.

The publisher has used its best endeavours to ensure that the URLs for external websites referred to in this book are correct and active at the time of going to press. However, the publisher and the author have no responsibility for the websites and can make no guarantee that a site will remain live or that the content will remain relevant, decent or appropriate.

Hodder Headline's policy is to use papers that are natural, renewable and recyclable products and made from wood grown in sustainable forests. The logging and manufacturing processes are expected to conform to the environmental regulations of the country of origin.

Impression number   10 9 8
Year   2014

Contents

Notes

As a mark of respect, Muslims may add 'Peace be upon him' when they refer to the Prophet Muhammad and other prophets. In this book it is abbreviated as ﷺ.

Dates from the Muslim calendar are shown as AH (*Anno Hegira*), others are shown as CE (Common Era) which is equivalent to AD in the Christian calendar.

Quotations from the Qur'an have been printed in italics, whereas teachings of the Prophet ﷺ himself are in normal script.

Acknowledgements

The publishers would like to thank the following for their permission to reproduce copyright photographs in this book:

Nadeem Khan – p. 23; Peter Saunders – p. 20; Rowland Box – p. 36. All the remaining photographs were supplied by the author.

Credits

Front cover: © Itani1o1/Alamy

Back cover: © Jakub Semeniuk/iStockphoto.com, © Royalty-Free/Corbis, © agencyby/iStockphoto.com, © Andy Cook/iStockphoto.com, © Christopher Ewing/iStockphoto.com, © zebicho – Fotolia.com, © Geoffrey Holman/iStockphoto.com, © Photodisc/Getty Images, © James C. Pruitt/iStockphoto.com, © Mohamed Saber – Fotolia.com

Only got a minute?

▶ Islam is one of three great interlinked faiths that worship the same Divine Being, the others being Judaism and Christianity.

▶ God is known in Arabic as 'al-Lah' or 'Allah' – the Almighty, the Creator and Sustainer of all that exists.

▶ Followers of Islam ('submission to God') are called Muslims – 'those who submit'.

▶ The first key belief, known as *tawhid*, is acceptance of the genuine existence of a Single Divine Entity (God).

▶ The second key belief is *akhirah*, or Life after Death. Life on this earth is regarded as a test, and after death comes judgement, and an eternal destiny in Heaven or Hell.

▶ The third key belief is *risalah*. People need to know God's will in order to do it. Therefore God sends chosen people called prophets or messengers.

▶ The Muslim holy book is the Qur'an, the revelation sent through the Arab prophet Muhammad ﷺ – 610–632 CE.

- The creed of Islam is the simple statement 'La ilaha ilallah wa Muhammadur rasul al-Lah' ('There is no God but Allah, and Muhammad is the messenger of God').

- Muslims try to keep God's will in all aspects of life, including ritual purity for prayer, choosing *halal* (accepted) foods and rejecting everything *haram* (forbidden) – which includes certain types of food, conduct, employment, relationships, etc.

- Muslims are requested to perform five religious duties, often known as the 'five pillars':
  - to bear witness to their belief (by faith, words and good living – *shahadah*)
  - to perform a special prayer five times per day (*salah*)
  - to fast throughout the daylight hours of the month of Ramadan (*sawm*)
  - to give up a fortieth of their saved wealth every year (*zakah*)
  - to make a pilgrimage journey to Makkah at least once in their lifetime (*hajj*).

Meet the author

Welcome to *Islam – An Introduction*!

I was born Rosalyn Rushbrook in 1942 – a white, English person. After graduating with a degree in Christian Theology at Hull University, I became Head of Religious Studies departments in inner-city Hull schools for 33 years, and was a pioneer for the inclusion of World Faiths into the syllabus. I converted to Islam in 1986, and I believe I was the first Muslim Head of RE in the UK. I was invited by Heinemann to write their textbook for GCSE Islam, and since then have written many more books. My best-known is probably *The Muslim Marriage Guide*. My website (www.ruqaiyyah.karoo.net) lists them all, and presents numerous articles on subjects I am passionate about: promoting the understanding of Islam in straightforward and accessible language; and countering the horrendous ignorance, extremism and terrorism with which some Muslims have blighted Islam. I retired from teaching in 1996, although I still tutor privately.

In 2001, I received the Allama Iqbal Award of Excellence for Creativity in Islamic Thought sponsored by *Muslim News*. In 2008 I received a Global Peace and Unity Lifetime Achievement Award for Literature, and was shortlisted for the Muslim Writers Award for Poetry. I continue to lecture when I can, and frequently still function as a 'cyber-counsellor'. My major (1 000 page) life's work on the life of the Prophet ﷺ is awaiting publication.

May God richly bless you and keep you in His care.

Wasalaam, Ruqaiyyah, 2010

1

Muhammad ﷺ

In this chapter you will learn about:
- *the main events of the Prophet's ﷺ life*
- *the significance of various historical events*
- *the four 'Rightly-Guided' Caliphs*
- *the conflict between the Prophet's ﷺ descendants and the Umayyads, and its consequences.*

The life of the blessed Prophet Muhammad ﷺ

HIS BIRTH AND EARLY LIFE

The Prophet Muhammad ﷺ was a direct descendant of the Biblical patriarch Ibrahim/Abraham ﷺ, through his eldest son Isma'il ﷺ. He was born in Makkah, Saudi Arabia, in around 570 CE, a member of the Hashim clan of the Quraysh tribe. His father, Abdullah, a merchant, died before he was born, and his mother, Amina, died when he was only six years old, leaving him an orphan. He was reared first by his grandfather, Abd al-Muttalib, a man famous for his saintly life, and then by his merchant uncle, Abu Talib. The only person with him from his first breath to his last was his Abyssinian nurse Barakah (Umm Ayman), who he always called 'Mother'.

> **Insight**
>
> Abdu'l Muttalib was the revered Guardian of the Ka'bah, a
> man famous for his visions, absolute faith in God, nobility
> and courage. He was a *hanif*, one of those untainted by
> paganism, who kept to the monotheism of Ibrahim ﷺ.

At this time, the people of Arabia were mainly superstitious
pagans with a few notable monotheist exceptions, such as Abd
al-Muttalib. There were also considerable numbers of Jews and
Christians in Arabia, especially on the border with Syria, the
north-east, and Yemen. Many Arabs lived nomadic lives on
traditionally claimed territories, and there were only a few key
cities such as Makkah, Yathrib and Taif. Makkah was a wealthy
trading post that also happened to be the most important shrine
for the Arab idols.

The cube-shaped Ka'bah temple claimed a very ancient history; the
site was said to have been consecrated in the first place by Adam ﷺ,
the first prophet, and then rebuilt by Ibrahim ﷺ and his son
Isma'il ﷺ (Heb. Abraham, Ishmael). Originally dedicated to the
One True God, over the centuries it had been utilized by polytheists
and by the time of the Prophet ﷺ it was said to have contained 360
statuettes and cult objects to minor deities, including not only the
moon-god and other astral 'deities', but also icons of the Virgin
Mary and Jesus ﷺ, and the Prophet Ibrahim ﷺ.

Muhammad ﷺ grew up a particularly devout and honourable man,
a believer in One God, like his grandfather. He worked first as a
shepherd, and then as a merchant, working for his uncle, Abu
Talib. He became well known and well liked, and earned the
nickname 'al-Amin' ('the Trustworthy One') for his piety, honesty,
fair dealing, and practical common sense. He was a founding
member of an Order of Chivalry (the Hilf al-Fudul) dedicated to
bringing justice and protecting the rights of the poor and weak.

Later, he was employed by a wealthy tradeswoman, Khadijah,
who, after a short while, offered herself in marriage to him,
although she was in her forties and he was about 25 years old.
She had been married twice before and had at least five existing

children. Despite the age difference, they were very happily married and had at least six children of their own. Their two sons (Qasim and Abdullah) died as infants, leaving Muhammad ﷺ with four daughters – Zaynab, Ruqaiyyah, Umm Kulthum and Fatimah. Only Fatimah survived him, and only by a few months.

He fostered two boys, his cousin Ali from the age of four, and a slave Zayd ibn Harithah from the age of 14. In due course Ali married Fatimah. Even though polygamy was normal among Arabs at this time, Muhammad ﷺ never considered any other marriage while Khadijah lived.

HIS CALL TO BE A PROPHET

His new wealth and security gave him much more time to devote to prayer and meditation. It had been his grandfather's practice to withdraw to the solitude of the mountains around Makkah, often staying away for several days, and remaining in this seclusion during the entire month of Ramadan, and now Muhammad ﷺ was able to do the same. He particularly used to favour the Cave of Hira on Jabal Nur (the 'Mount of Light') overlooking Makkah, a two-hour climb up for those fetching his provisions. During the Ramadan month of the year 610 CE, when he was around 40 years old, something happened that changed his life completely.

A presence he identified as the angel Jibril (Gabriel) was suddenly there with him, and he was shown words and ordered to recite them. He protested that he was not a learned man and could not read them, but the angel insisted, and suddenly Muhammad ﷺ was given to understand what the words said. He was ordered to learn them, and repeat them to others. Thus came the first revelation of the verses now collected in book form, known as the Qur'an (the Recitation).

..

Insight

Jibril (Bib. Gabriel) represents the 'presence of God', and functions as the chief intermediary between the non-material Divine Being and the material world. Often referred to in the Qur'an as the 'Holy Spirit' or 'Spirit of God', 'he' is God's means of communication with us, but not a part of a 'holy trinity'.

..

The night this happened was towards the end of the month of Ramadan, which later became the Islamic month of fasting. The night is known as *Laylat ul-Qadr*. It is usually celebrated on the 27th night of Ramadan, although the exact date is not known.

From this moment of calling, Muhammad's ﷺ life was no longer his own, but in the hands of Him who had called him to be a prophet, and to spend the rest of his days in His service. Modestly, he commenced his mission by repeating the messages to a small circle of his family and friends, but reports of what had happened spread like wildfire.

The first convert was a woman, his wife Khadijah; the first male convert was Ali (then aged ten), and the first adult males were his best friend, the merchant Abu Bakr, and his foster son Zayd.

The way of life he taught became known as 'Islam', which means 'submission to the will of God', and his followers were known as Muslims, 'those who submit'. Allah, the Muslim name for God, simply means 'the Almighty'.

Insight

People are often confused by the terms 'Islam', 'Muslims', 'Muhammedans', and the old-fashioned 'Mahometans'. Islam is the actual faith, meaning 'submission to God'; Muslims are those who decide to submit themselves to God (with all their human frailties and limitations). The labels Muhammedans/ Mahometans are rejected by Muslims – they worship God, not Muhammad ﷺ. All who submit to God's will, including Jews and Christians, are counted as Muslims – but they vary in their beliefs and practices.

After the first few visions, and the initial whirlwind of excitement, everything stopped. To his dismay and embarrassment, the Prophet ﷺ spent the next two years with no further angelic visitation or message, a period of trial and testing when he was not sure of the implications of what had happened to him. Then, at last, the messages began again, and continued for the rest of his life, a prophetic ministry of some 23 years from the first revelation to the last.

THE REVELATIONS

The Prophet ﷺ did not always see the angel Jibril when he had his revelations, and when he did, the angel did not always keep exactly the same form. Sometimes the angel was huge, filling the horizon, and sometimes the Prophet ﷺ was only aware of eyes watching him. Occasionally, he just heard a voice speaking to him. Sometimes he revealed that the message did not come through clearly, but there was a sound like muffled bells, and this gave him a headache. At other times, the message was as clear and direct as if another person was just standing by him.

Insight

In accepting prophethood, Muhammad ﷺ accepted a 'guided life', waiting for 'the word of the Lord' to bring him specific instructions on a day-to-day basis. The angel's frequent attendance, plus the scrutiny of those determined to copy every detail of the way he lived, ended his privacy and that of his family.

Sometimes he received the revelations when he was in deep prayer, but at other times they occurred while he was engaged in everyday life, out riding, or involved in conversation concerning the subject.

Every time he received a revelation, there was no doubt either in his mind or the minds of those observing him – he would suffer physical symptoms, like heavy sweating or a trance-like state, and he reported that he frequently felt as if he was going to 'have his soul snatched away'. Those who were with him could tell quite clearly when his revelations started and when they finished.

Many of those who rejected belief in what was happening to the Prophet ﷺ accused him of being mad, demon possessed or suffering from a disease, such as epilepsy; but there is no evidence whatsoever of that. A study of his life as revealed in the *hadiths* (his own sayings, and reports of his teachings and way of life) show him to have been an immensely sane, kind, warm-hearted, down-to-earth person, and later an eminent and astute leader of his nation.

At first, the Prophet ﷺ did not preach in public, but spoke privately to those who were interested, or who had noticed the change in him. The particular way of Muslim prayer was revealed to him, and he began to practise this daily, which again drew comment from those who saw him. When he was given the instruction to begin preaching in public, he was ridiculed and abused as people scoffed at what he was saying and doing.

Also, many of the Quraysh tribesmen – who had a vested interest in the Ka'bah shrine, since they provided the many pilgrims with food, water, lodging and protection en route – were seriously alarmed as they realized his insistence on the One True God would undermine the prestige and credibility of the shrine, if people were converted to the Prophet's ﷺ ways and began to abandon the worship of idols.

Some of the Prophet's ﷺ own uncles (such as Abu Lahab) became his chief opponents, vilifying and ridiculing him, and stirring up trouble for those who had been converted. There were many instances of torture and abuse, particularly against slaves and women who joined the 'new' religion. The first martyr of Islam was a slave woman, Sumayyah, and the first *mu'adhin* (caller to prayer) was a negro slave, Bilal, who was rescued by Abu Bakr from being left to die in the blazing sun with a huge rock on his chest.

Two groups of early Muslims migrated to Abyssinia, where they took refuge with the Christian ruler, the Negus, who was so impressed with their teachings and way of life that he agreed to protect them, and later became Muslim himself.

The Quraysh tribes decided to boycott the Prophet's ﷺ entire clan (the Hashimites), and for three years they were excluded from all trade, help, business and marriage arrangements, and were refused access to Makkah. It was a very difficult time, and many Muslims were reduced to absolute penury and near starvation. Abu Bakr risked his life and devoted his entire fortune to keeping them secretly supplied with food.

THE YEAR OF SORROW

In the year 619, the Prophet's ﷺ beloved wife, Khadijah, died. She had been his most ardent supporter and helper. In the same year his uncle Abu Talib, an eminent sheikh able to protect him from the worst persecution of the tribes, also died. The grief-stricken Prophet ﷺ left Makkah and tried to make a fresh start in the town of Taif, but was also rejected there.

Now aged 50, he had no wish to re-marry but struggled as the 'single parent' of his teenage daughters and foster sons. A female friend arranged for him to marry a devout widow, Sawdah, who was a suitable person to look after them and had been one of the first Muslim converts. She also suggested Aishah, the little daughter of his friend Abu Bakr, who the Prophet ﷺ had known and loved since the day she was born. She was far too young for physical marriage at this time, but was engaged in a non-physical relationship that was quite traditional.

THE 'NIGHT OF ASCENT'

It was during this same year that the Prophet ﷺ experienced the second most important night of his life, the *Laylat ul-Miraj* or 'Night of Ascent'.

This experience bore no resemblance to the Christian belief in the Ascension to Heaven of the body of Jesus ﷺ after his death and resurrection. The Prophet's ﷺ experience occurred during his lifetime. It is not clear whether it was a vision, dream or psychic happening, but in it he was woken from where he lay sleeping, and taken by a *buraq*, a miraculous beast, to Jerusalem. (Marks or impressions of footprints 'marking the spot' are symbolic of where he stood, not miraculous imprints.) From the ruins of the old Jewish Temple on Mount Zion, a way was opened for him through the heavens until he approached the Throne of God, in a region which even he and the angel Jibril, who was accompanying him, were not allowed to enter.

Figure 1.1 The dome of the Rock Mosque, Jerusalem (also known as al-Quds).

It was during this night that the rules for the compulsory prayer five times per day (the *salat*) were revealed to him. They became the central part of the faith and have formed the keystone for Muslim life ever since.

> **Insight**
>
> The Dome of the Rock is believed to be the site of the Holy of Holies of the Jewish Temple, the shrine of the Ark of the Covenant.

He was also said to have seen and spoken to the still-existing souls of other prophets from the past, including Jesus, Moses and Abraham (Ar. Isa, Musa, Ibrahim – peace be upon all of them ﷺ), and left interesting descriptions. The experience brought great comfort and strength to the Prophet ﷺ and confirmed that Allah had not deserted him, or left him to suffer alone. After this night, he lived for another 12 years, with no similar experience.

> **Insight**
>
> Muhammad ﷺ commented that the prophet who looked most like himself was Ibrahim ﷺ, and that Jesus ﷺ had a fresh-faced complexion like someone who had just showered, and freckles.

THE HIJRAH – MIGRATION TO MADINAH

The Prophet's ﷺ fortunes now changed drastically. Although he was still persecuted and ridiculed in Makkah, his message had been heard by people outside the region. Some of the elders of the town of Yathrib invited him to leave Makkah and move to their town, where he would be honoured as their leader and judge. This town was the home of both Arab and Jewish people and there had been constant conflict between them. They hoped Muhammad ﷺ would bring them peace.

The Prophet ﷺ immediately advised his Muslim followers to move to Yathrib, while he remained in Makkah as long as possible to allay suspicions. Their empty houses were soon noted, however, as they slipped away. He was almost the last Muslim to leave. Without the restraining hand of Abu Talib, he knew the Quraysh would feel free to attack him, even to kill him, and this is what he realized they intended to do. They had no intention of letting him leave the city, or be received with honour anywhere else.

The Prophet's ﷺ move was not without some drama. Ali bravely volunteered to stay in his bed as a decoy, and the Prophet ﷺ left with Abu Bakr. A price was put on their heads. On a couple of occasions the Quraysh nearly succeeded in capturing him, but eventually they arrived at the outskirts of Yathrib. This emigration was known as the *hijrah*.

So many people rushed out to offer him refuge in their homes that he was embarrassed by their kindness, and left the choice of place to his famous camel *al-Qaswah*. Where it stopped and sat down he would make his home. The camel hesitated a few times, then finally stopped by a place where dates were spread out to dry, and this was instantly offered to the Prophet ﷺ. He insisted on buying the land which was to become his mosque and his home. The town took a new name – *Madinat al-Nabi*, the 'town of the Prophet' – which is now shortened to Madinah.

The Muslims who had preceded him from Makkah and made their
own *hijrah* were known as *Muhajirun*, the 'emigrants'. They were
in the position of refugees, having left all their belongings behind.
The Prophet ﷺ appealed to the people of Madinah to take them in
and offer them homes. Those who volunteered to help the Makkan
Muslims were known as *Ansars*, the 'helpers'.

THE PROPHET ﷺ AS RULER

The Prophet ﷺ then set about creating a charter which would
enable all the disputing tribes and factions in Madinah to accept
him as head of state and abide by his decisions. He ruled that all
the citizens should be free to practise their own religion in peaceful
co-existence, without fear of persecution or ill-favour. He asked
only that if there was any aggression or tyranny, they should join
together and cooperate in the face of the enemy. The whole text
of the Charter was recorded, word for word, by Ibn Ishaq and
Abu Ubaid in their respective books from the original preserved
by Ibn Abi Khithamah.

The previous tribal laws of both Arabs and Jews were replaced by the basic principle of general justice for all, irrespective of class, colour or creed. At first, the Jewish tribespeople of Madinah accepted the Prophet's ﷺ rule; no Jew was ever forced to become a Muslim, and they were treated as equal citizens of Madinah and their own faith was protected. Later, trouble broke out when two Jewish tribes did not keep the principle of supporting Madinah against attacks from outside, and those individuals were condemned as traitors.

THE PROPHET'S WAY OF LIFE

Every act and detail of the Prophet's ﷺ life was of the greatest interest to those around him; his recorded deeds and sayings, the *hadiths*, ran into many thousands.

Although he was now ruler of a city-state, and in receipt of increasing wealth and influence, the Prophet ﷺ never lived like a king. His home consisted of simple mud-brick houses that were built for his wives; he never actually had even a room of his own. Adjacent to these little houses was a courtyard with a well that became the mosque, the meeting place for the Muslim faithful.

It was taken for granted that the Prophet's ﷺ life was 'public property'; the origin of the *hijab* or 'veil' grew out of the habit of the public claiming constant access to him and his hospitality, and the need to allow his family a little privacy. The original veil was a curtain separating their private quarters from the area where people came and went. The Prophet ﷺ later taught that no one had the right to enter, or even to look into, other people's houses without permission.

He believed strongly in good manners, always greeting people kindly, showing respect to elders, and balancing his serious teachings and reprimands with gentle good humour. He once said: 'The dearest of you to me are those who have good manners; the most offensive to me are the most boring and the long-winded!'

He was never arrogant or superior, despite his position as leader; he never made people feel small, unwanted or embarrassed. He urged his followers to live kindly and humbly, releasing slaves as far as they were able, and generally showing practical charity, without thinking of reward. He said: 'Feed, for the love of Allah, the destitute, the orphan and the prisoner, saying: We feed you for the sake of Allah alone, desiring no reward from you, or thanks.' Much of his time was spent visiting the sick, comforting the bereaved, and counselling people with personal, family and marital problems.

His personal habits were extremely abstemious; he ate little, only simple food, and made it his practice never to fill his stomach. He slept using his cloak as a blanket on a very simple mattress on the floor, and allowed little in the way of home comforts or decorations. He did not regard it as right to sit down idly while others were working, and used to join in the housework with his wives, and helped in the various labour projects of his friends.

He was sent many rich garments but did not keep them; he used to sew and patch his old clothes and shoes whenever the need arose. He regarded all material things as being no more than loans from Allah, to be used in His service, so whenever he was given anything, he usually gave it away to the needy. He and his family supervised the distribution of food and charity on a daily basis.

Insight

Some think of the Prophet ﷺ as an austere person, stern and unbending. In fact, Aishah recorded that 'he was a man just like you – except that he is always smiling!' He was considerate and generous, and a welcome guest in countless households.

All his recorded words and actions reveal him as a man of gentleness, kindness, good humour and excellent common sense, who had a great love for animals and for all people, especially children. He had an implacable sense of justice, but ruled with humility and compassion. He was not only treated by his followers with enormous respect – he was deeply loved.

Insight

Once he missed the old lady who used to sweep out his mosque, an ex-slave from Abyssinia. He found she had died, and no-one had told him. He went immediately to pray at her tomb.

THE PROPHET'S LIFE OF PRAYER

The Prophet's 卐 life was spent virtually in a constant state of prayer, and in teaching his followers. Apart from the five compulsory prayers, which he led in the mosque, the Prophet 卐 also spent many hours in private prayer and contemplation, sometimes during the greater part of the night.

Insight

Allah was not the moon-god, as sometimes suggested, but that same God who called Ibrahim 卐 and the other prophets away from the worship of idols and astronomical features such as the sun and moon.

His wives prayed some of the extra night prayers with him, but after they had retired to sleep he could be found standing or sitting in contemplation for many hours, snatching a little sleep towards the end of the night, before being woken for the pre-sunrise prayer (the *fajr*).

Like many in the hot climate of the Middle East, the Prophet 卐 made up for loss of sleep by taking a siesta during the heat of the day, after the midday prayer (the *zuhr*). Late afternoon was the time when the heat dropped again, and a major time of prayer – with the *asr* as the light began to change, and the *maghrib* after sunset. The last formal prayer was during the hours of darkness, the *isha*.

Figure 1.2 A pilgrim making personal prayer.

One of his most famous prayers is known as the 'Prayer of Light':

> O Allah, place light in my heart, light in my sight, light in my hearing, light on my right hand and on my left, light above me, light below me, light behind me and light before me. O Allah, Who knows the innermost secrets of our hearts, lead me out of the darkness into the Light.

THE PROPHET'S FAMILY

In the last ten years of his life, after Khadijah's death, the Prophet ﷺ took at least 12 other women and their children into his household, all but one of whom had suffered the loss of their original spouses through death or divorce. (The Prophet ﷺ took on four small children when he married Umm Salamah, for example, and Sawdah may have had six.) In three cases, the wives were daughters of eminent defeated enemies. Two of his wives were Jewish, one was a Christian.

14

Insight

It is worth making the comment that sometimes people have accused the Prophet ﷺ of being a sexual athlete, seeking intimacy with a selection of pretty girls. (If so, he was lucky to have started being such an athlete when he turned 50, having turned down any previous opportunity for a second wife besides Khadijah, or sexual intimacy with slaves and captives.)

Unlike Khadijah, the later wives of the Prophet shared his life as ruler of Madinah. However, they had no luxuries but were expected to follow his devout and simple way of life, and to make enormous personal sacrifice. They became known as the 'Mothers of the Faithful', and lived in their row of tiny houses along the wall of the Prophet's ﷺ mosque, at the centre of the Muslim religious community.

It is on record that all of these wives were once offered the free choice of whether they wished to live like this, or to leave him, and chose to stay, even those with whom he had no sexual relationship at all.

By these later wives, the Prophet ﷺ only had one further child of his own, a son Ibrahim, who, like his two sons by Khadijah, died in infancy.

His four daughters all married and three of them bore children. Of them, the most famous was his youngest daughter, Fatimah, who married Ali and gave him two grandsons, Hasan and Husayn, and two granddaughters, Zaynab and Umm Kulthum.

THE PROPHET'S ﷺ WIVES

1 *Khadijah bt. Khuwaylid*
2 *Sawdah bt. Zama'a*
3 *Aishah bt. Abu Bakr*
4 *Hafsah bt. Umar*
5 *Zaynab bt. Khuzaymah*
6 *Hind (Umm Salamah) bt. Abu Umayyah (his cousin)*
7 *Zaynab bt. Jahsh (his cousin)*

8   *Juwayriyyah bt. Harith*
9   *Ramlah (Umm Habibah) bt. Abu Sufyan*
10 *Zaynab (Safiyyah) bt. Huyayy (a Jewish rabbi's daughter)*
11 *Rayhanah bt. Zayd (a Jewess)*
12 *Maymunah bt. Harith (a half-sister of 5 Zaynab)*
13 *Maryam Qibtiyyah (a Christian)*

> ## Insight
> Of these wives, 1–7, 9 and 12 were among the very first
> converts to Islam. They all married the Prophet ﷺ after
> divorce or in widowhood, except Aishah and Maryam.

Khadijah and Zaynab bint Khuzaymah both died before the
Prophet ﷺ. Some scholars debate the status of Rayhanah and
Maryam Qibtiyyah as full wives. Before Islam, men did take
advantage of sexual intimacy with their servants, but this was
forbidden to Muslims. If they married a servant ('one whom their
right hand possessed'), she might receive her freedom in lieu of the
dowry given to free women upon marriage.

JIHAD

The Prophet ﷺ was a man of peace and reconciliation, and would
have preferred it if he had been left in peace in Madinah, but sadly,
the opposition from the Quraysh tribes continued and he was
obliged to take part in sporadic warfare. Even so, the total amount
of time he spent fighting only came to a few months.

His two most important early battles – Badr and Uhud – only
took a single day. The Muslims won the first, but the second was
a stalemate. As a result of this warfare, the many rules of conduct
of war and treatment of prisoners were laid down for Muslims,
the rules of *jihad*.

> ## Insight
> The battles the Muslims fought to defend themselves from the
> Makkans were particularly traumatic for both sides, as the
> warriors had to confront and perhaps kill their own relatives.

Jihad was never to be military activity for the sake of nationalism, tyranny or aggrandizement, but primarily for defensive reasons, and only until the enemy could be brought to peace. During the Prophet's battles, many of the enemy were converted to his side, impressed by the Muslim chivalry, courage and faith in God.

In March 627, Abu Sufyan, the chief sheikh of Makkah, raised a massive force of 10,000 men and advanced on Madinah, buoyed up by support from a Jewish tribe in the Madinah outskirts that had agreed to the charter, but then turned traitor and decided to oust the Prophet ﷺ. This was called the Battle of the Trench, since the Prophet had a huge ditch speedily constructed to protect the city. After a two-week siege, the opposition withdrew, giving the Prophet ﷺ a moral victory, for the eyes of Arabia had been upon him, and he had shown that even this vast army could not defeat him.

In the aftermath, the renegade Jewish tribe was dealt with severely. The Prophet ﷺ always counselled mercy for defeated enemies, and never forced anyone to accept the faith of Islam against their will. On this occasion, however, it was a serious matter because these citizens of Madinah had agreed to let in the enemy to destroy Muslims so long as they were spared, even though they had signed the pledge of loyalty. The Prophet ﷺ agreed to spare their lives so long as they repented their treachery and agreed to abide by the laws of Islam, but they refused.

They were then allowed to appoint their own judge; but this judge had been so shocked by their treachery that he said he would apply their own ancient law to them, and quoted Deuteronomy 7:2:

When the Lord your God gives them over to you, and you defeat them, then you must utterly destroy them, and make no covenant with them and show no mercy to them.

All the unrepentant men of the tribe were then put to the sword. In a way, it helped to underline the point the Prophet ﷺ was trying to make: that the laws of Islam should supersede those from the ancient past.

The incident had nothing to do with anti-Semitism, and shortly
afterwards, as if to prove the point, the Prophet ﷺ married two
of the Jewish widows, Zaynab the daughter of a chief rabbi –
thereafter known as Safiyyah, and Rayhanah bint Zayd. No Jews
who accepted the charter were persecuted, or pressured to leave
Madinah or to accept Islam.

PILGRIMAGE TO MAKKAH

In March 628 the Prophet ﷺ dreamed of returning to Makkah, and
decided to make this dream reality. He set out with some 1,400
followers, all unarmed, in pilgrim dress of two simple white cloths.
Although an increasing number of the citizens of Makkah had by
now accepted Islam, the Prophet's ﷺ followers were still refused
entry. Instead of making trouble, they offered their sacrifices
outside Makkah, at a place called Hudaybiyah. The Quraysh chief,
Suhayl, who had replaced Abu Sufyan, came out and negotiated a
treaty to keep the peace for ten years.

The Muslims repeated the pilgrimage in 629, and this time were
allowed to visit the ancient tribal holy places undisturbed while
the Makkans vacated the city and watched them from the hills.
The impressive Muslim behaviour made many new converts.

THE SURRENDER OF MAKKAH

The Prophet ﷺ then began to plan for the spread of Islam. He dictated
letters to the celebrities of the surrounding kingdoms, inviting them to
consider Islam – the Roman Byzantine Emperor, the Persian Emperor,
the rulers of Egypt, Abyssinia and many leading chiefs – but of these
only the Abyssinian Negus accepted and was converted. However,
many Christian Arabs soon converted. It is claimed that some of
these letters still exist, notably the letter to the Muqawqis of Egypt
which may be seen in the Topkapi Museum, Istanbul.

The truce of Hudaybiyah did not hold; in November 629 the Makkans attacked one of the tribes that allied with the Muslims. By 630, the Prophet ﷺ, who now had grounds for marching on Makkah, gathered a force of 10 000 men, the largest army that had ever left Madinah. They marched to Makkah, camped outside the city, and Abu Sufyan (whose widowed daughter Umm Habibah had become one of the Prophet's ﷺ wives) came over to his side. The Prophet ﷺ promised a general amnesty if the Makkans would formally submit, declaring that all who took refuge with Abu Sufyan or who shut their doors on the battle would be safe. In the event, there was only one skirmish in which 11 people lost their lives before the surrender.

Insight

The capture of Makkah was an amazing contrast to the bloodthirsty massacres, rapes and enslavements that usually followed the conquests of those times.

The Prophet ﷺ entered the city in triumph, went straight to the Ka'bah, and performed the ritual circumambulation seven times. He then entered the shrine and destroyed all the idols.

All the hereditary territories were left in the hands of their accustomed guardians, and the Prophet ﷺ asked his followers whose abandoned property in Makkah had been seized when they moved to Madinah not to claim it back. Uthman ibn Talhah, who had once refused Muhammad ﷺ entry to the Ka'bah and persecuted him, was given back the key to the shrine, and it remains with his family to this day. One by one the Quraysh swore their fealty to the Prophet ﷺ, and were pardoned. Only ten people who were also guilty of murder or incitement to murder were condemned to death, but of these only four were actually executed.

THE FINAL PILGRIMAGE AND THE LAST SERMON

The Prophet ﷺ did not live long to enjoy a peaceful rule. His army was obliged to conduct further warfare against tribes that attacked them – tribes that had been shocked by the desecration of their idols at Makkah, but he was soon able to return to his home in Madinah.

Events outside Arabia worked to the advantage of Islam. The western part of the Roman Empire was overrun by barbarians, and in the east the Byzantines at Constantinople had fallen into confusion through internal conflicts and inefficient rule. The Persian Sassanid Empire (which covered today's Iraq, Iran and Afghanistan) had engaged the Byzantines in conflict for some 30 years, and had successfully captured Jerusalem, but by 630 the Byzantines had retaken it and Persian influence was low, leaving a political vacuum for the warriors of Islam to occupy.

In March 632 the Prophet ﷺ made his one complete Muslim *Hajj* to the Ka'bah shrine, known as the *Hajjat ul-Wida*, the Final Pilgrimage. During this pilgrimage the revelations about the rules of the Hajj were given to him, which are followed by all Muslims to this day. Up to this time pagans had been allowed to visit the Ka'bah as well as Muslims, but now all pagan influence was removed, and only Muslims were allowed into the city.

Figure 1.3 Pilgrims gather at the Ka'bah.

When the Prophet ﷺ arrived at Mount Arafat for the 'Stand before Allah' (see page 111), he delivered what is known as his 'Final Sermon'. The summarized text of this famous teaching can be found in mosques all over the world:

> O people, listen carefully to what I say, for I do not know whether, after this year, I shall ever be amongst you again. Listen carefully, and report my words to those who cannot be here today.
>
> Regard the life and property of every Muslim as a sacred trust ... Hurt no one, so that no one may hurt you. Remember that you will indeed meet your Lord, and that He will reckon your deeds ... You will neither inflict nor suffer injustice ...O men, remember that you have rights with regard to your women, but they also have rights over you. Remember that you have taken them as your wives only under Allah's trust and with His permission ... Treat them well and be kind to them, for they are your partners and committed helpers ...
>
> O believers, worship Allah, say your five daily prayers; fast during the month of Ramadan, and give your wealth in zakah. Perform Hajj, if you can afford to ...
>
> An Arab has no superiority over a non-Arab; a white has no superiority over a black, nor a black over a white, except by piety and good deeds. Every Muslim is a brother (or sister) to every other Muslim ...
>
> No prophet or apostle will come after me, and no new faith will be born ...I leave behind me two things, the Qur'an and the Sunnah; if you follow these, you will never go astray.[1]

Insight

So far as we know, Muhammad ﷺ was indeed the last prophet called by God. Since his time, there have of course been many inspired teachers and charismatic leaders, but no further prophets.

[1] Shi'ite sources specify the two things as the Qur'an and his descendants.

At the end, he received his final revelation:

Today I have perfected your religion for you, and I have completed My blessing upon you; and I have approved Islam as your religion.
(Surah 5:5)

There was a silence, and then the voice of Bilal rose over the hushed enormous crowd, calling them to prayer.

THE DEATH OF THE PROPHET

When he returned home to Madinah, he began making preparations for an expedition to repulse a huge Byzantine army on the Syrian border, but he became ill and developed a heavy fever.[2] He continued to attend and lead the prayers in the mosque as far as he was able, supported by Ali, and when too ill he requested Abu Bakr to take his place. The army was entrusted to Usamah, the 17-year-old son of Zayd by the Prophet's ﷺ nurse Umm Ayman.

He did not recover, and eventually collapsed. His wives realized that he wished to be with Aishah, and moved him to her room, where he died in her arms[3] on 8 June 632 (12 Rabi'ul Awwal, 11 AH, in the Muslim calendar).

Insight

Some people believe their faith can protect them from harm or misfortune. Islam teaches that even prophets (persons much cherished by God) face tests of suffering, misfortune, betrayal, illness, wounding and death.

He was not an old man – only 63 years old. (Many of his friends lived into their 80s.) His last words were said to have been: 'I have chosen the most exalted Companions, in Paradise.'

Umar and other Companions found it hard to believe their Prophet ﷺ could have died like a mortal man, but Abu Bakr reminded them of the revelation after Uhud:

[2]He and his friend were served poisoned lamb by a Jewish widow, and although he never swallowed it, and forgave the woman, his friend died and he was never fully well afterwards.
[3]Shi'ite sources state he died in Ali's arms. Both were present at this sad time.

Muhammad is but a messenger, and messengers have passed away before him. If he die, or is slain, will you then turn back?

(Surah 3:144)

He was buried in Aishah's room, which is now a shrine and part of the modern mosque complex at Madinah. May peace be upon him.

Figure 1.4 The Prophet's mosque. The dome covers the site of his tomb, Madinah.

The succession

THE 'RIGHTLY-GUIDED' CALIPHS

After the death of the Prophet ﷺ the new caliph (successor) was to be someone who had been with him in both Makkah and Madinah, qualified to pass on correct *hadiths*, and whose life was so similar to the Prophet's ﷺ that it exemplified the *sunnah*. Such a person would be able to make decisions as binding as those of Muhammad ﷺ himself; the majority of Muslims believe that the first four caliphs fulfilled these criteria, and are therefore known as the 'Rightly-Guided' Caliphs or *Rashidin*.

Although the caliphs increasingly had access to enormous wealth, the first four continued to live simple lives, as the Prophet ﷺ had done, and were famous for their saintliness and humility.

Abu Bakr (632–4)

During his lifetime the Prophet ﷺ had given several indications that Ali should have been the next leader, but he requested Abu Bakr to lead the prayer when he was too ill, and there was strong feeling that the leadership should go to one of the 'elders' in the traditional Arabic manner. Tribal leadership rarely passed to eldest son, but to the most capable and reliable candidate, chosen by consultation. Abu Bakr, then in his sixties, had been the Prophet's ﷺ life-long best friend and supporter, was his first adult male convert and was the father of his dearly loved wife Aishah. He was respected not only for his closeness to the Prophet ﷺ but also for his gentleness, wisdom, piety and humility. As caliph, he was known as As-Siddiq (the Witness to the Truth) and Amir ul-Muminim (Ruler of the Believers).

Some of the most respected Companions of the Prophet ﷺ (including his cousins Talhah and Zubayr) were unhappy that Ali had not been chosen, and criticized Abu Bakr's election as being rushed through while Ali was attending to the Prophet's ﷺ funeral. It was Ali's supporters who were to become known as the *Shi'at Ali* (party of Ali) or Shi'ites.

Nevertheless, Abu Bakr was elected. His short reign consisted largely of warfare (known as the Riddah Wars), because the allegiance of some Arab tribes had been political rather than of religious conviction, and once the Prophet ﷺ had died they decided they need no longer pay the *zakah*. Abu Bakr successfully brought these tribes back into the fold of Islam.

On his deathbed, Abu Bakr did not give the community the chance to elect the next caliph, but nominated Umar – also one of the senior Companions. Ali was disappointed, but accepted the decision.

Insight

Family connections – the Prophet ﷺ married Abu Bakr's daughter Aishah and Umar's daughter Hafsah. Uthman married two of the Prophet's ﷺ daughters – Ruqaiyyah and Umm Kulthum, thus gaining the nickname 'He of the two lights'. Ali married the Prophet's ﷺ youngest daughter Fatimah. When the Prophet ﷺ died, all his children but Fatimah were already deceased, and Fatimah died (it is said, of grief) shortly after her father. Aishah lived as a widow into her sixties. Ali married many more times and had some 30 children.

Umar (634–44)

Umar's caliphate saw the rapid spread of Islam, and war with surrounding territories. However, most of the populaces felt liberated and were happy to accept Muslim rulers instead of the previous cruel and corrupt rulers. Damascus was taken in 635, and Mu'awiyah became governor there in 640. In the Battle of Yarmuk (636) the Byzantine Emperor Heraclius sent a vast army of 200,000 men against the Muslims, and thousands were killed – but the Muslims won.

The battle of Qadisiyah (636–7) saw the defeat of the Persian Emperor Yazdigard, whose flight ended the rule of the Sassanians. One of his daughters was captured, and became the bride of the Prophet's ﷺ grandson Husayn.

Jerusalem fell in 638, the Christian ruler Sophronius declaring that he would surrender to none other than Umar himself. Umar behaved with great consideration to the Christians by refraining from offering prayer in the Shrine of the Holy Sepulchre, so that it was not turned into a mosque. The Byzantine Viceroy of Egypt was defeated in 639.

Although the Muslim army conquered territory successfully, no individual was forced to be converted to Islam at the point of the sword, as is often suggested. The Qur'an specified quite clearly: *'Let there be no compulsion in religion. Truth stands out clear from error.'* (Surah 2:256). The formula was 'accept Islam, pay alliance tribute, or face the sword', the sword being reserved for those who refused to pay the appropriate taxes. Those who did convert to Islam lived tax-free, but paid the *zakah*.

In 644 Umar was assassinated by a Firoz, a Persian Christian slave, who had been brought to Madinah to embellish the simple mud dwellings that had been the home of the Prophet ﷺ. Umar was stabbed six times at the dawn prayer, and died three days later.

Uthman (644–56)

As Umar lay dying, he elected a *shura* (consultation group) of six people to choose the next leader, one of whom was Ali, but again, one of the Prophet's ﷺ senior contemporaries, Uthman, was chosen. In his reign the Muslim empire spread west across North Africa and east to the boundary of China and the Indus Valley.

Although Uthman was a saintly man, he was also a wealthy member of the Umayyad clan of the Quraysh, and in setting up governors for the newly acquired territories, he promoted too many of his own relatives, and was accused of nepotism. For example, his cousin Mu'awiyah, the son of Abu Sufyan, was created Governor of Syria, and another cousin, Amir, was Governor of Egypt. He also treated some of the most respected of the Prophet's remaining Companions harshly.

The Muslims of Kufa and Fustat protested, and tried to persuade the 80-year-old Uthman to abdicate. Uthman refused and preached a fiery sermon against them, in the face of all good advice. Soon afterwards, while he was reading his Qur'an, a group of Egyptians killed him. This Qur'an, marked with his blood, still exists in Tashkent.

Insight

Uthman's last wife Nailah, a converted Christian, tried to protect him, and in the attempt her fingers were cut off. She sent them, with her plea for help, to Mu'awiyah in Syria. They were displayed in the mosque in Damascus.

Uthman's murder led to the Fitnah Wars, the first inter-Muslim fights, which resulted in the deaths of all the Companions who had been at Badr, and moved the capital away from Madinah. It also resulted in the emergence of the Kharijite sect ('those who went out from the community').

Ali (656–61)

Twenty-four years after the Prophet's ﷺ death, Ali (also known as Asadullah – the Lion of God) claimed to be the rightful successor, but Aishah still opposed him, supported by Talhah and Zubayr. Aishah accused Ali of being lax in applying justice to those responsible for plotting Uthman's murder (two of his sons, for example, were supposed to have been guarding him). When Ali also began deposing Uthman's provincial governors (including Mu'awiyah who had successfully ruled Syria for 20 years) opposition to his leadership grew. The deposed officials joined Aishah. Mu'wiyyah would not take the oath of allegiance to Ali, and may even have secretly recognized Zubayr. Aishah personally led an army against Ali in 656, the Battle of the Camel (named after her magnificent animal, al-Askar – the warrior), but was defeated and captured. She was treated with respect and returned safely to her friends in Madinah, where she lived until she died. Talhah and Zubayr were both killed, but Zubayr's son Abdullah lived to claim the caliphate later.

Insight

Aishah led her own troops, the traditional tribal practice of bold Arab women inciting their men to fight bravely, as Mu'awiyah's mother Hind had done years before. Aishah's unfortunate camel was hamstrung to bring it down, by which time her red mail-covered howdah was covered in arrows 'like a porcupine'.

Next, Ali was opposed by Mu'awiyah. There were attempts to negotiate, but their armies met at the Battle of Siffin in 657, a battle that lasted for weeks and saw the slaughter of a vast number of men (some said Mu'awiyah lost 45,000 and Ali 25,000). It ended when Mu'awiyah's troops put leaves of the Qur'an on the end of their spears, and Ali's soldiers refused to strike them. Ali agreed to accept arbitration, in which both sides should stand down and face new elections, but this was tantamount to accepting that he was not the rightful caliph. His most pious warriors were so shocked that Ali should have agreed to this that they seceded from his ranks, becoming known as the *Kharijites* (Seceders – the fore-runners of later extremists who were prepared to kill or die rather than compromise their sectarian attitudes and beliefs).

In 658 Ali's forces attacked a large force of Kharijites at Nahrawan, one of the survivors being Ibn Muljam – the man who would shortly assassinate him.

Ali was given many premonitions of his fate, including even the name of the man destined to kill him. Despite this he refused to hide or run away and was struck down while praying in the mosque at Kufa. During the three days it took him to die, he protected and fed his assassin, ordering that he should be spared if he lived, and killed with one stroke if he died. He was buried at Najaf.

MU'AWIYAH AND THE UMAYYADS

The Muslim split resulted in Mu'awiyah seizing the chance to have himself elected as fifth caliph, whereas the Shi'ites made Ali's eldest son Hasan caliph in Iraq. But instead of fighting, Hasan agreed to waive his rights and accept a pension, and Ali's second son, Husayn, agreed to leave his claim until the death of Mu'awiyah. Instead of caliph, both Hasan and Husayn took the title *Imam*.

Insight

Mu'awiyah's mother was the fiery Hind, infamous for her bare-breasted exhortation of the Makkan army against the Prophet ﷺ and the slaying of his uncle Hamzah (whereupon she mutilated his corpse and chewed his liver). She accepted Islam when Makkah fell, and ended up – as mother of the caliph – as the most powerful Muslim woman of her time.

Mu'awiyah decided not to leave Damascus and move to Madinah, so Damascus became the new capital of the Muslim world. He reigned for 19 years, during which time Islam reached Sind, Bukhara, Samarkand and North Africa. On his deathbed, instead of nominating Ali's son Husayn as promised, he put up his son Yazid as successor, and from then on the Sunni caliphate became hereditary, the first dynasty being known as the *Umayyad*.

Husayn's supporters never accepted Yazid. The Shi'ite revolt peaked with the Battle of Karbala.

The martyrdom of Husayn

In 680 CE/61 AH, Husayn and his small band of supporters were surrounded by Yazid's huge army of 4,000 warriors at Karbala. For eight days they tried to negotiate Husayn's unconditional surrender, but his belief in his right to be caliph was so strong that he refused to give way, even when it meant his defeat and death. Husayn had already foreseen his martyrdom in a vision. They were in sight of the River Euphrates, but Yazid's army tormented them by denying them any access to the water and watched as they began to die of thirst. When Husayn held out his baby son Ali Asghar for mercy, an arrow fired through the baby's neck and pinned him to Husayn's arm.

Husayn knew it was the end. He gave one night for any who wished to leave him to go, but as day broke he found no-one had gone but some of the enemy had come to join him.

On 10th Muharram, he put on the mantle of his grandfather the Prophet ﷺ, and went out to die. Hopelessly outnumbered, he and his followers (including some 70 of the Prophet's ﷺ relatives, several of them children) were slaughtered.

The Prophet's ﷺ family was almost wiped out. Only a few women (including Husayn's sister Zaynab), Husayn's son Ali Zayn al Abidin, who had been too ill to go out on the battlefield, and Ali Zayn's four-year-old son Muhammad al Baqir, remained. The body of Husayn, riddled with arrows, was trampled in the mud. His head was hacked off and taken to Damascus.

Yazid spared the survivors, but took them prisoner. Ali Zayn might have been killed, but Zaynab threw herself upon his body and the soldier held off. She nursed him back to health, and acted as leader of the Shi'ites until he recovered, becoming famous for her impassioned speeches which moved crowds to tears, throughout her journey to prison.

The shrine where Husayn was buried, at Karbala, became a holy place that rivalled Makkah. Shi'ites hold a ten-day festival there every year, in remembrance of his martyrdom. During the festival the people weep for the seeming triumph of tyranny and evil (symbolized by the corrupt, cynical Yazid) over the good (symbolized by the piety and refusal to compromise of Husayn). They pledge themselves to keep up the fight to defend their faith and principles.

Insight

The 'wounds' from the horrors committed at Karbala still remain unhealed and largely unforgiven by Shi'ites. Many Sunni Muslims do not even know the details, and regard all the history after the Prophet's ☪ lifetime as irrelevant to Islam.

The main feature of the festival, which takes place in the month of Muharram, is a series of processions and passion plays commemorating the terrible deaths of Husayn and the Prophet's ☪ family. There are daily gatherings, or *rawdahs*, in which emotions are stirred up until everyone weeps and dedicates their lives anew (see Ashura, Chapter 3).

Sometimes the men in the processions gash themselves with knives and beat their backs with chains, in memory of the martyr's wounds.

SHI'ITE ISLAM

Some 20 per cent of the world's Muslims are *Shi'ites*. Shi'ites claim that *Sunni* Islam is the creation of the lax and worldly Umayyad caliphs backed up by the eminent but rather pedantic Muslim jurists of the ninth and tenth centuries CE, and that Shi'ite Islam is actually older and more closely based on the actual teachings and practice of the Prophet ☪. Sunnis reject this point of view, and claim that they represent authentic Islam – which is practical, tolerant and compassionate – and that the Shi'ites, in their quest for personal purity and interest in the theology of that which lies beyond human understanding, have developed a speculative and extremist form of Islam.

Both Sunni and Shi'ite extremists are frequently regarded as troublemakers in the West because they will not compromise or accept a status quo that goes against their principles; their zealots preach revolution against tyranny and corruption, and have stirred up numerous uprisings and civil wars, interpreting the verses about *jihad* in the Qur'an to mean that they should put all their energy into conversion of the world by driving away the devil and all his works. (The West has typically been regarded as corrupt – through sexual freedoms, drugs, and American politics – and known as 'the Great Satan'.)

Shi'ite Muslims claim that the Prophet ﷺ had always intended Ali to be his successor after his death, and had declared it at a huge gathering at Ghadir Khum after his final pilgrimage. They therefore reject the caliphate of Abu Bakr and his successors. Sunnis interpret the speech at Ghadir Khum as being no more than an acknowledgement of Ali's merit, and not a nomination for succession.

Ever since the caliphate passed to Mu'awiyah and other Umayyads after him, who were not direct descendants of the Prophet ﷺ, the Shi'ites have agitated to replace them with a true descendant on the throne of a united Islamic Empire.

They reject the Sunni principle of 'the consensus of the community' (*ijma*) and substitute the doctrine of the *Imam* or spiritual head directly descended from Ali. Shi'ites believe the choice of these Imams was divinely ordained, not left to human error, and that they were blessed with divinely inspired knowledge, which was infallible.

The Shi'ites later divided into two major branches known as Seveners or Twelvers according to whether they believed that either the seventh or twelfth descendant Imam mysteriously disappeared without dying and now follows the course of history in a mystical way. They believe that their 'Hidden Imam' (or Mahdi) is forever present in the world, although unseen, appearing to the faithful in their times of need and sending out his light to convert all mankind. He appears to people in prayer and strengthens the faithful in times of persecution.

> ### Insight
> One famous Mahdi was Muhammad Ahmad, who led the Sudanese revolt against General Gordon of Khartoum. The 49th Isma'ili Imam is the Aga Khan, an eminent worker for many charities. His grandfather Aly Khan hit the headlines when he married the film star Rita Hayworth.

The Mahdi will eventually return to establish righteous rule and bring about the end of the world. The Seveners and Twelvers then split into further sub-sects, notably the Isma'ilis.

> ### Insight
> Some Muslims believe the Mahdi who will return just before the end of the world will be the Prophet Jesus ﷺ, returning for his 'second coming'.

Other key Shi'ite differences from Sunni Islam are their belief that God has foreknowledge of all human action, but does not predestine it; a different form of call to prayer and ritual ablution before prayer; the permission of temporary marriage (*mutah*) which was repealed by the Prophet ﷺ after initially allowing it; the veneration of shrines and tombs of Imams (seen as *shirk* by Sunnis), and the permission to conceal their beliefs (*taqiyya*) in order to avoid persecution and suffering, or argument with the mainstream Sunni, who regard all these things as incorrect.

> ### Insight
> Sunni purists reject Shi'ism because of its developing doctrines, and what is considered over-veneration of the Prophet's ﷺ descendants.

Iranian Shi'ism (perhaps from a Persian Zoroastrian background) draws sharp boundaries between the worlds of light and darkness, black and white, *haq* (truth) and *batel* (falsehood), and is undergirded by a conviction that the world is unsafe for Shi'ites. Neither the Prophet ﷺ, His family, nor any of the 12 Shi'a Imams died a natural death (they believe the Prophet ﷺ also died a martyr, the result of poisoning), which contributes to the tendency to feel relentlessly persecuted.

The chief Shi'ite holy cities are Najaf in Iraq, (the burial place of Ali – the tomb is located four miles from Kufa where Ali was felled by Kharijite assassins in 661), and Karbala, the site of the martydom of the Prophet's ﷺ grandson Husayn.

10 THINGS TO REMEMBER

1 *The Prophet* ﷺ *(570–632 CE) was a descendant of Ibrahim/ Abraham, born in Makkah.*

2 *An exceptionally noble man, famous for his life of prayer, kindness and wisdom, he was called to Prophethood at the age of 40 in 610 CE.*

3 *He was persecuted in Makkah, accused (quite wrongly) of fraud, insanity, demon-possession, epilepsy, personal ambition, and desire to pervert the youth and split families.*

4 *The* Laylat ul-Miraj *was the night of his ascension through the heavens from Jerusalem – either a vision or a 'miraculous journey' that occurred while he still lived in Makkah.*

5 *The people of Yathrib oasis invited him to abandon Makkah and become their ruler, and he migrated there (the* hijrah*) in 621 CE. Yathrib became known as Madinah.*

6 *Islam spread very rapidly, and although the Makkans carried on attacks for 8 years, Makkah became a Muslim city in 630 CE.*

7 *His teachings and example (the* sunnah*) were recorded in statements and recollections known as* hadiths*. His way of life was and still is the pattern for all Muslims.*

8 *By the time he died (aged 63 in 632 CE), the whole of Arabia had accepted Islam and it was spreading farther afield.*

9 *The leader of Islam after Muhammad's* ﷺ *death had the title of* caliph *or* khalifah*.*

10 *The first four caliphs were chosen from his closest companions: Abu Bakr (ruled 632–4), Umar (634–44), Uthman (644–56) and then his son-in-law Ali (656–61). These four were known as the 'Rightly Guided' or* rashidun.

2

The Qur'an and its teachings

In this chapter you will learn about:
- *the Qur'an*
- *the* hadith *collections*
- *the key beliefs of Islam –* tawhid *(the reality of the One Almighty God),* risalah *(the channel of prophecy),* akhirah *(the judgement and life to come) and* qadr *(free-will and predestination).*

The Qur'an

WRITING DOWN THE REVELATIONS

The *Qur'an* was revealed to the Prophet ﷺ bit by bit over a period of 23 years. Muslims believe that it is the Word of Allah, exactly as the Prophet ﷺ received it, and in this sense it is different from any other of the world's holy books, since they were all created by human authors many years after the deaths of the prophets involved, and were then edited and revised and added to by disciples. The Qur'an contains nothing but the direct revelations from Allah, through the angel Jibril, not one word of it being the creation of the Prophet ﷺ. He was nothing more than the transmitter. (The Prophet's ﷺ own teachings and sayings run into many thousands and are known as *hadiths*.)

As each revelation was given, the verses were learnt by heart and
jotted down on whatever materials came to hand: dried-out palm
leaves, pieces of broken pottery, ribs and shoulder bones of sheep,
bits of animal skin and flat stones.

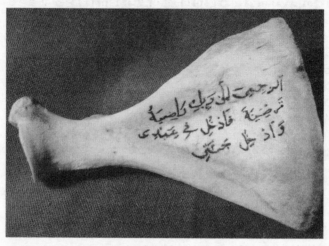

Figure 2.1 A verse of the Qur'an on a sheep's shoulder bone.

A single verse is known as an *ayah* (meaning a 'sign'), and a
chapter is a *surah* (a step up). There are 114 surahs of varying
lengths (all except the ninth beginning with the words '*In the
Name of Allah, the Most Compassionate, the Most Merciful*'),
and 6,616 ayahs – a total of 78,000 words in Arabic.

The surahs are not in chronological order, however. It is generally
accepted that the first words are in surah 96:1–5 and the final
words are in surah 5. The order was also something revealed to the
Prophet ﷺ, who had to recite the whole collection revealed so far
to the angel every Ramadan, and the entire text was checked with
the angel twice, shortly before the Prophet ﷺ died.

The first surah is called *al-Fatihah* (the Opening). Each surah is named after some striking incident or word in it, so some have strange names like *al-Baqarah* (the Cow) and *al-Ankabut* (the Spider). Others have names of Allah, for example, *al-Nur* (the Light), *al-Rahman* (the Merciful). The Cow is actually about religious duties, divorce laws and rules governing fair conduct of war.

COMPILED AS A BOOK

Islam began at a time when books were the property of only the rich, and people had the habit of learning a great deal by heart. Anyone who knew the full text of the Qur'an was known as a *hafiz* (pl. *huffaz*).

After the Prophet's ﷺ death, Abu Bakr requested that the Prophet's scribe Zayd ibn Thabit put together the first complete written version in one book. Zayd had been the Prophet's ﷺ secretary from the age of 12. He was reluctant to do something the Prophet ﷺ had not authorized, but was eventually persuaded, and gathered the text 'from the leaves of the date, and white stones, and the breasts of people that remembered it', of whom he was one.

He did not alter the messages in any way; no explanations or
editorial comments were added. The pages of this text were kept by
Abu Bakr, passed to Umar, and then to his daughter, Hafsah the
Prophet's ﷺ widow, and were known as the *mushaf* of Hafsah.

Uthman's 'recension'

When many of the original huffaz had passed away, and Muslims
were beginning to write down verses in their dialects, this brought
with it the danger of personal interpretation, misinterpretation
and alternative versions (*qira'ah*). Uthman realized the Revelation
might become corrupted, since all translations and editions were
dependent upon the skills of the translator or editor; so in 651 he
ordered that all texts which individuals owned were either checked
for full agreement against Hafsah's text, or destroyed.

Uthman had six copies of this 'standard' text inscribed on the
specially prepared skins of sacrificed goats. He kept one for himself
in Madinah, and sent the others to the chief Muslim centres –
Makkah, Kufa, Damascus, Cairo, and Sana. Since then all texts
have been identical, and handed down unaltered; and there is
probably no other book in the world which has remained
12 centuries with so pure a text.

If non-Arabic-speaking Muslims wish to read the Qur'an translated
into their own languages, it is best done with the original Arabic
alongside. Muslim scholars all try to master Arabic, and those with
no Arabic usually refer to several translations.

THE ART OF CALLIGRAPHY

Calligraphy means 'beautiful writing'. The early scribes
concentrated on finding styles worthy of the words they were

putting down. Master writers believed that a person's handwriting revealed their inner character and nature, so only a spiritually pure person should attempt the task.

The earliest scripts were the *Ma'il* (slanting) and the *Mashq* (extended), and the most famous are *Kufic* (from the Islamic centre at Kufa) and *Naskhi* (inscriptional). Eighth century Kufic has formal, simple lines easily drawn on parchment or inscribed on stone, but is so angular and ornamented that only a practised eye can read the script. The more cursive Naskhi style is easier to understand, and more easily done with pen on paper. It largely displaced the Kufic script and became the standard for most Qur'ans from the eleventh century onwards, and is the script used for virtually all printed Qur'ans today.

Insight

Arabic writing at the time was an incomplete script that did not include vowel markings or other diacritics needed to distinguish between words. Hence, if there was any question about the pronunciation of a written verse, the memorized version was a better authority than a written one.

The first handwritten Qur'ans had no artwork, because the scribes believed it was wrong to make representations of heavenly (or even human) beings; and they did not wish people to pay attention to the decoration rather than the content of the verses. Later, the wealthy sultans commissioned lavish and colourful Qur'ans resplendent in gold, green, red and blue. A superb Qur'an in gold script on blue vellum survives almost intact from Kairouan in Tunisia where it was originally inscribed in the late ninth or early tenth century. The bulk of it is preserved in the National Library of Tunisia (a number of leaves removed from it are in other public libraries and private collections).

The fate of the oldest Qur'ans

Leaves of the six special copies prepared under the official supervision of Uthman still exist, but the one sent to Makkah was destroyed by fire in 683 CE, and those commissioned for Madinah and Kufa were also lost irretrievably.

> **Insight**
>
> Some handwritten copies on vellum are huge books which can be a metre high. As distinct and valuable as handwritten Torahs and Bibles, many still exist.

One codex was found in Iraq by the conqueror Tamerlane who took it to his capital, Samarqand, where it remained from c.1485–1868 CE, and was then removed to St. Petersburg/Leningrad. Fifty facsimilies were prepared at the request of Czar Nicholas the Second in 1905, and the original sent to Uzbekistan. This is now kept in the Soviet State Library at Tashkent. It is incomplete, with only about one-third (some 250) of the original pages surviving, written in a bold Hejazi script, similar to Kufic script. It has eight to 12 lines of script to the page. Many pages are mutilated.

Critics often point out that there are many references to claims made in different parts of the Muslim world to possess not only one of Uthman's copies, but even his own copy stained with the blood of his assassination. In fact, the Tashkent text does appear to have the bloodstain, on Surah 2.137.

Another ancient manuscript is kept on public display in the Topkapi Museum in Istanbul, and another manuscript at the al-Hussein mosque in Cairo, the stack of leaves standing a staggering 50 centimetres high.

Modoern technology has now taken over the task of the copyist; the Tashkent Qur'an has recently been photocopied.

> **Insight**
>
> Robert of Ketton was the first person to translate the Qur'an into a Western language (Latin) in 1143. The oldest surviving Qur'an for which movable type was used was printed in Venice in 1537. The first English version was by Alexander Ross, in 1649.

HOW RESPECT IS SHOWN TO THE QUR'AN

The Qur'an is not just a book, but the Sacred Text. If Muslims have the space, their Qur'an may be kept in a special room which is kept clean and used only for prayer and reading the holy Text.

When a Qur'an is in the room, Muslims are expected to behave with reverence, so it would not be proper to act indecently, rudely, cruelly or selfishly. The Qur'an imparts an atmosphere of prayer – it is the silent reminder of the Muslim submission to Allah. If a TV or video is in that room any crude, violent or abusive programme content would not be suitable.

While the Qur'an is being recited aloud, Muslims should not speak, eat or drink, smoke, or make any distracting noise. Before touching the Qur'an, Muslims should be in a state of *wudu* (see page 80), or at least wash their hands. Muslim women would usually cover their heads as for prayer, and a woman who is menstruating or has recently given birth should not touch it.

Before beginning to read, Muslims 'prepare the heart' by consciously thinking about Allah and seeking refuge from Satan (Surah 16:98). They adopt a special position, so that the body is disciplined and alert, often sitting on the floor with the Qur'an on a special stand (called a *rehl* or *kursi*) in front of them. It is disrespectful to place the Qur'an on the floor.

Insight

Imam al-Ghazzali recommended that in order to read the Qur'an, one should perform ablution, be soft spoken and quiet, face the qiblah, keep the head lowered, and should not sit 'in a haughty manner' but as one sits humbly before a master.

Reading with heart, soul, mind and strength is known as *tilawah*, and the practice of correct pronunciation (usually learned in the mosque school or *madrassah*) is called *tajwid* (from *jawad* – to make well, make better or improve). Many Muslims do not speak Arabic, and some initially learn how to recite the verses without understanding what they mean. However, as they progress in Islam they should also learn the meanings, and see how the messages apply to them and how they should alter their own lives. Muslims try to recite or read the entire Qur'an each Ramadan.

Figure 2.2 Muslims start their studies at an early age.

Insight

It is said that *tajwid* is emitted from 17 places in the neck and lower head: regions of the throat, tongue, lips, nose and the mouth as a whole.

When the reading is finished, the Qur'an is put away carefully. It should not be left casually on a table, where someone might put something down on top of it! Muslims are sometimes shocked and offended to see Qur'ans kept and handled in shops, libraries and classrooms.

Translations of the Qur'an into other languages are not regarded as being quite the same thing as the Qur'an itself, and most Muslims in countries where printed books are commonplace are used to the idea of translations being treated casually. It is perhaps important to realize, however, that a Muslim might be horrified rather than flattered by a non-Muslim, not in *wudu*, pulling a Qur'an out of his pocket to have a quick read in the pub!

Figure 2.3 Studying the Qur'an.

INSULTING THE QUR'AN

As the direct Word of God, Muslims react strongly when they see or feel that the Qur'an has been treated with insult or disrespect.

Muslims object to anything that contains God's name or revealed words being misused, as in advertisements; one outrage was a design that looked strikingly similar to the Arabic name of God on the sole of a sports shoe. To be 'under the feet' has been a gross insult in the Middle East for centuries. Another design, tactfully withdrawn, was the Burger King logo for its ice cream cups.

Insight
The Prophet ﷺ said: 'Read the Qur'an, put it into practice, do not abandon it, do not make others resent it, do not exploit it in order to gain food and wealth.' (Ahmad).

Deteriorating or no-longer-usable worn-out Qur'ans are either buried or stored in a special room or 'grave' (like the Jewish *genizah*), as in the Sana collection. Even newspapers in Muslim societies are disposed of carefully, in case they have the name of God or Qur'anic text in them. They may be buried, burnt or binned – but never left around to be used on wet floors or for other undignified purposes. Even a piece of jewellery inscribed with the name of God or Qur'anic text would be taken off before entering a toilet. In 2005 a soldier in the Guantanamo Bay prison camp reportedly flushed a Qur'an down a toilet after urinating on it, sparking off a huge outcry.

The sunnah – the Prophet's ﷺ way

Show us the Straight Way, the way of those on whom You have bestowed Your grace, whose (portion) is not wrath, and who do not go astray. (Surah 1:6–7)

The life and example of the Prophet ﷺ is known as the *Sunnah*. The *Shari'ah* is the general title for Islamic law. The *din* (pr. *deen*) is the complete Islamic way of life. The sunnah is known from a study of the *hadiths*, the sayings and teachings of Muhammad ﷺ himself and narratives about him recorded by his friends and handed down to later generations. (In this book, all quotations from the Qur'an are given in italics, and Muhammad's ﷺ teachings in normal script.)

Although the hadiths are not part of the Qur'an revelation, nevertheless they are regarded as vitally important for the full understanding of Islam. They often explain matters or give extra information about the matters ordained by Allah. Once, his wife Aishah was asked about the Prophet's ﷺ customs and way of life. She replied: 'His way of life IS the Qur'an.'

The Qur'an is roughly the same length as the New Testament. The teachings of Muhammad ﷺ himself, if all put together, would work out about the size of the *Encyclopedia Britannica*.

THE HADITH COLLECTIONS

The Prophet ﷺ actually disliked the writing down of his teachings,
lest anyone should mistake them for the Qur'anic revelations. The
difference had to be made absolutely clear. The Companion Abu
Sa'id al-Khudri commented that what the Prophet ﷺ particularly
objected to were hadiths being recorded on the same piece of
parchment that had Qur'an on it.

The importance of checking

The Prophet's ﷺ disciples used to make a conscious effort to
memorize his sayings accurately. The Companions used to sit in a
circle to recount hadiths to each other from memory; sometimes as
many as 60 people joined these circles.

The Prophet ﷺ gave a very stern warning to those who might be
tempted to make things up or exaggerate: 'Whoever intentionally
ascribes to me what I have not said, then let him occupy a place in
Hell-fire.' (Bukhari)

The Companions were prepared to go to enormous lengths to check
the hadiths. Jabir once undertook a month-long journey to Syria
to hear a single hadith. Abu Ayyub once travelled to Egypt just to
check the exact words of one hadith, and when he was satisfied set
off home again without even entering the house for refreshment.

By the third century AH there was a vast amount of material in
circulation, and unfortunately it is a well-known fact that by
then many hadiths were pious fabrications. It is on record that
one man was executed for inventing some 4,000! The scholars
developed very strict rules for deciding whether a hadith was

sahih (authentic), *da'if* (weak), or *ma'udu* (doubtful). The chain of transmitters was always carefully examined. Out of tens of thousands scrutinized, only a limited number were selected for the compilations and, of those selected, the scholars could only count on their own judgement, which was not infallible.

> ### Insight
> A chain (*silsilah*) started with the person who had actually heard the Prophet ﷺ state something, and learned it. His transmitter would then say: 'I heard so-and-so say: "I heard the Prophet ﷺ say ..." and so on. These chains may seem cumbersome, but give important information.

The two most important collections of hadiths are those of Imam Muhammad b. Isma'il al-**Bukhari** (d.870 CE), which is regarded as the most authentic (a collection of 7,563 hadiths, covering a vast range of subjects), and **Muslim** b. al-Hajjaj (d.875 CE) containing 7,422 hadiths. It is easier to read than Bukhari's collection because it arranges all the sayings relevant to one issue together. There are four other collections considered authentic – Ibn Majah (d.886 CE), Abu Dawud (d.888 CE), Tirmidhi (d.892 CE) and Nisa'i (d.915 CE), and all hadiths in them are accepted as being genuine by virtually all Muslims.

Imam Malik took 40 years to put together a very early collection known as the Muwatta, representing the 'well-trodden path' unanimously agreed upon by the people of Madinah. The reason it was not included in 'the Six' was simply that it predated much of the methodology developed by the classical hadith scholars.

> ### Insight
> A hadith qudsi is a saying Muhammad ﷺ received from God that was not included in the Qur'an. There is a famous collection of 40 of them.

Weak and suspect hadiths
How can Muslims tell if a hadith is genuine? It is vital to realize that if a hadith is not in keeping with the words or principles of the

Qur'an, it cannot be considered genuine. The Prophet ﷺ said: 'After me many hadiths will be related. Thus, when something is said to be a saying of mine, check it against the Qur'an. If it agrees with the Qur'an accept it, and if it disagrees with the Qur'an, reject it.' (*Kitab al-tawdeeh wat-talweeh*).

Insight

Many favoured hadiths did not get included in the Six Authentic Collections. For example, of Aishah's known 2,210 hadiths, only 316 were selected by Bukhari or Muslim.

Insight

The most trusted traditions of Shi'ite Muslims were transmitted through their Imams, Muhammad's ﷺ descendants via his daughter Fatimah.

IS KEEPING THE SUNNAH COMPULSORY?

The vast majority of Muslims would never go against the teachings of the Prophet ﷺ as recorded in the hadiths; but occasionally reformers wishing to return to the fundamentals, or people wishing to 'update' Islam take the point of view that it is enough to study the Qur'an, and that if Allah had wished a thing to be known or done, He would have certainly included it in the Qur'an and not left it to chance.

The Prophet ﷺ himself was well aware that this would happen, and gave clear warning against it:

I have indeed been given the Qur'an and something similar to it besides it. Yet, the time will come when a man leaning on his couch will say: 'Follow the Qur'an only; what you find in it as halal, take as halal, and what you find in it as haram, take it as haram.' But truly, what the Messenger of Allah has forbidden is like what Allah has forbidden. (Abu Dawud and Darimi)

The Qur'an granted the Prophet ﷺ enormous authority:
Take whatever the Messenger gives you, and keep away from what he forbids you. (Surah 59:7)

The Prophet ﷺ specifically stated:

> **Behold, I have left among you two things; you will never go astray so long as you hold fast to them – the Book of Allah and my sunnah.**[4]

(Hakim)

Fard and sunnah

Many Muslims are so devout that they take all the Prophet's ﷺ *sunnat* (recommendations) as *fard* (compulsory obligations of Islam). However, scholars do make a difference between the two on these grounds: if a fard is missed, then the Muslim has committed a sin for which he or she would be accountable, and if the fard is done, they have done good for which they will be rewarded; but on the other hand, if a Muslim does something sunnah, he or she will be rewarded for it, but there is no punishment if it is omitted. This is a very important difference.

The key teachings of Islam

TAWHID AND SHIRK

There are three basic doctrines about God in Islam: One-ness, Transcendence, and Immanence.

God's Unity or One-ness is known as *tawhid*, 'There is no God but One'. Muslims reason that if God is the First Cause, Creator and Supreme Force in the universe, there can only be One by definition – it is impossible to have two 'supremes' or 'first causes'.

Nothing is remotely like God, and nothing can be compared to Him. Nothing shares His power, and He certainly does not have partners, or any kind of 'family'. The name al-Lah is the name also used for God by Arab Christians. It means 'the Almighty', 'the Supreme'.

---

[4] The Shi'ite version of this saying differs significantly. The two things mentioned are the Book of Allah and the Prophet's ﷺ descendants.

> *He is Allah (the Supreme), the One. Allah is Eternal and
> Absolute. None is born of Him. He is Unborn. There is
> none like unto Him.* (Surah 112)

God is only referred to as 'He' because it is traditional. 'He' has no
gender; this is why Muslims prefer to use the word 'Allah' rather
than 'God', which has a plural (gods) and a female form (goddess).
All the many 'names' of God revealed in the Qur'an are not really
names but reflect qualities or characteristics – for example, *al-Badi*
(the One Who creates out of nothing); *al-Batin* (the One Who
knows the latent and hidden properties of things); *al-Muqit*
(the Controller).

Many times Allah is called *Rabb*, or Lord; but never once in the
entire 23 years of revelations did He call Himself *Abb*, or Father.
This cannot have been accidental. The word 'Father' has human
and sexual connotations, and although Muslims are aware of God
in an intimate and personal way, they think of Him as Creator
rather than Father. To a Muslim, the concept of 'father' has
dangerous implications that can lead into *shirk* (the division of
the unity of God).

Allah, the Supreme knows and sees everything. He is totally 'other'
from His created universe, outside time, eternal, without beginning
or end.

> *No vision can grasp Him, but His grasp is over all vision. He is above
> all comprehension, yet is acquainted with all things.* (Surah 6:103)

He is beyond the limits of the human mind. It is impossible for humans to imagine what He is like, except as He chooses to reveal it. Our senses always present a limited picture of reality; for example, we think we can touch and see solids, but the microscope reveals something completely different. Allah revealed that He is absolute Order, Justice, Mercy, Truth and Love, and many other concepts.

> ### Insight
> The Qur'an does not teach that God does not know us, nor that He remains transcendent and unknowable. Quite the contrary – He is present everywhere, and closer to a human than his/her jugular vein.

As well as being transcendent, God is also immanent (*aqrab* – nearer), closer to us than our innermost thoughts, more bound up with us than our own bloodstream. He is near to every person equally, since He is everywhere, in the sense that there is no place that is without His presence.

He is the Owner of everything; what humans think they own is allotted to them by God's will, a gift, and should be used in order to do His will, and must be given back to God in due course.

THE LOVE AND COMPASSION OF ALLAH

God is not only Creator, He is also Judge, and the eternal fate of every living being lies in His 'hands'. Thankfully, the justice of Allah is not the same as that of human beings, who have incomplete knowledge, or who can be vengeful. God knows every thought and motive, every influence acting upon a person. The nature of Allah, repeated over and over again in the revelation, is Love and Compassion. (*Allah*, *ar-Rahman ar-Rahim*.)

> ### Insight
> The Prophet ﷺ often taught in simple, natural imagery. Allah is more caring of us than a mother bird sheltering her chicks. He mourns our loss more than a cow bewails the calf that

has been taken away. If we remember how we feel when our camel wanders off and leaves us lost in the desert, and what joy fills our hearts when we see it coming in the distance – why, Allah is more joyful to see our return than we would be to see 10 magnificent camels!

His mercy is far greater than any humans have the right to expect, or that they show to each other.

> *If God punished us according to what we deserve, He would leave on earth not one living thing.* (Surah 34:45; 16:61)

> *O My servants, who have transgressed against their own souls! Never despair of God's mercy, for Allah forgives all sins. He is the Compassionate, the Merciful.* (Surah 39:53)

Insight

The Qur'an teaches that God will respond to anyone who cries out to Him in distress, and mercifully provides guidance to humanity so that we can follow the 'straight path'.

Many humans, of course, find this hard to accept, either because they are too proud, or too hard-hearted, or too despairing, or for many other reasons. Nevertheless, Allah assures us of His mercy constantly throughout the Qur'an and hadiths.

> *O child of Adam – so long as you call upon Me and ask of Me I shall forgive you for what you have done ... Were you to come to Me with sins as great as the earth itself, and were you then to face Me, ascribing no partner to Me, I would forgive you in equal measure.* (Hadith Qudsi, Tirmidhi, Ahmad)

Similarly, Muslims are expected to forgive those who sin against them, to treat them with gentleness and 'cover' their faults (Surah 3:159).

THE UNSEEN

The universe consists of that which is seen and understood by our five senses, and that which is unseen (known as *al-Ghayb*). What we see and understand is only the tip of the iceberg in the vastness of God's creation. The two most important non-physical created entities are angels and *jinn*.

Angels are the agents and servants of God, the means by which He governs the universe and the channels by which humans become aware of Him. They do not have free-will, but carry out God's wishes. They are sometimes seen by people in times of crisis; many sensitive people feel aware of their presence when they pray and meditate. They may take any shape or form.

Each human is assigned two special angels as guardians and 'recorders'; they activate a person's conscience, so that the human is aware they are about to make a right or wrong choice, and they note down every response, every good and evil deed, in each person's 'book', the record which they will see and understand, and on which they will be judged on the Day. All good deeds are recorded for ever, but if a person repents, the record of the evil deed is wiped out.

> **Surely those who say 'our Lord is Allah' and who follow the straight path, the angels descend upon them saying: 'Fear not and do not be sad ... we are your protecting friends in this life and in the next.'**
> (Surah 41:30–1)

Insight

Our 'record books' are not kept in order to give information to God upon which He may judge us – He already has full knowledge of everything, our circumstances, character, motivation, tendencies, etc. It is to justify the resulting decision to us – and show us the consequences of everything we did.

A few angels are named and have specific roles: Jibril (Gabriel) brings messages to the chosen ones, and is frequently referred to as the 'holy spirit' in the Qur'an; Mika'il (Michael), is the protector of holy places and life-sustainer in times of trouble; Azra'il takes away the souls of the dying; Israfil is the angel who calls the souls on Judgement Day; Munkar and Nakir are the questioners; Malik, the keeper of Hell; Ridwan, the keeper of Paradise.

Jinn are also non-physical beings, and they can be either good or evil, having free-will like humans. They are thought to inhabit unclean places, and can often frighten and confuse human beings by involving themselves in their lives and homes. Occasionally they attempt to possess human bodies and have to be exorcized. They are not always malevolent, however, and Surah 72 mentions jinn that were converted to Islam.

The Devil (*Shaytan* or *Iblis*) is not a fallen angel in Islamic tradition, but the chief of the jinn. He became the origin of evil through pride, disobedience and rebellion when he refused God's command to honour the newly created humans because he thought he knew better than God. Out of jealousy, he became the enemy of all humans, determined to lead people's hearts and minds away from God. (See Surah 15:28–31; see also 2:36; 3:36; 4:117–120; 5:94; 7:200–1; 8:48; 15:17, 34; 16:98–100; 22:52–3; 24:21; 35:6; 36:60.) Evil is never equal to Good.

Huris

Another order of beings mentioned in the Qur'an are the *huris*, or 'pure companions' of Paradise. These are not our loved ones made young again, nor a supply of virgins to gratify the lusts of the deceased, but 'spirit beings' who know us as our soul-forms, who both miss us when we live on earth, and welcome us when we return to our eternal abode. (Surah 56:22)

So far as we know, human beings are the highest physical creations of Allah, and possess both material and spiritual characteristics. Each being has a distinct individual soul (the *rouh*). It is the soul, and not the body the soul lives in, that is the real person.

Every human being consists of 'earth' – that is, material stuff that is constantly coming into being, 'dying' and being replenished – in order to be the temporary 'body' of an individual soul. Keeping this body alive requires continual interaction with the environment (through breathing and eating, for example), and when the soul departs, all the constituent parts of each body become separate again, disintegrate and are recycled by the 'earth'.

Insight

Four mysteries of the unknown are the origin of matter itself, the origin of life, the origin of sexual difference (since simple cells merely divide and are identical), and the origin of death.

Adam and Eve, or evolution?

Muslims believe that human beings are all descended from an original soul created by God and then divided into male and female (Surah 4.1). As regards the theory of evolution, it is as yet unproven and remains no more than a theory, for which there is debatable evidence; apes were created in their own image, and still exist as apes, and so on. Many Muslims accept the notion of 'intelligent' or 'guided evolution', but believe that all scientific theories should be studied with an open mind, since today's 'facts' are often quickly out of date with new discoveries.

It is usually accepted that the first created humans were Adam ﷺ and Eve. The Qur'an does indeed state that Adam ﷺ was created without parents, from 'clay', which may symbolize that human beings are made of or dependent upon humus. The tradition about the woman being created from Adam's ﷺ rib is not part of the Qur'an; the Prophet ﷺ referred to it with some humour when counselling male Companions not to try straightening them, as they would snap.

The Qur'an also states that Allah chose a human, Adam, ﷺ and called him to be His *khalifah* or deputy on Earth, responsible for the care of the planet (Surah 2:30–2). Humans have an allotted time-span of life on earth, over which they have no control. They are created with equal rights and are equally loved by God, but do not have equal talents or characteristics. Because they exercise free-will they can love and be kind, or hate and be destructive. Their worth in Islam is not measured in intelligence or status, but in submission to God and right living.

Insight

Muslims regard Adam ﷺ as the first prophet. Perhaps he represents (or was) the first morally conscious human being; having been made aware of the existence and presence of God set him apart as vastly different from any humanoid animals that preceded him.

TESTS

Life is not seen as random with no point, but as a period of training and testing for the life to come. We are allotted circumstances, talents, and so forth, and are tested in the use we make of them.

We shall certainly test you with fear and hunger and with the loss of goods or lives or the fruits of your toil. But give encouragement to those who patiently persevere, and, when calamity befalls them, say: 'We belong to Allah, and to Him do we return.'

(Surah 2:155–6)

Some are tested with poverty or ill health – will they become despairing and dishonest, or show patience and faith? Others are tested by being rich – what use will they make of their riches? Will they become selfish and greedy, or act with responsibility? It is pointless to bewail one's lot – all situations can be reversed in a second if God wills; the Muslims' duties are to accept, remain firm, patient and faithful, and seek to do God's will in whatever circumstances they find themselves.

If the Muslim's duty is to serve God and do His will, it is God's duty to explain clearly what that will is, otherwise the individual cannot be held responsible for their choices (Surah 17:15). *Risalah* is the channel of communication from Allah. A prophet who merely taught and did not leave writings is a *nabi*, and one who left writings is a *rasul*.

The chain of prophecy

Before the Blessed Muhammad ﷺ there was a whole chain of prophets, including the 26 named in the Qur'an, that were sent to people of all times and races with messages suitable to those who heard them. These include 23 celebrities known from the Bible; Noah (Nuh), Abraham (Ibrahim), Moses (Musa), John the Baptist (Yahya ibn Zakriyah), Jesus ('Isa), and many others. Only three are not named in the Bible – Hud, Salih and Shu'aib – though this last is believed to be the same as Jethro, Moses's father-in-law (may peace be upon all of them). The great leaders of other monotheistic faiths may have been among the thousands of unnamed prophets.

Holy books mentioned in the Qur'an

Four Divinely Revealed books are mentioned in the Qur'an: the *Sahifa* or scrolls dictated to Abraham, the *Tawrat* (or Torah) revealed to Moses ﷺ, the *Zabur* (or Psalms) of David ﷺ, and the *Injil* (or Gospel) revealed to Jesus ﷺ. The first is completely lost, and Muslims believe that the others are not to be identified with the contents of today's Bible, which are compilations and editions written many years after the prophets lived.

Insight

The contents of the 66 books in the Bible were all written by humans, perhaps utilizing ancient documents and selecting various passages (i.e. human choice from the available sources), edited many times by people with differing motives, and so on. Perhaps the nearest we get to the original prophetic message is where the actual words: 'Thus says the Lord' are given.

WAS MUHAMMAD THE GREATEST PROPHET?

It is considered inappropriate to try to guess who were the best prophets, or to elevate any messenger above the human status.

Say: 'We believe in God and that which has been revealed to us, and (also) that which was revealed to Abraham (Ibrahim), Ismail (Isma'il), Isaac (Yizhaq), Jacob (Yaqub) and the tribes, and in that given to Moses (Musa), Jesus ('Isa), and (all) the prophets from their Lord. We make no distinction between any of them, and to God do we submit our will.'
(Surah 3:84)

All the prophets were messengers from the One and the same God, a single 'chain' or prophecy, and all are to be respected and believed. Jesus ﷺ was the most famous as a miracle worker; Muhammad ﷺ is regarded as the 'seal' of the prophets, and the last messenger. Although many other great teachers have inspired the world throughout history since then, there have been no further prophets in the chain bringing direct revelation from God. Muhammad ﷺ said:

My relationship to the other prophets before me is that of a man who has expertly and beautifully built a house, except for the placement of one brick in the corner. People pass by and wonder at its beauty, but say: 'Would that this final brick be put in its place!' I am that brick, and I am the last of the prophets.
(Bukhari 4.735)

JESUS ﷺ

Jesus ﷺ is regarded by Muslims as one of the greatest of all prophets, the miracle worker. It is always made very clear in the Qur'an that he was not to be thought of as Divine, a Son of God, in the Christian sense. Muslims believe in his virgin birth, but that this was a miracle of God in creating a child without a father, not that it made the miraculous child in any way a part of God.

Insight

Muslims do not refer to themselves as 'sons' or 'children' of God, as in the Lord's Prayer ('Our Father, who art in
(Contd)

Heaven'); rather, they believe we are all the servants of
God. Jesus ﷺ and Muhammad ﷺ were two of the very best
examples of servants of God – and both were bin Adam ﷺ
(i.e. A son of Man, not of God).

Muslims believe Jesus ﷺ was the Messiah (Ar. *Masih*), the
messenger to the tribes of Israel. The vast majority of his recorded
teachings would be accepted as Islamic (especially such well-known
passages as the Sermon on the Mount, the Lord's Prayer, the
parables of the Prodigal Son, the Sheep and the Goats, etc.), which
teach clearly that God always forgives the genuine penitent, and
that we will be judged on the efforts and actions of our lives,
a judgement tempered by Allah's grace and mercy.

Basically, Muslims believe what Jesus ﷺ taught but not the later
doctrines taught about him. They can never accept the Church
Creeds formulated around a Trinitarian theology during the three
to four centuries after Jesus' lifetime. Throughout the Qur'an there
are verses reminding Muslims that to believe that God has partners
or a family is *shirk* and a fundamental misunderstanding of the
nature of God.

Insight

If Jesus ﷺ did say 'No man comes to the Father but by me'
(John 14.6), this may have been true in his lifetime, when
he taught people to believe in God and in 'him who He had
sent'. But this does not mean that six centuries later, after
doctrinal aberrations, God could not send another messenger.

Jesus the saviour?

The Qur'an indicates that Jesus ﷺ was not overcome by death, and
this is taken to mean either that God rescued him from crucifixion,
or that he physically survived the crucifixion, and then ascended
alive into Heaven (Surah 4:157). Another possible interpretation
was that by God's will, death could not kill him. Christian theories
in the centuries before Islam included Docetism (that Jesus ﷺ was
never fully human), or that God somehow substituted another to

die in his place (for example, Simon of Cyrene, Judas Iscariot). These theories also exist in Muslim folklore, but not in the Qur'an.

Jesus' ﷺ function can never be seen by a Muslim as a redeemer or saviour, except in the sense that those who follow his teachings will be 'saved'. He cannot be a sacrifice to save people from their sins – for every person will be judged as an individual, and no one will bear the sins of another. He was a messenger of God and his life was dedicated to showing the way to God. Islam teaches that Jesus ﷺ the masih will return before the end of the world and the Day of Judgement.

If Jesus ﷺ ever did say 'No man can come to the Father but by me' (John 14.6), this is balanced by the Islamic teaching: 'No one can come to Me unless the Father who sent Me draws him.' (John 6.44).

Insight

In two of his most famous parables, Jesus ﷺ taught that the son who had gone wrong was forgiven unconditionally when he returned repentant, and that we will be divided into 'sheep' and 'goats' by the Divine Farmer according to how we lived and behaved in our Earthly lives.

AKHIRAH – LIFE AFTER DEATH

Muslims believe that the human soul lives only once on Earth, and after death faces a Day of Judgement, and an eventual fate in either Paradise or Hell (*Jannam* and *Jahannam*).

After death the body is buried, but the soul of the good person may experience expanded horizons without limit, while the bad person is cramped in the grave. On the Day, God will resurrect all people, and may choose to recreate their decomposed bodies, down to the details of their individual fingerprints (Surah 45:24; 75:1–4). None will escape this, if God wills, no matter how they died or what happened to their bodies.

Heaven and Hell are frequently described in graphic physical terms; Heaven, or Paradise, being like a beautiful garden, where people become young again and enjoy untainted pleasures, and Hell being a terrible, scorching place of torment, sorrow and remorse. Although many Muslims take the descriptions literally, there are also clues in the Qur'an that they should rather be considered symbolically, since Heaven and Hell are not physical dimensions at all, and our future state lies beyond the scope of our limited human knowledge.

> *In Heaven, I prepare for the righteous believers what no eye has ever seen, no ear has ever heard, and what the deepest mind could never imagine.* (Hadith Qudsi, and Surah 32:17)

> *We will not be prevented from changing your forms and creating you again in forms you know not.* (Surah 56:60–1)

Islam teaches that God does not wish to send anyone to Hell, and they will only be obliged to go there if they insist on evil living without repentance, and treating the truth of God as a lie.

Some Muslims even interpret Hell as being rather like a hospital, where the cure may be painful and drastic, but in the end the patient is made whole. Most accept that the state will be eternal.

> *Their status in Heaven or Hell may last for eternity – but this is subject to God's will and mercy.* (Surah 11:106–8)

Insight

Muslims do not believe in reincarnation (souls living a series of lives in different bodies), but no person may suggest a limit for what God might choose to do. The notion of reincarnation is rejected as there is no textual evidence for it in the Qur'an or hadiths.

AL-QADR – PRE-DESTINATION

Muslims believe that the entire universe is under God's control and direction, therefore nothing can take place without His ordaining it. There cannot be such a thing as a random or chance event (see Surah 35:2; 57:22). Muslims accept that things happen according to our destinies; one often hears the phrase 'It is written' (Ar. *maktub*).

Everything is known (even the number of hairs on your head or how many breaths you will take in your life), and everything that happens is an expression of His will, and has purpose and meaning. God alone is the source of benefit or harm, and to turn to anything else for protection or help is futile.

This idea of pre-destination is notoriously difficult to reconcile with the concept of free-will, but Islam should not be considered a fatalistic religion. The whole point of sending messengers from God to give revelations is to allow humans to use their free-will; the whole point of human life is a test, which would be totally pointless if God had pre-destined human choices.

Indeed Allah declared He would not alter the condition of humans until they changed what was in themselves. (Surah 13:11; 8:53)

Early sectarian disputes included the question of whether sinning believers would have eternal punishment in Hell? The Kharijites deemed a sinner to have become an unbeliever and therefore would be condemned to Hell; the Murjites accepted that all humans are weak (which Allah knows) and therefore even though sinful, if they believe they are still Muslims and will not go to Hell. Mu'tazilis took the middle ground that God's justice demanded that sinful Muslims were destined for punishment, but that they occupied a 'middle ground' – they could be prayed for and forgiven, if God willed.

Fatalism renders people helpless and weakens their sense of responsibility, a criticism frequently made of Muslims who misunderstand the importance of revelation and free-will.

The doctrine of Divine Justice ('adl) suggests that the inequalities in human fortunes and the calamities that befall people are an integral part of the test of life. The powerful, rich and healthy will be questioned about their responses to the blessings and bounties they enjoyed, and whether they used them in order to alleviate the sufferings of others; and the less fortunate will be questioned on their response to their sufferings and whether they maintained faith and patience, having been given the knowledge that there would be absolutely just recompense to come.

Although everything in the universe is governed by natural law, human beings are not governed in the same way that the Sun and Moon are, for example. We are warned that we are under Law, and the breach of Law brings penalty. This applies on both the physical and moral levels; if we do not wish to be burned, we must keep our hands out of the fire. It makes no difference whether or not we knew in advance that fire would burn.

Muslims accept that every breath we take is a gift from God, and He alone knows how many breaths he has allotted to us. Can a person cheat God's will and die at a time other than the one allotted? Muslims accept there is a difference between dying (which happens when God wills) and killing – which is governed by human free-will and natural law (see pages 278–9).

10 THINGS TO REMEMBER

1 *The Qur'an was revealed verse by verse over 22 years, and recorded on bits of pot, bone and stone, and in the memories of Muslim 'learners'.*

2 *Muslims always treat Qur'ans with respect as regards their storage and disposal when fragile with age, and as regards behaviour in their presence.*

3 *It is vital to preserve the original text in Arabic, as translations are always only as good as the skill of the translators.*

4 *The recorded sayings of the Prophet ﷺ (the hadiths) are kept scrupulously separate from the Qur'an.*

5 *The* hadiths *all involve the individual memories, interests, opportunities and interpretations of the recorders and transmitters, and are not always reliable.*

6 *The basic rule for judging if a* hadith's *teaching is genuine is whether or not it is compatible with the words and/or spirit of the Qur'an.*

7 *The three basic theological concepts in Islam are* tawhid *(One-ness),* akhirah *(Life after Death) and* risalah *(Prophecy, or Revelation from God).*

8 *God (al-Lah, the Almighty or Supreme) is the One, the Alone, the First Cause, the Creator and Sustainer of the universes.*

9 *Humans can only know and understand a fraction of what is – there are realms beyond human comprehension, known collectively as* al-Ghayb *(the hidden).*

10 *Muhammad's ﷺ special status lies in his being the last of the prophets, the seal of all that was revealed before. His function was to transmit God's exact words, to be preserved for ever.*

3

Islamic worship

In this chapter you will learn about:
- *worship and prayer*
- *the importance of helping others and fasting*
- *Hajj – pilgrimage to Makkah*
- *jihad*
- *festivals and special days.*

Worship – ibadah

Ibadah comes from the word '*abad*', meaning a slave or servant. Ibadah is therefore service of Allah, or slavery to Him. Basically, it is what Muslims mean by 'worship'. However, for Muslims, worship is not something confined to special days or particular prayers, but a conscious awareness of God throughout the day, every day, and a conscious desire to carry out His will in every sphere of activity.

THE CONCEPTS OF WORSHIP

Ihsan
Muslim worship really begins with the concept of *ihsan* or realization. It is perfectly possible for a human being to go through all sorts of forms of worship, prayer and other ritual without really

being truly aware of the presence of God. Human nature being what it is, this rather barren worship can happen to anybody from time to time. However, ihsan implies that a person really is making a conscious effort to be 'in communication' with God.

Insight

If we pray with ihsan, it means that we are conscious that Someone is actually hearing us. We do not need to give God information, but should listen and try to deduce what He wishes us to do in any situation.

There is a very famous hadith recorded by Caliph Umar that describes ihsan. One day the Prophet ﷺ was approached by a traveller in very white clothing, who sat down with him knee to knee, and asked him to tell him about Islam. This traveller was the

Figure 3.1 'In communication with God' – this Muslim girl wears a prayer veil.

angel Jibril, the very one who had revealed the messages of the Qur'an to the Prophet ﷺ. One of the direct questions he asked was for a definition of ihsan. The Prophet ﷺ replied that it meant you should worship God as though you could see Him, for He sees you even though you do not see Him.

Awareness of God (also known as *taqwa* or God-consciousness) leads to deepened consciousness of the importance and meaningfulness of the gift of human life, and the desire to make the very best of it while one has the chance. Awareness of God creates a shield against wrong-doing. Sometimes it is translated as 'fear of God' – but those who are aware of God serve Him from love, not out of fear. The phrase 'Guard (or protect) yourself from Allah' should rather be 'Take Allah as your Protector (or Guardian)'.

Insight

Taqwa involves being sensible, cautious and wary. If you are walking through sharp thorns, take precautions and be careful not to get pricked or get your clothes torn. To be a 'God-fearing' person means being reverent towards God, respectful and humble because of His great love and generous goodness, rather than being afraid.

Iman

The word *iman* means 'faith'. When the same traveller (Jibril) asked the Prophet ﷺ to define iman, he replied that it was to believe in God, His angels, His books, His prophets, and the Last Day and the decreeing of both good and evil. We have already considered the implications of iman in previous sections.

Amal

Amal means 'action'. Muslims see no point in academic beliefs or doctrines unless they are translated into action. The whole point of Islam is to submit to Allah and direct your life into carrying out His will to the utmost of your ability.

The concept of amal can actually be divided into two categories. The first is to obey the commands of Allah, as in the practice of the five disciplines known as the 'Five Pillars', which will be described shortly. The second is to do one's best in every aspect of daily life and routine to follow the *sunnah* or practice of the Prophet ﷺ, or at least the principles behind the sunnah (if one is dealing with some aspect of modern society that was beyond the personal experience of the Prophet ﷺ) so that every single thing one does is for the greater glory of God. That way, the Muslim believes he or she will keep on the right path, and will find peace, satisfaction, justice and happiness.

Insight
Amal is a sense of social responsibility growing from our religious convictions. The Prophet ﷺ taught that someone who saw a hungry person and did not feed him, was not 'one of us'.

Din (pr. *Deen*)
Putting faith and way of life together is known as the *din*, the total desire to commit to Islam.

Jihad
Jihad is often thought to mean military activity, and obviously it can have a military context, but this is not the true meaning of the word. The definition of jihad according to Qur'an and sunnah is a struggle or an effort that is exerted in order to attain some end or result, any kind of striving which involves either spiritual or personal effort, material resources, or lastly, military means.

A jihad or struggle in the cause of Allah (*fi sabi'l illah*) involves an unceasing effort to eliminate evil in the form of wrong beliefs, ideas, and values that are projected via thoughts, words and deeds – things like racism, abuse, selfishness, laziness, miserliness, aggression and oppression. It could also be a personal struggle involving some form of hard work or effort to accomplish something of value for Allah's sake – such as studying, teaching others, caring for others in trying circumstances, facing up to bullying, even trying to eliminate some harmful personal habit, such as smoking or obesity. (For more details, see later in this chapter.)

Insight

Islam consists of these five core subjects – iman (faith), amal (Islamic action), ummah (sense of community), adl (justice) and jihad (struggle).

THE GREATER JIHAD

The true jihad is the battle against what Muslims call *dunya* (literally 'the lusts and degradations of worldliness'). The jihad against selfishness, ignorance and corruption is the 'inner' or 'major' jihad (*jihad al-akhbar*) because all evil arises from the desire of the *nafs* or human soul to put self before Allah. Ignorance, arrogance and lack of compassion lie at the root of all evil, are the causes of all corruption, and the sources of all suffering. The opposite of ignorance is knowledge (*ilm*) that gives rise to wisdom (*hiqmah*). This jihad is therefore an act of devotion with the same significance as the Five Pillars of Islam, so much so that it is often called the Sixth Pillar. 'Striving after (the jihad for) knowledge,' said the Prophet ﷺ, 'is the sacred duty of every man and woman' (Ibn Majah).

Insight

The struggle for justice can be fought on many fronts or levels – political, economic, educational, intellectual and social.

While the sacrifice of struggle of jihad 'with the sword' is a great act when it comes to defending Islamic lives and values, or in protecting the innocent and defenceless from unjustified aggression, the jihad 'with the word' (*dawah*) to spread the teachings and values of Islam to the ignorant is far greater. It was the first command to the Prophet ﷺ, (i.e. the command '*Iqra*!' meaning 'recite' or 'tell them') and many verses of the Qur'an start with the word '*Qol*' – 'speak' or 'say to them'. The Prophet ﷺ faithfully obeyed this charge laid upon him until his life's end, transforming people into a devout and virtuous community.

Dunya

Dunya (literally, 'the world'), as creation of God, is not in itself an evil thing or place, but there are certain aspects of material existence which are directly opposed to God's will.

The Prophet ﷺ said:

> **It is not poverty which I fear for you, but that you might begin to desire the world as others before you desired it, and it might destroy you as it destroyed them.** (Bukhari and Muslim)

The most basic wrong thing is obsession with self. The self is a creation of Allah, and something to be loved, cherished, cared for and respected. But when a person becomes selfish then they are putting their own base greeds and desires before right living, and love of self has become a form of *shirk*. People who are selfish are worshipping themselves rather than God; they are certainly putting themselves before their duties towards God, which are generally expressed in our love and concern towards others, whether people or animals.

Thus, dunya represents the lure of the world's luxuries and lusts that lead people away from the right way and influence them to become miserly, greedy, cruel, cowardly, arrogant, callous and so on. Jihad is the fight against this tendency.

> *The life of the world is but a past-time and a game. Lo! Real life is the Home of the Hereafter, if you but knew it.* (Surah 29:64)

The Prophet ﷺ taught:

> **Riches are sweet, and a source of blessing to those who acquire them by the way; but those who seek them out of greed are like people who eat but are never full.** (Bukhari)

> **Richness does not lie in an abundance of worldly goods, but true richness is the richness of the soul.** (Muslim)

Ummah

The Prophet ﷺ was told by Allah as part of His revelation to say:

O humanity! I am the messenger of God to you all!   (Surah 7:158)

Believers are one single community (ummah), so make peace and reconciliation between two contenders, and have reverence for Allah, that you may receive mercy.   (Surah 49:10)

The faith of Islam is a universal faith, intended for all people. The worldwide community of Muslims is known as the *ummah*. It extends across all places and ethnic groupings. Believers belong to local ummahs, or Muslim communities, but the entire worldwide Muslim community follows the same faith, shares the same basic values, and has sworn allegiance to the will of Allah and obedience to the Prophet ﷺ. When Muslims travel around the world, they find they can mix very easily with other Muslims, even if they do not understand their language.

Insight

An ummah can be small – just one or two people – or it can be as large as a whole society. It can be local, national or global. Its foremost purpose is to advocate justice, and bring about change where injustices abound.

Ibadah

Declare your jihad on thirteen enemies you cannot see – egoism, arrogance, conceit, selfishness, greed, lust, intolerance, anger, lying, cheating, gossiping and slandering. If you can master and destroy them, then you will be ready to fight the enemy you can see.   (al-Ghazzali – note: the thirteenth 'enemy' is not listed)

Taking all these concepts together, ihsan, iman, amal and jihad make up the Muslim concept of *ibadah*; worship of Allah. This is why Islam is not just a matter of ritual, prayers or fasting or feasts; it is the conscious bringing of every moment of the day, every decision, every detail of one's thoughts and actions, into deliberate line with what one accepts as being the will of Allah.

Bearing witness and prayer

The faith and practice of Islam is often said to rest upon five pillars: bearing witness, prayer, fasting, charity and pilgrimage (shahadah, salah, sawm, zakah and Hajj).

SHAHADAH – BEARING WITNESS

Shahadah is belief in the heart and bearing witness to the faith. It is a simple statement of creed that falls into two parts: that there is no God but Allah (the Almighty, Supreme, the One), and that Muhammad ﷺ is His genuine messenger. It comes from the word '*ash-shadu*' which means 'I declare' or 'I bear witness'.

In Arabic, the words are:

Ash-shadu an la ilaha illallah wa Muhammadar-rasulullah.

When people make this declaration and truly believe it in their hearts, then they have entered the faith. There is no ceremony like a Christian baptism; what counts is the conscious awareness and firm conviction that one genuinely does hold these two beliefs.

Insight

Although not a necessity, it sometimes saves a lot of hassle when visiting Muslim countries, or seeking entrance to certain mosques and shrines, if the new Muslim is given a 'certificate of conversion' from the mosque.

Sometimes a new Muslim will talk things over with an *imam* (teacher), or have a course of study sessions; once the new Muslim takes the decision to become Muslim (or realizes that he or she is Muslim), they should declare the faith publicly, in front of two witnesses. From that moment of public witness, they have started on the path of submission to God. Some new Muslims, particularly white ones, like to have a certificate for occasions when proof might be needed. However, shahadah is not just a matter of reciting words; it is something that has to be believed with all one's heart, because following this declaration Muslims are intended to trust God completely, and hand over their lives to His service.

Insight

Converts to Islam often refer to themselves as reverts, from the feeling that this is what they have always believed in their hearts, and they have 'come home' after perhaps years of wandering. Tears, and the feeling that a great burden has been shed, are not uncommon.

Making this decision can cause some pretty drastic changes. It involves far more than words; your whole life must back up what has been declared. Most people coming into Islam in the Western world have to change a great deal of their diet and lifestyle; they have to give up pork products, any animal products that are not *halal* (permitted), alcohol, entertainment based on the social giving of alcohol, immodest dress, and so forth. They also have to give up arrogance, selfishness, deceitfulness, lust and indecency and many other weaknesses of character.

The call to prayer

The shahadah is also used for the call to prayer five times per day. If the mosque has a tower, a man known as the *mu'adhin* (or *muezzin*) climbs up and calls aloud:

> *Allahu Akbar!* (four times)
> *Ash-hadu an la ilaha illallah* (twice)
> *Ash-hadu ana Muhammadar-rasulullah* (twice)
> *Hayya ala-salah* (twice)
> *Hayya ala-falah* (twice)
> *Allahu Akbar* (twice)
> *La ilaha illallah.* (once)

Insight

The freed Abyssinian slave Bilal was the first mu'adhin. His voice had such a hypnotic ethereal quality that people stopped in their tracks to listen. The most sublime call I have heard was in Regent's Park Mosque, London, given by the converted pop star Cat Stevens, who became Yusuf Islam.

In English, these words mean:

> **God is the Most Great!**
> **I bear witness that there is no God but Allah.**
> **I bear witness that Muhammad is the Prophet of Allah.**
> **Come to prayer!**
> **Come to success (or salvation)!**
> **God is the Most Great!**
> **There is no God but Allah!**

At the end of the first prayer of the day the phrase 'It is better to pray than to sleep!' is added – '*as-salatul khairum min an-naum*'.

This call to prayer is known as the *adhan*, and it gives Muslims time to get ready if they are going to attend at the mosque. Just before the actual start of the prayers, a second call to prayer is uttered before the congregation, known as the *iqamah*. It is the same as the adhan, except that the words '*qad qamatis salah*' – 'The prayer has begun' – are added before the final *Allahu Akbars*.

Other times that the shahadah is pronounced are at the birth of a new baby, first thing on waking and last thing before going to sleep at night and, if possible, they are the last words in the hearing of a dying person.

SALAH – PRAYER

> **O you who believe! Be steadfast in prayer and regular in**
> **charity, and whatever good you send forth for your souls**
> **before you, you shall find it with God; for truly God sees all**
> **that you do.** (Surah 2:110)

Prayer is the second pillar of Islam. Prayer in general terms means being conscious of God and communicating with Him in some way or another, and Muslims try to maintain an attitude of prayer and be constantly aware of God throughout the day. However, the prayer ritual of *salah* is somewhat different from the casual making of appeals to God of a personal nature. It is perhaps better translated in English as 'worship' rather than 'prayer'.

Salah is a ritual of movements and words (each full sequence of which is called a *rakah*), some of the words repeated as part of the regular routine, and others chosen from the Qur'an by the Muslim as he or she wishes. This prayer is one of the five duties laid down as *fard*, or 'compulsory', for a Muslim. Allah requires those who submit to carry out this prayer five times per day, at certain set times.

Prayer times

The five daily prayers are now known as *fajr* (the morning prayer between dawn and sunrise), *zuhr* (just after the height of the midday Sun), *asr* (during the afternoon when the shadows have lengthened), *maghrib* (just after sunset), and *isha* (during the hours of darkness).

Insight

Fajr commences with the first break of the light, long before sunrise. One way of telling the time is to listen for the birds – their waking praises often commence with a single blackbird or thrush, and within moments the air is reverberating as they sing their hearts out – the dawn chorus.

The prayer times deliberately avoid the exact times delineated by sunrise, midday and sunset because of their pagan connotations of Sun worship. At those exact times, Muslims are actually ordered not to pray. However, the times are obviously related to the Sun's progress through the day, and since times of sunrise and sunset change according to the seasons and the country in which one lives, these days Muslims usually have timetables for each region showing the exact moments when the prayer times begin and end. (In the United Kingdom sunrise comes very early in summer months; Muslims are allowed to go back to bed after they have performed their fajr prayer.)

Since many Muslims go to the mosque to pray together, they also have timetables for congregational prayer, for obvious practical reasons. Many mosques set up clock faces showing these times, five for the daily prayers and one for the special Friday prayer.

Muslims regard it as preferable that men meet together in congregation to pray, but women are generally encouraged to pray in the home. However, there should be nothing to prevent women coming to congregation if they so wish, and it is not compulsory for men to attend every single prayer in the mosque if they prefer to pray elsewhere.

Figure 3.2 Young men praying together.

Salat al-jama'ah

Only one congregational prayer in the mosque is regarded as compulsory, the midday prayer on Fridays – *salat al-jama'ah* – also known as *salat al-jumah*. The word '*jama'ah*' means 'congregation' or 'gathering', and the word '*jumah*' simply means Friday. All adult male Muslims are expected to attend, and are thought to have left Islam if they do not attend for more than three weeks. In Islamic countries all shops and businesses close during this time, so that men can go.

> *O believers, when proclamation is made for prayer on the Day of Congregation, hasten to God's remembrance and leave business aside; that is better for you, did you but know.* (Surah 62:9)

Even Muslim men who are negligent about the other daily prayers make an effort to gather at the mosque on Fridays. During the special service, the key features are the two *khutbahs* or sermons given by the imam. The Congregational Prayer itself consists of only two *rakat*. After this, people can pray individually, and then go back to work. Having allowances made for Friday prayer is one of the difficulties confronting workers and students in non-Muslim countries where Friday is not a day off.

It is sometimes possible to make up a congregation in the workplace or school, but Muslims always consider it preferable to meet together in the full congregation at the mosque, wherever possible.

Individual devotion, not priests

In the age-old conflict between 'priestly' religion and personalized and accountable faith, Islam comes down solidly behind the latter. Historically, organized religion always seems to have been a battle between those who claim that only special priestly figures, with special knowledge of how to perform the ritual and carry out sacrifices accurately, are effective, and those who claim that such formalism is meaningless before a God who requires personal morality and devotion. (Some people in the Christian faith would no doubt see the historical conflict between the 'Romanism' of Roman Catholics and the 'Protest' of Protestants in the same terms.)

For many simple folk in pre-Islamic times, worship had become little more than a vast system of sacrifice, the value of which depended not so much upon the moral conduct of the individual worshipper as on the qualification of the officiating priest. Priests monopolized the number, length and terminology of prayers, the liturgies and dogma, and were largely responsible (even if unintentionally) for the notion that an individual could turn up to a congregation once a week to make up for the spiritual and moral deficiencies of the other six days.

There are no priests in Islam. No monopoly of spiritual knowledge or special holiness intervenes between believer and God. No sacrifice or ceremonial is needed to bring the anxious heart nearer to the Comforter. Each Muslim is his or her own priest, no individual being denied the possibility of drawing near to God through his or her own faith. Islam recognizes the dignity and responsibility of every individual human soul; each person faces God on a one-to-one basis, in worship which is a most heartfelt outpouring of devotion and humility before God.

Insight

Muslims do not feel the need for an intermediary like a priest, and have no sacraments. Any male who can recite some Qur'an may lead the prayers, his function being to keep everyone in unison.

The practice of the Prophet ﷺ has, however, attached certain rites and ceremonies to Muslim prayer, and this is the most obvious aspect of it to an observer; it should be pointed out in unmistakable terms that it is to the devotional state of the mind that the Searcher of the spirit looks. Prayer without the presence of the heart is to no avail; devotion without understanding is a useless empty formalism and brings no blessing. Mere external or physical purity does not imply true devotion, but rather a sense of pride and religious hypocrisy. It is purity of heart and mind, and humility of spirit that bring an individual close to God.

Imams

The person who stands before the congregation leading the prayer is not in any sense a priest, but simply a person who has volunteered to lead, someone who is respected, has good knowledge of Muslim faith, and who knows enough of the Qur'an to recite during the prayer. Most mosques have a regular *imam* these days, but this is not a compulsory requirement, and any

Muslim may lead the prayer in his absence, or when the prayer is being carried out elsewhere, for example, in the home.

If men and women are praying together, the leader is always a man; it could even be a very young man – there are *hadith* showing how a seven-year-old boy led prayers during the Prophet's ﷺ lifetime.

Insight

Salamah b. Qays had learned verses of Qur'an from passing camel drivers, and was the most knowledgeable in Islam of his newly converted tribe. When he led the prayer for the first time his tunic was so short his congregation nearly saw more of him than they wished – so his aunt made him a new one. He commented that nothing ever made him more proud than that garment. He kept it – and retained his post as imam – for the rest of his life.

If women are praying together, one of the women leads from the middle of the row, and is in effect a female imam (see Female imams page 368). A male imam stands just in front of the other worshippers, who form lines behind. If there are only two worshippers, the imam stands on the left with the other worshipper on the right-hand side, just a few inches back.

The purpose of prayer

Muslim prayer is intended to purify the heart and bring about spiritual and moral growth. The aims are to bring people close to Allah; to bring a sense of peace and tranquillity; to encourage equality, unity and brotherhood; to develop gratitude and humility; to demonstrate obedience; to train in cleanliness, purity and punctuality; to develop discipline and will-power; to draw the mind away from personal worries, calm down passions, and master the baser instincts.

Preparation for prayer

NIYYAH

The first part of prayer is *niyyah* or intention. By closing the mind to all worldly distractions (whether pleasant or unpleasant ones), the worshipper begins to make ready for prayer. Although prayer can be said at any time in any place, the Muslim prepares for *salah* by making his or her own body physically clean, and by selecting a clean place in which to pray, if possible. If one prays in the desert or by the roadside, one is not able to dictate conditions, but in Muslim countries there are usually little areas marked out and set aside for prayer and kept in a clean condition. In the home, or at the mosque, prayer is usually said on a carpet. It may be an individual prayer mat or, at the mosque, the floor is usually carpeted or covered with rush-matting, with lines marked out on it so that the worshippers may arrange themselves in orderly fashion.

Prayer mats are usually small colourful rugs, decorated with abstract designs or depicting some holy mosque. They frequently show the Ka'bah or the mosque at Madinah where the Prophet ﷺ is buried. The only significant point about the design is that it should not depict living beings. Otherwise, any mat will do.

Insight

Prayer mats are not compulsory – they aid cleanliness, comfort and orderly spacing. If used, they are treated with respect and folded up after the prayer and not walked on like normal carpets.

CLOTHING

Muslims should wear clean clothes for prayer, as far as possible. They remove their shoes, but it is not necessary to remove socks, stockings or tights. Men must be covered at least from waist to knee, and women must completely cover themselves, leaving only face and hands visible, and should not wear perfume. It is preferred if women do not wear make-up, and nail polish is not accepted as it prevents full *wudu*, although staining the nails with henna is acceptable.

It is not compulsory for men to cover their heads, but many wear a special prayer cap, often of white lace.

Figure 3.3 Many people wear prayer caps.

Insight

Before my conversion, I once had dinner with a group of women and was baffled when they disappeared one by one for a few minutes. I discovered they were sharing one special set of prayer garments – a head-veil and a wrap-round skirt – and were taking it in turns to use them.

WUDU

There is a difference between everyday washing away of dirt and becoming purified for prayer. Purification (*taharah*) is a mental as well as a physical cleansing. Before prayer, Muslims perform the ritual wash known as *wudu* (some Muslims pronounce it *wuzu*), cleansing certain parts of the body in running water.

> *O you who believe! When you rise up for prayer, wash your faces and your hands as far as the elbows, and wipe your heads and wash your feet to the ankles; and if you are under the obligation to perform a bath (i.e. ritually unclean after sex, menstruation or childbirth) then go through the complete wash; and if you are sick, or on a journey, or have come from the toilet or have been intimate with a woman, and you cannot find water, then take clean earth and wipe your faces and your hands with it. Allah does not wish to put you into difficulties, but He wishes to purify you that He may complete His favour on you.*
>
> (Surah 5:6)

The Prophet ﷺ expanded:

> Wash your hands up to the wrists three times; rinse your
> mouth three times with water thrown into your mouth with
> the right hand; sniff the water into the nostrils and blow it out
> three times; wash the entire face, including the forehead, three
> times; wipe the top of the head once with the inner surface
> of both hands together; wash your ears with your forefingers
> and wipe the back of the ears with your thumbs, and wipe the
> back of your neck once; wash the right foot and then the left
> foot up to the ankles three times; let the water run from your
> hands up to your elbows three times.   (Bukhari)

The washing is always done in a quiet, prayerful manner, for it
is in itself part of the act of worship. While washing, Muslims
pray that they will be purified from the sins they have committed
by hand or mouth, that they will be empowered to do good and
refrain from evil, and that they should walk on the right path and
not go astray.

Insight

In the Turkish attempt to force secularization, men were
ordered to wear 'Western' caps with a peak at the front. They
solved the problem of not being able to put their foreheads to
the earth during prayer by simply turning them back to front.

If water is not available, the worshipper can perform a dry wash
known as *tayammum*, which simply involves touching clean earth
and wiping over the face, hands and arms in an imitation wash.

Muslims are not required to make a fresh wudu before every prayer
if they have remained 'in wudu' between times. Wudu is broken if
a person has sexual intercourse, or if any discharge leaves the body
(such as blood, seminal fluid, urine or faeces, or wind), or if the
person has lost consciousness through sleep or other cause. Women
who are menstruating, or are in the days after childbirth, cannot
enter wudu and are excused from salah prayer at these times. A full
bath, known as *ghusl*, is necessary after sexual intercourse, when
menstruation has finished, and after contact with dead bodies.

If socks are worn, it is not considered necessary to wash the feet every time; so long as they are in wudu at the first wash, Muslims may simply wipe over the socks with wet hands the next time, although many Muslims regard this as laziness.

QIBLAH

The *qiblah* is the direction faced during prayer. All Muslims, when they pray, turn to the direction of Makkah. They usually know its position in advance, but if they are in a strange place they can ask, work it out from the position of the sun, or use a small compass.

There is a consolidating effect in fixing a central spot around which to gather the religious feelings of Muslims throughout the world. Muslims do not believe that God somehow lives at Makkah, or in the Ka'bah sanctuary, or could be 'confined' to any temple made with human hands, much less that they are worshipping the famous black stone set in one of its corners. In the spiritual sense, the true qiblah means to turn the heart in the direction of God – and He, of course, cannot be located in any physical direction whatsoever.

THE BARRIER

It is bad manners to pass in front of someone at prayer. If they are praying in the open, Muslims usually mark off the area of their prayer with a barrier, or *sutrah*, which separates them from any people or animals passing in front of them. The Prophet ﷺ used to stick his staff into the ground, just to the right of him, in case there might be any thought that he was in some way bowing down to it as one might bow down to an idol.

Figure 3.4 The Mihrab and Minbar, Zagreb, Croatia.

The practice of prayer

The series of movements and accompanying words is known as a *rakah* (pl. *rakat*). These always follow a set pattern.

During the rakah there are eight separate acts of devotion. The first, after *niyyah* (conscious intention), is *takbir* or glorification, the deliberate shutting out of the world and its distractions, delights and miseries. Muslims stand to attention, and raise their hands to the level of their shoulders, and acknowledge the majesty of God. They say 'Allahu Akbar' – 'God is the Most High'.

Second, they place their right hand over the left on the chest, and say in Arabic 'Glory and praise be to You, O God; blessed is Your name and exalted is Your majesty. There is no God other than You. I come, seeking shelter from Satan, the rejected one.'

After this comes the recital of the first *surah* in the Qur'an, *Surah al-Fatihah* – the translation is:

> *In the name of Allah, the Compassionate, the Merciful. All praise be to Allah (the Almighty), the Lord of the Universes, the Most Merciful, the Most Kind, Master of the Day of Judgement. You alone do we worship, and from You alone do we seek help. Show us the next step along the straight path of those earning Your favour. Keep us from the path of those earning Your anger, those who are going astray.*

Next, another passage from the Qur'an is recited, the choice of the prayer leader. It can be long or short, but the Prophet

Figure 3.5 Muslims carrying out rakah.

recommended keeping recitals short for public prayers (where people in the congregation might be suffering discomfort, illness, coping with children, or have business to attend to), and whatever length you liked for private prayers.

A favourite short surah is *al-Ikhlas* (the One-ness):

> **He is God the One; He is the Eternal Absolute; none is born of Him and neither is He born. There is none like unto Him.**   (Surah 112)

Next comes *ruku*, the bowing. Men rest their hands on their knees and bow right over with a straight back; women do not bow quite so deeply. This bow is to show that they respect as well as love God. They repeat three times:

> **Glory be to my Great Lord, and praise be to Him.**

Insight

It is considered better to pray together at the mosque than on your own, but it is not always possible, and not compulsory.

The next state is *qiyam*, when they stand up again and acknowledge their awareness of the presence of God with the words:

> **God always hears those who praise Him. O God, all praise be to You, O God greater than all else.**

Next comes the humblest of all positions, the *sujud* or *sajda*. Muslims prostrate themselves upon the ground, touching the ground with their hands, forehead, nose, knees and toes. Their fingers face *qiblah*, and their elbows are raised and not lying on the ground. They repeat three times:

> **Glory be to my Lord, the Most High. God is greater than all else.**

Then they kneel up again in a sitting position known as *julus*, palms resting on the knees in a moment of silent prayer, before repeating *sujud* again.

There is a set number of rakat for each prayer; *fajr*, the dawn prayer requires two, the *zuhr* and *asr* have four; *maghrib* has three and *isha* has four. At the end of the compulsory sequence they pray for all the brotherhood of the faithful, the congregation gathered there, and for the forgiveness of sins. When they pray for forgiveness, they place their right fist on right knee and extend the forefinger. The last action is to turn the head to right and left with the words:

> **Asalaam aleikum wa rahmatullah – Peace be with you, and the mercy of Allah.**

This is known as the *salaam*, and acknowledges not only the other worshippers, but also the attendant guardian angels. Some Muslims can be seen sighing, and wiping their hands over their faces to end their prayer session.

Prayers not done together

Sometimes you see Muslims praying on their own, or praying 'out of time' with the other Muslims there. This is because many Muslims pray extra non-compulsory rakat before and after salah, at their own speed, following the practice of the Prophet ﷺ. It is normal to pray two rakat upon entering a mosque, before the congregation is ready. You always know when the compulsory prayer is ready to begin because someone will make another call to prayer (the *iqamah*) and everyone will line up behind a leader. When Muslims join the prayer lines late, they usually make up the missed part of their prayer after the main prayer is finished. Many Muslims finish the set prayer, then change their position to indicate this, and then pray as many more rakat as they like.

Insight

The amount of time spent praying is not necessarily an indicator of a Muslim's real piety. Someone who prays a lot could also be selfish, mean, spiteful, lazy, neglectful of others or dishonest. Allah knows best.

Figure 3.6 Du'a, after Salah prayer.

The *Tahajjud* prayer is an optional prayer that is supposed to be performed in the middle of the night. It can be performed anytime between isha and fajr.

Du'a – personal supplications

Private prayer requests are known as *du'a*. These may be said at any time. They include private thanksgivings for some blessing received (such as childbirth, passing exams, recovery from sickness, and so on), requests for help, please for forgiveness or guidance.

....
Insight
A Muslim prayer is not 'Dear God, please do this for me...', but 'Dear God, please show me what is Your will in this situation.'
....

TASBIH (SUBHAH)

Sometimes worshippers carry a string of 99 or 33 beads, and can be seen praying quietly while passing the beads through their fingers.

These beads are called *tasbih* or *subhah*. They are divided into three sections by larger beads. While praying, the Muslim may say *Subhanallah* (Glory be to Allah), *Alhamdu lillah* (Thanks be to Allah), and *Allahu akbar* (God is Most Great) 33 times, as they pass the beads.

Figure 3.7 Bosnian Imam with tasbih.

Helping others and fasting

ZAKAH – THE RELIGIOUS TAX

By no means will you attain to righteousness until you spend (in the way of Allah) out of that which you cherish most. (Surah 3:91)

The third pillar of Islam is *zakah* from the word *tazkiyah* meaning 'to cleanse, bless, purify, increase and improve'. Virtually every time Allah asked for the practice of regular prayer to be said by believers, He also asked for Muslims to give material help to those less fortunate than themselves. The Qur'an actually specifies the categories of those people who should be helped by this giving:

Zakat are for the poor and the needy, and (to pay) those employed to administer the funds; for those whose hearts have been (recently) reconciled (to Truth); for those in bondage, and in debt; in the cause of God; and for the wayfarer; (Thus is it) ordained by God, full of knowledge and wisdom. (Surah 9:60)

Purifying your attitude towards money means being prepared to sacrifice it for God rather than clinging to it selfishly. Zakah discourages hoarding and miserliness. It blesses the wealth from which it is taken, and the person who makes the sacrifice.

Muslims regard everything in the universe as belonging to God, including all the things humans usually count as their own possessions or earnings. If all our belongings are only loans in trust by God, then when anything is sacrificed for the sake of God it is only being given back to its rightful Owner.

God alone has the choice of who is to be born rich or poor; therefore all Muslims have a duty towards others. The wealthy have an obligation to give; it is not a matter of personal choice.

Insight

Muslims living in hope of an eternal future know there is no point in clinging foolishly to possessions or, even worse, letting them become your masters.

Muslims have a duty to look after themselves and their families and dependants; but after that is taken care of, Allah requires that they should look at their surplus money, capital or goods, and give up one fortieth of it (or 2.5 per cent) to God's service, asking neither recompense nor thanks (Surah 26:109). This is a reasonable amount and is not usually a massive sacrifice. However, if the person is extremely wealthy, they can afford to give more. Alms are due only when the property amounts to a certain value, and has been in the possession of the person for a whole year. Alms are not due on cattle employed in agriculture, or used for the carrying of burdens.

Basically, Islam is against the idea of hoarding. All of Earth's commodities, including cash, should be in use, or in flow. Any time an individual hoards something, this is disapproved of in Islam, because it is a selfish misuse of that commodity, and deprives others who might be able to put it to use. Zakah taxes collected by an Islamic treasury are used to provide for the needy, including the poor, elderly, orphans, widows and disabled. An Islamic government is also expected to store food supplies in case of famine or other disaster. In effect, it provides for a 'welfare state'.

Insight

Paying zakah allows wealth to circulate more fairly in society, and in paying it Muslims purify both themselves and their wealth. It helps Muslim donors to fight greed, and the recipients to fight jealousy, envy and hatred.

It is not only the poor who are helped by receiving zakah; it is also a means of helping rich people to carry out their responsibility towards others honourably, since Muslims believe that the rich person is only so by the grace of God, and his or her riches are only given in trust to them, to be used properly and not in a miserly fashion.

People giving zakah normally do it anonymously, so as not to cause embarrassment. The only time giving is done with publicity is if that would help and encourage others to give also (see Surah 2:271). The Qur'an disapproves of people who make a show of their giving:

> *Don't nullify your charity by reminders of your generosity, or by holding it against those you give it to – like those who give their wealth only to be seen by others ... They are like hard, barren rock on which is little soil. Heavy rain falls on it and leaves it just a bare stone.*
> (Surah 2:264)

There is no authority to force any Muslim to pay this; it is entirely up to the conscience of the individual whether or not he or she pays it; nobody checks, and it is not a state tax even in Muslim societies – although the Muslim authorities will collect and distribute moneys when required. Therefore, zakah is very much a test of sincerity, as well as unselfishness. Being willing to pay it shows that your heart is clean of the love of money and the desire to cling to it. It shows that you are prepared to use your money for the service of humanity, and the promoting of good and justice in the world.

The Prophet ﷺ stated:

He is not a believer who eats his fill while his neighbour remains hungry by his side. (Muslim)

Insight
The amount disbursed to individuals should be sufficient to cover their basic needs, including food, clothing and housing, for one year. These rates are determined according to the prevalent customs of the time and place.

Sadaqah – charity
Giving zakah is not to be confused with the sort of charity giving that is called forth by public response to tragic catastrophes in the news today. That is quite a different sort of charity, known in Islam as *sadaqah* or 'righteousness'. Zakah is a regular, sacrificial giving that depends on motives quite different from sympathy and charity. Sadaqah indicates the sincerity (*siddiq*) of the almsgiver's religious belief, a choice of his/her own free-will. Without that free choice it is not considered an act of merit.

'Every good act is charity,' said the Prophet ﷺ. 'Smiling upon your brother is charity; urging others to do good is charity, helping the blind is charity, removing stones, thorns and other obstructions from the road is charity, giving water to the thirsty is charity.'

Insight
Giving out of compassion in response to some catastrophe is known as sadaqah. It can be interpreted to include any act of kindness, however small.

SAWM – FASTING

O believers, you must fast so that you may learn self-restraint.
Fasting is prescribed for you during a fixed number of days,
so that you may safeguard yourselves against moral and
spiritual ills.

(Surah 2:183–4)

The fourth pillar of Islam is to fast during the ninth month of the
Muslim year, *Ramadan*. Many Muslims fast at other times too,
and some fast one day every week.

Insight

Ramadan is a period of spiritual training in which Muslims
devote much of their time to intensive prayer, study of
the Qur'an and giving charity. Muslims are expected to
control their tongues, eyes, ears, thoughts and deeds, and
do everything possible to seek God's pleasure.

Ramadan and the seasons

The Arabs kept the lunar calendar – 12 months of 28 days. This
comes to 336 days, which is 29 days shorter than the solar year.
Every three years they would intercalate a 29-day month, to bring
the calendars back in line.

Ramadan was not one of the months regarded as sacred by
the pagan Arabs, but monotheists (like the Prophet's 🕮
grandfather) used to keep it as a special time to withdraw
from the world and draw closer to God in peace, prayer and
contemplation. The Prophet 🕮 himself withdrew to solitude the
entire month.

Originally Ramadan fell in March–April, before the rains ended
for the drought months. It was a time also significant for Jews and
Christians, as the Jews kept their feast of Passover on the night of
the full moon, and Christians kept Easter on the first Sunday after
the full moon following the spring equinox.

The reason it became so special and significant for Muslims was that it was during this month that Allah chose to call Muhammad ﷺ to be a prophet, and sent down the first revelations of the Qur'an. Therefore, Ramadan is seen as the most significant of months.

Insight

The month of Ramadan was not originally a sacred month to Arabs. What made it special to Muslims was the giving of the first revelation to the Prophet ﷺ and the start of his ministry. The orders to fast were not given until after he had moved to Madinah.

Shortly before he died, the Prophet ﷺ abandoned intercalation, so thereafter the Ramadan month travels through the secular calendar, coming around ten days earlier each year.

Ramadan has basically three aspects – it is a time of physical discipline and self-control, a time for withdrawing from the world and drawing closer to God in peace and prayer, and thirdly, it is a time for making extra effort to reach out to the world, and if possible to touch the lives of others in spreading love, peace and reconciliation.

The physical discipline of Muslim fasting involves giving up all food, liquid, smoking and sexual intercourse during the time from the first light of dawn to sunset, for the entire month.

Insight

Muslims do not starve to death, because eating, drinking and marital intimacy are all allowed after sunset, until the first light of the next day's dawn when a black thread can be distinguished from a white one.

However, it is not just a question of going without food and drink; that is only one aspect of it, and indeed, it is not the most important aspect. Breaking the moral codes of Islam break the fast just as much as eating or drinking. Allah pointed out that if a person could not give up evil ways, violence, greed, lust, anger and malicious thoughts, He had no need of their giving up food and drink. It would be meaningless.

There are many who fast all day and pray all night, but they gain nothing but hunger and sleeplessness. (Abu Dawud)

Insight
Around the equator the fasts are always around 12 hours. Elsewhere, when Ramadan falls during the winter months the fast is fairly easy, because the daylight hours are short. However, in the summer months the reverse is the case, and the fast is very strenuous indeed.

Long fasts can be very strenuous. In the UK, for example, the fast on 1 July starts at 2.55 a.m. and finishes at 9.40 p.m. demanding considerable self-control. Muslims are often asked what happens in places like the Arctic Circle, the land of the 'midnight sun'. In those places, Muslims either follow the same hours as the nearest Muslims outside the polar zones, or follow the practice of Makkah, which is 6 a.m. to 6 p.m. fast. The object of the fast is not to make people suffer, but it is intended to make them realize what it is like to go without, and to share just for a little while the deprivations of the poor, so that a more sympathetic attitude is engendered.

Withdrawal
The second aspect is the withdrawal from the everyday world, with all its commitments and anxieties, to deliberately cultivate a peaceful and prayerful attitude of mind.

Tarawih prayers
Muslims spend more time in prayer and study of the Qur'an in Ramadan, many reading through the entire Qur'an. There are special extra voluntary prayers at the mosque each evening when the day's fast ends. These special prayers take about two hours, and are known as *tarawih* (pauses or sections); the Qur'an is divided into 30 sections – so that by the end of the month the entire text will have been recited. Mosques may call on the services of visiting *huffaz* (not necessarily trained imams but pious visitors

from 'back home' who know the Qur'an by heart) to help lead these special prayers. These voluntary prayers consist of either eight extra rakat after the compulsory isha prayer (if Muslims are following the sunnah of the Prophet ﷺ), or 20 extra rakat (the practice started by Caliph Umar).

I'tikaf

Some Muslims withdraw altogether from ordinary life and go into retreat for the last ten days of Ramadan to devote their entire time to prayer and reading the Qur'an. Men sometimes live and sleep in the mosque in order to do this, and women withdraw from normal life at home.

....

Insight
Women can usually only practise *i'tikaf* if they are supported by other family members who can prepare their food and so on, so the whole family feels involved.

....

Laylat ul-Qadr

No Muslim knows for certain which is the night of the Descent of the Qur'an, but traditionally it is celebrated on the 27th Ramadan. Scholars admit, however, that it could have been any one of the odd nights during the last ten days of Ramadan.

A large number of Muslims spend this entire night in the mosque, reading the Qur'an and praying together. Indeed, the mosque is usually completely packed. Muslims believe that if they spend the whole of this night in prayer and meditation, they will be granted the blessings as if they had prayed for a thousand nights.

People excused from fasting

Any person who would undergo real suffering if made to fast is excused from doing it. This applies to people who need to be nourished, such as small children and old people, and expectant and nursing mothers, and those with a medical condition requiring food, liquid or medicine. They perform their fasts by *fidyah*, feeding a poor person twice a day for the month, or paying the cash equivalent.

Also excused are people whose condition would be made worse by fasting: menstruating women, soldiers in battle, people on long journeys, and the mentally ill – if they cannot understand the religious reasons behind the fast. All the people in these categories should, however, make up the fasts missed as soon as it becomes practicable to do so. If this is impossible, then they should donate to charity the equivalent cost of two meals for each fast-day they have missed, if they can afford it.

Children generally start fasting when they are quite young, perhaps just missing a dinner; they are expected to be able to take an adult role when they are around 12 years old.

Breaking the fast

Although fasting makes people feel very tired and quite weak, food is prepared very carefully during Ramadan, an extra sacrifice on the part of those preparing it, who must be very tempted to eat a little. If a person breaks the fast by accident in a moment's forgetfulness, like taking a taste of something while cooking, this is not counted as breaking the fast so long as it was not done deliberately. That day is still credited to them. If one sees someone doing this, it is not good manners to comment on it, or draw it to their attention. The fault is 'covered'.

Breaking it deliberately, however, means making up for it by paying a penalty (*kaffarah* – compensation, or 'action to cover the fault') – generally the price of two meals a day for 60 poor people, or 2 kg bread-flour, or equivalent in cash. The alternative is two months' consecutive fasting.

A time of joy

The fast is not dreaded by Muslims, but looked forward to as a time of great joy, family celebration, entertaining of guests, and reconciliation. It is a very special month, and has a very special atmosphere for the Muslims who keep it.

When the fast starts very early in the morning, it is quite normal for Muslims to stay up during the previous night, and then go to bed after they have prayed the dawn prayer and started their fast. In Muslim countries they are sometimes woken up by a drummer, or someone firing a cannon. In the family, it is often the mother who is up and awake first, who has the job of rousing her family and getting them to take the *suhur* or early breakfast before dawn. Light nourishing foods are generally eaten at this meal, and spicy things (which make people feel thirsty) are avoided.

As soon as the sun sets, when the time to end the fast draws near, people feel excited, hungry, proud of their achievement. The time is sometimes signalled on TV or radio, or by the call to prayer from the *minaret*. Muslims usually break the fast with a sweet drink and some fruit, frequently a few dates because this was the habit of the Prophet 🕌. It is not sensible to fall upon a heavy meal and devour it without giving the stomach a little preparation first; people who do this are often sick, and regret it.

Insight

In my first Ramadan I was still a smoker – it was extra hard to go without not only coffee but also cigarettes. I also learned – the hard way – that it was not a good idea to gobble down food and light up eagerly as soon as the fast ended.

After the little meal, known as *iftar* (breakfast), the *maghrib* or evening prayer is said, and only then will the Muslims eat the main meal. This can be quite an occasion, as friends and relatives are often invited, and any poor people or strangers welcomed and included if possible. Many mosques run a communal kitchen paid for by donated money, where people may eat for free. Those who are single, lonely and needy are particularly encouraged to come, and it is quite a party atmosphere.

Figure 3.8 Sharing food together.

Insight

I once had the task of cooking 400 pakoras for one night's iftar. I wondered how my English versions would go down – to my surprise they went down in around 30 seconds!

Ramadan manners

It is considered to be very bad-mannered to eat or drink or smoke in front of a person who is fasting. In some Muslim countries people would be arrested if they did this, and even kept locked up until the fasting month was over. Some tourists in Muslim countries feel they should still be catered for, even though the people are fasting, and this can cause problems. Tourists are usually aware of Ramadan, and often choose not to go to Muslim countries in that month. However, those that enter the religious spirit often find the experience and camaraderie wonderful.

General problems

People who do not fast, or who think that the Muslim fast is not particularly strenuous or is even hypocritical or 'cheating' because they can eat at night, often do not realize the effects it can have. The first week is often the worst, until the body gets used to the new regime. Symptoms may include headaches, dizziness, nausea, light-headedness and faintness. It is especially difficult for Muslims who are addicted smokers, because they have to give up their cigarettes as well as food and drink (in fact, it is a very good time to try to kick the habit!). By the fourth week, some fasters are considerably weakened, and have little or no energy. Muslims frequently need to take rest and lie down, and because of the broken nights and little sleep, they try to catch up on some sleep during the day if possible. Muslim children at school should be excused heavy activity, such as PE, if they cannot cope with it. They are grateful when schools provide somewhere they can pray and rest, away from those munching through lunch. Other Muslims reap considerable physical benefit from the discipline and self-denial.

WHY ARE THEY SPITTING?

Some Muslims take an extreme point of view, refusing even to swallow the saliva already in their mouths, and spit it out into cloths or handkerchiefs. Some will not clean their teeth or take showers in case they swallow some water, and they may refuse to have medicine or injections during the fast time. In fact it is allowed to swallow saliva already within the body, and if a person would be harmed by not taking medicine they are excused fasting – all sick people are, and there is little point in actually making a person ill by deprivation of medical aid.

Insight

Sometimes fasting Muslims are embarrassed because fasting makes their breath smell. This is to be expected. The Prophet ﷺ cheered his followers by commenting that the unpleasant smell was better in the sight of God than the sweetest scent.

Benefits of fasting

Muslims maintain that there are numerous benefits to be gained from fasting. Some maintain it is a healthy time anyway, as the stomach is rested and Muslims eat more fruit and fewer spices than they might do normally. However, the main benefits are spiritual and mental. First, it is excellent discipline and training in self-control. The Muslim becomes master of his or her own body and appetites.

There is a wonderful feeling of community and togetherness. Muslims are sharing an experience, and they are also sharing their food together at night. It is a particularly lovely feeling when a wealthy person can sit down with needy people, feed them and eat with them. The fast makes people appreciate what things they do have, particularly the blessings of food and drink.

Insight

Innovative ideas to share the meaning of Ramadan with non-Muslims include raising money for local charities, inviting the local poor in for a meal each night, taking food to hostels, having a fast-a-thon, or being sponsored for each successful day.

People who come from affluent societies gain at least a little knowledge of what it is like to do without. It makes them more sympathetic and understanding, and generous when they are in the position to be.

Figure 3.9 Eid Mubarrak: Muslims greeting one another after the Feast Prayer.

Hajj – pilgrimage to Makkah

It is the duty of all believers towards God to come to the House a pilgrim, if able to make their way there. (Surah 3:91)

The fifth pillar of Islam is somewhat different from the other four, in that it involves a complete upheaval of the individual's life for the space of a few days. The *Hajj* (which means 'to set out with a definite purpose') is the pilgrimage to Makkah, the 'Mother-town' of Islam, and it is compulsory for every adult Muslim who can afford it, and who is able to go, once in a lifetime. If any Muslim cannot afford to go, or if it would cause hardship to their dependants, they are excused from making the journey. Some Muslims make the Hajj many times, but this is not encouraged nowadays because the vast number of pilgrims is causing considerable difficulties.

Anyone who wishes to make their pilgrimage more than once is encouraged to go at some time other than the Hajj time, when the pilgrimage is known as the Lesser Pilgrimage, or *umrah*. The true Hajj takes place at a specific time in the Muslim calendar, in the month of *Dhu'l Hijjah*, two months and ten days after Ramadan.

Making the Hajj used to be a considerable sacrifice and effort, some people travelling for months and even years overland to reach Makkah. Sometimes people save for a lifetime to make the trip, and when at last they have enough money, they are too old or infirm to go. Any Muslims who cannot make the Hajj are encouraged to pay instead for another person. Sometimes a family or community will club together in order to be able to send one representative on their behalf.

Insight

Pilgrims should settle any debts before they go on Hajj, and should not leave any of their dependents in difficulties or unprovided for. Pilgrims are not entitled to spend money on benefiting themselves while they are in debt to others.

As always in Islam, the real worship and sacrifice is of a spiritual nature rather than the physical show. If, for example, a person who had saved up for Hajj decided to donate that money instead to some unfortunate person in dire need, God would accept the *niyyah* or intention of their Hajj, and it would be counted for them as if they had done it.

PEOPLE EXCUSED FROM HAJJ

Pilgrims have to be Muslim (it is not a tourist attraction), of sound mind and of the age of reason. They must be able to understand the religious significance of the experience. Children might be taken along with the family, but it does not count as their own Hajj until they have reached adulthood. Pilgrims have to have enough money to pay for the trip and keep up all their duty payments towards their dependants. If any person gained money to pay for the Hajj by dishonest means, their Hajj would be invalid.

Insight

Many people die on Hajj, so before setting out pilgrims should make wills and say goodbye to their relatives and friends, and seek forgiveness for any hurts committed. It is possible they may not see them again.

Pilgrims should realize that they have to be reasonably fit to cope with the strenuous conditions. In view of the numbers and circumstances, many people do pass away while on Hajj – through accident, sickness or old age. Those who leave for Hajj do it knowing they may never return.

The sacred place

Makkah is regarded by Muslims as a specially holy place, and no non-Muslim is allowed to enter it. It is *haram*, which means both 'sacred' and 'forbidden'. When travellers come to Makkah by road, they will arrive at places where their passports will be checked, to make sure that they are genuine Muslim pilgrims and not just curious tourists.

BACKGROUND TO THE HAJJ

The Hajj pilgrimage celebrates three particular events in Muslim history. The first is the reunion and forgiveness of Adam ﷺ and Eve (there is no doctrine of an original sin passed on to descendants to be redeemed from); the second is the Prophet Ibrahim's ﷺ sacrifice of his eldest son Isma'il ﷺ, and the third is the life of obedience of the Prophet Muhammad ﷺ.

Adam ﷺ and Eve

According to the Qur'an, when Adam ﷺ and Eve – the original human couple created from the division of the original soul – gave in to the temptation of Satan, they were cast out of Paradise and obliged to wander the Earth in grief, hardship and pain. Not only had they lost God, they had also lost each other, and they were in great confusion and terrible unhappiness. But God had not abandoned them – He watched over them, waiting for the moment when they would turn back to Him and exchange their defiance for the desire for forgiveness. The moment they came to their senses and realized what they had done, God forgave them, and they were reunited on the plain of Arafat, where there is a small hill, Mount Arafat, also known as Jabal ar-Rahman, the Mount of Mercy.

Insight

Islam has no doctrine of inherited original sin that needs a divine saviour to cancel it. Allah, the Compassionate, always forgives those who are sorry.

Muslims believe that for any pilgrim to be on that Mount of Mercy on the ninth Dhu'l Hijjah brings total forgiveness of all one's past sins, and enables life to begin again. The stand there is called the *Wuquf*.

The Ka'bah

Nearby, they built a simple shrine in gratitude – the area known as the *Ka'bah* sanctuary. This is now the sacred shrine of Islam, the *qiblah* towards which all Muslims turn in prayer five times per day. The word 'Ka'bah' means 'cube', and it gets this name from the fact that it is a simple, cube-shaped building, some 15 metres high, built of stone blocks. According to Muslim belief, since the first shrine of the Ka'bah (also known as al-Bait al-Haram – the Holy House) was built by the first human, it is therefore the first shrine for the worship of God on Earth.

Ibrahim 🕮 and Isma'il 🕮

Ibrahim 🕮 was known as the Friend of God (al-Khalil). Although his family (from Ur in Iraq) had been worshippers of the Moon, he had vowed to devote his life to the One True God who had called him to leave his country, travel to Harran, and thereafter live as a nomad. He was a most humble and devout man, even though he was the wealthy owner of vast herds of sheep and goats. He lived peacefully with his childless wife Sarah and a second wife, an Egyptian woman called Hagar (or Hajarah) who had given birth to his son Isma'il 🕮.

The famous story of Ibrahim's 🕮 sacrifice of his son is quite different from that presented in the Bible (Genesis 22:1–14, where God tested his obedience by asking him to sacrifice his son Isaac) 🕮.

The Qur'an reveals that Ibrahim 🕮 dreamed that God wanted him to sacrifice Isma'il 🕮 (Surah 37.102). He informed Isma'il, 🕮 and the youth agreed that he should do whatever he believed to be God's will.

Tradition added details that heightened the drama. Ibrahim 🕮, his wife Hajarah and Isma'il 🕮 were all troubled by a stranger – an old man (who was Satan in disguise), who tried to persuade them that they were being misled. Only the devil would ask Ibrahim 🕮 to do such a wicked thing. They all resisted this thought, still believing it was God's will. In the end, all three of them took up stones and threw them at the unwelcome stranger, driving him away.

Isma'il 🕮 was so determined to submit to the will of God that he made his father place him face down, so that he should not be overcome with grief when he saw his face. However, Ibrahim 🕮 had been mistaken and the sacrifice of his son was not God's will. At the last moment God told Ibrahim 🕮 he had long since fulfilled the purpose of that dream, i.e. to show his obedience (37:105).

A ram was sacrificed instead, and became the origin of the 'tremendous sacrifice' of *Eid ul-Adha* at the end of Hajj.

The reward of Ibrahim was that his barren wife Sarah at last gave birth to a son of her own – Isaac ﷺ (Surah 37:100–13).

Later, Sarah's jealousy on behalf of her son caused the family to split up and Ibrahim ﷺ left Hajarah and Isma'il ﷺ to God's care beside the ancient shrine. Here Hajarah was tested again, for although the place was on a caravan route, no water-carrying caravans came by, and they began to suffer severe thirst. When Isma'il ﷺ was on the point of death the angel Jibril (Gabriel) appeared and opened a spring – the well now called Zamzam.

Later the family was reunited and on finding the sanctuary now known as the Ka'bah suffering from flash-flood damage, Ibrahim ﷺ and Isma'il ﷺ rebuilt it together. For the last 4,000 years or so the Ka'bah has always been reconstructed on the same foundations, and the faithful have always gone there on pilgrimage.

THE MAQAM IBRAHIM ﷺ
In the courtyard of the mosque is a stone known as the *maqam Ibrahim* ﷺ, which marks the spot where he used to stand to direct building operations.

THE GRAVES OF ISMA'IL ﷺ AND HAJARAH
The semi-circular enclosure in front of the Ka'bah marks the traditional site of the graves of Hajarah and Isma'il ﷺ.

Ibrahim ﷺ himself, his wife Sarah, his son Isaac ﷺ, Isaac's wife Rebekah, Isaac's ﷺ son Jacob and Jacob's wife Leah are all buried at Hebron in Palestine. Jacob's ﷺ other wife Rachel is buried just outside Bethlehem.

THE RITES OF HAJJ

It is compulsory for each pilgrim to do four things on Hajj: to enter the state of *ihram* and put on ihram clothing, to perform the circling of the Ka'bah (*tawaf*), to make the stand at Arafat (*wuquf*), and to circle the Ka'bah again, after returning from Arafat. When the pilgrim has done all these four things, he may take the title *hajji* (a female pilgrim is a *hajjah*).

Ihram

Ihram literally means 'consecration', to be *haram* (forbidden to or separated from the world) and it is a special state of holiness, expressed by three things: the complete purification of the body with full bath; the casting aside of normal garments in order to wear special clothes; and the keeping of the ihram rules of conduct.

Women may wear any plain, loose, full-length clothing and a head veil, so that every part of them is covered except the face, hands and feet. They often choose to wear white. Men have to put on two simple pieces of unsewn white cloth, one wrapped around their waist which reaches to their ankles, and one thrown over the left shoulder. They wear nothing else (see Figure 1.2). The object of ihram garments is both purity and equality, single-mindedness and self-sacrifice. Clothing frequently indicates rank, special career or high office; in ihram, no matter how wealthy the pilgrim or how highly born, everyone is dressed the same in these simple unsewn clothes, and they stand before God as equals.

The places where it becomes obligatory to put on these garments are known as *miqat*, around 4 km from the Ka'bah shrine. These days many pilgrims put on ihram even before they board their planes.

Rules of ihram

Once Muslims pass miqat, they say two rakat, and they have entered the state of ihram. From this moment they must not do anything dishonest or arrogant, but behave like true servants of Allah. Normal marital relations are set aside, and all flirtatious thoughts about the opposite sex are forbidden. One may not get engaged, marry or have sexual intercourse on Hajj. If any pilgrim did, their Hajj would not be valid. To express confidence and the atmosphere of purity, and to show that all lustful thoughts have been put aside, women should not cover their faces, even if they normally did so.

Insight

The Ka'bah is usually draped with a veil (in hijab, like a modest woman). During Hajj, the huge black cloth is lifted. Similarly, ladies on Hajj must unveil their faces, even if they normally cover them.

Men must not wear jewellery or rings, and women may wear wedding rings only. No one may use perfume or scented soap (unscented soap is on sale for pilgrims). Men must leave their heads uncovered to express their humility, but they are allowed to carry umbrellas to shelter from the sun. To express simplicity, everyone must go barefoot or in sandals that leave the toes and heels bare.

To express non-interference with nature, no one must cut hair or fingernails. To curb aggression and feel unity with God's creatures, no blood must be shed by killing animals, except fleas, bedbugs, snakes and scorpions. To develop mercy, no hunting is allowed. To feel love for nature, no plants may be uprooted or trees cut down. Muslims strive to keep their minds at peace, and not lose their tempers, quarrel, or get exasperated by difficulties. They have to turn their minds completely to the will of Allah.

Talbiyah

On arrival at Makkah, Muslims start reciting the *talbiyah* prayer, a deeply moving experience as each individual among the thousands and thousands of pilgrims cries to Allah that he or she has arrived, in His service.

Insight

A most moving aspect of Hajj is being conscious that, among the millions there, God knows that you have come, that He sees and 'greets' you, and that all your past inadequacies are 'washed away' by His blessings, and you start life again with a 'clean heart'.

The translation is:

> **At Your command, here I am, O God, here I am! At Your command I am here, O Thou without equal, here I am! Thine is the kingdom and the praise and the glory, O Thou without equal, God Alone!**

This is the pilgrim's personal answer to the divine call to come. Some pilgrims are overcome with emotion at this point. Some shout out joyfully, and others weep. As they enter Makkah, they pray this prayer:

> **O God, this sanctuary is Your sacred place, and this city is Your city, and this slave is Your slave. I have come to You from a distant land, carrying all my sins and misdeeds, as an afflicted person seeking Your help and dreading Your punishment. I beg You to accept me, and grant me complete forgiveness, and give me permission to enter Your vast Garden of Delight.**

Tawaf

The first thing all pilgrims are required to do on arriving at the Ka'bah is to encircle it seven times in an anticlockwise direction – the *tawaf*. (They try to run for the first three circuits if they are able.) They do this, no matter what time of day or night they arrive. If they can reach the black stone (*al-hujr al-aswad*), they will touch or kiss it, or raise their hands in salute if they cannot get near. Invalids and old people are carried on specially constructed stretcher-chairs. An example of the prayers prayed is this one, used on the fourth circuit:

> **O God, Who knows the innermost secrets of our hearts; lead us out of the darkness into the light!**

At the end of the circling, they go to the Station of Ibrahim ☙ to pray two rakat.

al hujr al-aswad

This is the black stone set in one corner of the Ka'bah. It was said to have been sent down from heaven, and is probably a meteorite.

There are numerous traditions about it, one being that it was originally white in colour but it turned black in sorrow at the world's sin (in reality, shiny as it entered the Earth's atmosphere, and black now).

Figure 3.10 The black stone in the Ka'bah.

It now has a silver surround, but it is still open to the touch. The deep hollow in the middle has been worn away by the millions of pilgrims who have touched and kissed it. It is not, however, an object to be worshipped.

Al-Kiswah
The Kiswah is the black cloth that covers the Ka'bah shrine. It is traditionally made afresh each year in Cairo by male embroiderers. Verses from the Qur'an are embroidered around it, in gold thread. It is draped over the Ka'bah like a veil and, like the women's veils, is lifted up during the Hajj. At the end of Hajj it is taken down and cut up into small pieces, which become souvenirs or gifts for special pilgrims. Pieces are sent to mosques throughout the world, and many Muslims frame their piece and hang it on the wall as a reminder.

Figure 3.11 The black cloth over the Ka'bah.

Inside the Ka'bah

People rarely go inside the Ka'bah through the huge door. It has remained empty ever since the Prophet ﷺ cleansed it of its 360 idols. Inside, there are no *mihrabs*, since the Ka'bah itself is the 'centre of the world' and all Muslims pray towards it. It is decorated simply, with texts from the Qur'an on the walls.

Sa'i

The *Sa'i* is the ritual of running or walking briskly seven times between the two small hills of Safa and Marwah (now a passageway enclosed within the Ka'bah shrine). Any invalids, old people, or those who cannot walk have a special protected wheelchair path down the middle. This ritual is in commemoration of the desperate trail of Isma'il's ﷺ mother, Hajarah, between these two viewpoints, when looking for caravans carrying water. It symbolizes the soul's desperate search for that which gives true life.

The well of Zamzam represents the truth that when all seems lost, God is still present, with healing and life for the soul. The well is still there in a chamber under the courtyard. Pilgrims drink some of the water, and might even collect some in bottles (these can also be bought as souvenirs). Some pilgrims dip their ihram cloths in the water intending to keep them and use them as their shrouds, when they die.

When Muslims have done both tawaf and Sa'i, they have completed *umrah*, the lesser pilgrimage. After this, male pilgrims either shave their heads, or at least cut their hair, and women cut off an inch or so of their hair. Then, they are allowed to put on their normal clothes again.

Mina

On the eighth day of Dhu'l Hijjah, the pilgrims take a full bath and put on ihram again, and proceed to the valley of Mina some 10 km away. This used to be a walk into the desert, but now the town of Makkah reaches virtually as far as Mina, and there are special walkways to make it easier for the huge crowds. It was in the underground walkway that there was a horrific accident with hundreds being suffocated and crushed a few years ago.

There are a few hotels in Mina, but most pilgrims stay in a huge city of tents. Some pilgrims now miss out Mina and take modern transport straight to Arafat, because of the sheer numbers involved.

Wuquf

On the ninth day, all the pilgrims have to reach the plain of Arafat (24 km east of Makkah) and make their stand before God on or surrounding the Mount of Mercy. They have to be there between noon and dusk. Some arrive in good time, but others come rushing up from Mina, having made their dawn prayer there. If they do not arrive for the Standing in time, their Hajj is invalid.

Insight

The Wuquf is a personal challenge under the blazing sun. Some do allow themselves the shade of an umbrella. This ordeal, coming to its climax with the vast crowd united in silent prostration before God, feeling the joy of achievement and release from any burden of sin, is the spiritual climax of Hajj.

This is really the most important part of the pilgrimage. The pilgrims must stand in the sweltering heat, bare-headed (for men), thinking about God and praying for His mercy. It is a time of great mystical and emotional power, and there is a tremendous sense of release – being totally wrapped in love, totally 'washed', totally cleansed.

It is an amazing sight to see over 2 million pilgrims perform the zuhr and asr prayers here, especially the moments of prostration and total silence as they bow before Allah.

Muzdalifah

By sunset, the pilgrims begin to head back to Muzdalifah, between Arafat and Mina. There they say the maghrib and isha prayers, and collect small pebbles. They arrive back at Mina by the morning of the tenth Dhu'l Hijjah.

Stoning the Jamrat

Next comes the ritual of casting their pebbles at Satan, in remembrance of the temptations of Ibrahim ﷺ and his family. There are three pillars set up at representative places, known as *jamrat*, and pebbles are hurled at each one. While doing this, pilgrims rededicate themselves to Allah and promise to do their utmost to drive any evil out of themselves. Muslims are reminded, incidentally, to be careful when hurling these pebbles, so that no one gets hurt.

These days police are in attendance to keep an eye on over-enthusiastic pilgrims. Despite the recent improvements and precautions over 350 pilgrims were crushed to death there in the Hajj of 2006. Some scholars feel it would be better to make this ritual symbolic only.

The sacrifice

After all this, on the tenth Dhu'l Hijjah, the pilgrims who can afford it buy a sheep, goat or young camel, to make their animal sacrifice. This is a three-day festival to commemorate Ibrahim's ﷺ willingness to offer his son's life, but Allah making the substitution of a ram at the last moment.

The animals provide a huge amount of meat to be consumed, so not every person does this. Some pay a cash equivalent. The sacrificer may use two-thirds of the meat for himself and those with him, and a third of it is given away to those too poor to buy their own animal. After the sacrifice the meat is roasted and eaten. The vast number of animals slaughtered presented quite a problem until the Saudi authorities stepped in to organize the disposal of the carcasses. It is impossible for all the meat to be eaten, even if it is shared, so modern technology freezes and processes all the excess meat for distribution further afield.

This is the festival known as *Eid ul-Adha*, the major festival (see page 127), and at the same time as the slaughter, Muslims all over the world are keeping the feast.

Final rites

After this festival, male pilgrims can again shave their heads or shorten their hair, and females trim their hair again. This is done by someone not in ihram. When they return to Makkah they make the final tawaf, and then the pilgrimage is complete.

Insight

When Hajj is complete, Muslim men have their heads completely shaved, and women cut about an inch of their hair. Some men also dye their beards a brilliant orange with henna.

MUSLIM 'TOURISM'

Most pilgrims also take the chance to visit sites in the neighbourhood connected with the Prophet ﷺ, and may also visit Madinah, where the Prophet ﷺ is buried in what used to be Aishah's room (the *hujurah*), along with his friends, Abu Bakr and Umar. Nearby is the cemetery of al-Baqi where many of his family and the early Companions are buried. Here one notices the extreme simplicity of the tombs, which are simply mounds of small stones. There had been grander mausoleums there in the past, but after being preserved for centuries they were destroyed by the strict Islamic Wahhabi sect in the reign of King Abd al-Aziz al-Saud, which disapproved of hero-worship or saint cults.

Pilgrims might also climb the hill Jabal Nur to see the cave where the Prophet ﷺ received his first vision, and Jabal Thawr where he hid from the Makkans. They might perhaps also visit some of the famous battlefields and mosques. The Masjid at-Tawqa (or Qiblatain), built when the Prophet ﷺ first entered Madinah, is interesting for having two mihrabs, one facing Jerusalem.

The Prophet ﷺ said:

> He who comes for Hajj and does not visit me is a miser. One that comes to my grave and gives me salaam, I say salaam to that person in reply.

Jihad

Jihad is one of the most misunderstood of all aspects of Islam. Most non-Muslims take it to mean military action for the purpose of forcing other people to become Muslims, but this is totally against the principle of Islam, which defends individual liberties. The fact that various persons claiming to be Muslim have acted incorrectly, some even to the extent of horrifying brutality, does not alter this fact, any more than one could judge Christianity by the atrocities of the Klu Klux Klan in the USA.

Islamic jihad in fact insists that oppression for the sake of religion is wrong. Religion should never become an oppressor. People should never be forced to accept things that they do not believe. The whole essence and reason for jihad is to be prepared to sacrifice one's own self in order to fight against tyranny and oppression, to bring freedom and justice and a just peace.

Insight
God does not require Muslims to try to conquer the world and bring everyone into Islam. Instead, God has granted to humans the free-will to accept or reject any faith, as they decide.

NO COMPULSION IN RELIGION

It is impossible to force anyone to believe or love anything. It is hopeless to expect conversions without education. Muslims are required to present the evidence, show the results and consequences of actions, present the proof – then leave it to people to believe or not. It is their choice. In any case, faith is not complete when it is followed blindly or accepted unquestioningly.

> *If it had been the Lord's will for all who are on earth to believe, they would have believed! How do you, therefore think you can compel people to believe against their will? No soul can believe except by the will of Allah, and He Himself places doubt (or obscurity) in the minds of those who do not wish to understand.*
>
> (Surah 10:99–100; see also Surah 18.29 and Surah 28.56)

Human beings need to build faith on well-grounded convictions beyond any reasonable doubt. The attempts of those who try to force a belief on someone are ridiculous and can only work through tyranny and aggression. The way of *dawah* in Islam is to make as clear as possible the evidence and proof – but every person must be allowed to believe or disbelieve what they want.

Insight

Trying to force someone to believe something they patently do not believe is as ridiculous as trying to force someone to fall in love with you. The more the force is applied, the less likely the hoped-for result.

PERSECUTING NON-BELIEVERS

Nowhere does Allah give permission to force or kill people who refuse to accept the message. On the contrary, believers are asked to be patient with those who do not believe:

> *Bear with patience what they say, and when they leave give a courteous farewell.*
>
> (Surah 73:10)

Deal gently with disbelievers; give them enough time (to change their minds).
(Surah 86:17)

Duty to warn, not enforce

All Muslims are required to do is give the message:

The delivery of the message is the duty for you, and the judgement is the duty for Us.
(Surah 13.40)

> ## Insight
>
> The Prophet ﷺ taught that all non-Muslims were not enemies but potential Muslims, and many who started out as his worst enemies ended up outstanding converts, and some even died as martyrs.

Allah is the Judge. It is for Him to decide, in ultimate terms, what the fate will be of those who reject the message, and not any zealot militia. It is up to Muslims to show that everything in the message is good, and promotes goodness and happiness and progress and peace, and that Allah never asked anyone to promote anything that was evil or harmful, or hurtful verbally, physically, mentally or morally. The message was and is all good.

MILITARY JIHAD

The much-used term 'holy war' is actually not found anywhere in the Qur'an. War with its awful devastation and suffering and death can never be a good thing (except in the circumstances to be mentioned shortly), and Allah denies Muslims the right to ever inflict suffering in order to take power, food, land or anything else, by force. One meaning of the word 'Islam' is 'peace'. The greeting used by all Muslims when they meet each other is '*salaam aleikum*' – 'May peace be with you.'

Whenever a tyrant is successful, even if there is no actual fighting there is no peace, because:

▶ *there is no security*
▶ *people feel dishonoured and ashamed in allowing the situation to continue*

- ▶ *people feel frustrated and helpless, and unable to do anything about it*
- ▶ *people feel ashamed because they think they have acted in a cowardly manner.*

Insight

Muslims are expected to be '*staunch in justice*' (Surah 7.29). Those who advocate social justice more often than not conflict with the hidden agendas of state authorities. They may pose a threat to the political elites, who may then try to persecute or purge such groups.

In fact, the Prophet ﷺ stated quite clearly that:

If anyone walks with an oppressor to strengthen him, knowing that he is an oppressor, he has gone forth from Islam. (Bukhari, Muslim)

Islam cannot acquiesce in wrong-doing, and this is where personal and political decisions could be interpreted differently – who is the oppressor and who the oppressed? It is regarded as weak and irresponsible cowardice to ignore tyranny, or to fail to try to root it out.

If God did not check certain people by using others, surely many monasteries, churches, synagogues and mosques would all have been pulled down. God will aid those who fight for Him. (Surah 22:39–40)

Jihad with the use of weapons is only to be resorted to by Muslims as a means of necessary defence against aggressors who have first attacked believers, or tyrants who have abused and corrupted others. However, once attacked, injustice would soon be triumphant in the world if good people were not prepared to risk their lives, and even sacrifice their lives, for a righteous cause.

Like Christianity, Islam permits fighting in self-defence, in defence of religion, or on the part of those who have been expelled forcibly from their homes. War is the last resort, and jihad subject to the rigorous conditions laid down by the sacred law, rules of combat that include prohibitions against harming civilians or destroying crops, trees and livestock, as far as is humanly possible.

Insight

Islamic military jihad is to bring freedom and justice, and a just peace. Although peaceful, Muslims are not pacifists – they believe it wrong to stand by and do nothing if people are being oppressed.

Rules for jihad

Jihad, therefore, does not mean every single battle fought by any Middle-Eastern soldier, who may be anything from a Marxist to a member of a private bodyguard, and not a martyr for God. Many battles have nothing whatever to do with Islam.

Islam placed legal restrictions upon the conduct of war. In general, Muslim armies may not kill women, children, seniors, hermits, pacifists, peasants or slaves unless they are combatants. Vegetation and property should not be destroyed, water holes should not be poisoned, and flame-throwers should not be used unless out of necessity, and even then only to a limited extent.

Torture, mutilation and murder of hostages are forbidden under all circumstances. One of the Prophet's ﷺ worst enemies, Suhayl, was captured – a man who had a cleft lower lip. Umar threatened to knock out his two front teeth, stating: 'Then his tongue will flop out, and he will never be able to speak against you again!' The Prophet ﷺ was not pleased. 'I will certainly not mutilate him,' he replied, 'for if I did, surely Allah would mutilate me, even though I am His Messenger. Think – it may be that one day he will make a stand for which you will not be able to find fault with him.' (Ibn Kathir 2.324) Suhayl did indeed convert and became a Muslim hero. The Prophet's ﷺ forward-looking and generous attitude is an important *sunnah* for those zealots who regard non-Muslim territories as Dar al-Harb (House of War), full of enemies who need conquering. The Prophet ﷺ, on the contrary, saw such territories as Dar al-Dawah (House of Missionary Preaching) full of potential converts.

> ## Insight
> The Prophet's ﷺ prisoners were amazed by the treatment they received, some stating they were fed and cared for better than in their own homes. If they could not arrange a ransom payment, many were released for token sums, or for performing some service such as teaching someone to read.

A jihad should be declared only:

- ▶ *in defence of the cause of Allah, not for conquest*
- ▶ *to restore peace and freedom of worship*
- ▶ *for freedom from tyranny*
- ▶ *when led by a spiritual leader*
- ▶ *until the enemy lays down arms.*

Jihad does not include:

- ▶ *wars of aggression or ambition*
- ▶ *border disputes or either national or tribal squabbles*
- ▶ *the intent to conquer and suppress, colonize, exploit, etc.*
- ▶ *forcing people into accepting a faith they do not believe*
- ▶ *acts of terrorism, suicide bombings, etc. (see page 353).*

National jihad has to be commanded by a leader who is accepted as a spiritual guide and supreme judge, who can assess the need, the cause, and give right guidance to oppose a clear unjust oppressor; someone not governed by personal ambition.

Sometimes after starting jihad in the correct spirit, a human leader then becomes ambitious. In this case, the qualification for leadership is lost and the community has the right to demand a change of his ways or his abdication, or even his death if he refuses to give way.

When to cease the jihad

All the following texts are direct orders to Muslims from the Qur'an:

The reward for an injury is an equal injury back; but if a person forgives instead, and makes reconciliation, he will be rewarded by God.
(Surah 42:40)

If two sides quarrel, make peace between them. But if one trespasses beyond bounds against the other, then fight against the one that transgresses until it complies with the law of God; and when it complies, then make peace between them with justice, and be fair.
(Surah 49:9)

....

Insight

Goodness and evil cannot be equal. Repay evil with what is better, then he who was your enemy will become your intimate friend.

(Surah 41:34)
....

The physical fighting is only allowed until the enemy seeks peace terms, and then it must cease.

Fight them until there is no more persecution, and religion is for God. But if they desist, then let there be no more hostility – except against those who continue to do wrong.
(Surah 2:193)

If they seek peace, then you seek peace. And trust in God – for He is the One that hears and knows all things.
(Surah 8:61)

The highest sacrifice

When all else fails, the highest sacrifice people can make is obviously of their actual lives. The Prophet Jesus ﷺ said: 'Greater love has no man than this – that a man lay down his life for his friends.' (John 15:13) He was talking about sacrificing his own life for the sake of those who followed him, because he loved God more than he loved himself. In Islam, people who are prepared to die because they love God more than their own lives are called *shahid*. By dying in Allah's cause they bear the ultimate witness to their faith in the existence of God and the Life to Come. Some believe and love God so much they do not even regard it as a sacrifice – but to those helped or protected by them no sacrifice could be higher, or more admired.

Festivals and special days

The Muslim word for a festival is *id* or *eid*, from the Arab word meaning 'returning at regular intervals'. The fact that they do occur in a regular cycle is important, for it gives a repeated opportunity for renewal, to forgive enemies, put right quarrels, do things you ought to have done but have perhaps put off or forgotten, and contact people you have not seen for a long time.

Although there are several special times in the Islamic calendar, there are really only two religious festivals. These are *Eid ul-Fitr*, the feast that breaks the fast at the end of the Ramadan month, and *Eid ul-Adha*, the feast of sacrifice that takes place during the Hajj. Eid ul-Adha is the major festival, and Eid ul-Fitr the minor festival.

Both of these feasts are times of celebration and joy, at the express command of Allah as revealed in the Qur'an, when family and friends get together and the local community feels a strong sense of fellowship with the whole Muslim world.

Insight

It is tricky to make advance arrangements for days off from school or work for Muslim Eids in non-Muslim countries, as they occur according to the lunar calendar and not the Western Gregorian one, which is solar. The festival dates on the Western calendar therefore change each year.

THE AIMS OF EID

The first aim of Eid is basically to praise and thank God for His many blessings, in particular those connected with the background of the feast, and to enjoy oneself and appreciate God's blessings.

The second basic aim is unity, to arouse a heightened feeling of *ummah* or one community. At Eid, Muslims are requested to bring loved ones to memory, particularly those who cannot be present because they live in far distant parts of the world. One should also think lovingly of all the members of the family of Islam, not just those in one's own family – whether known or unknown, rich or poor. Equally important are loved ones who have died. Eid is a time to think about them, and say prayers for their souls.

THE DUTIES OF EID

There are several aspects to Muslim duty at Eid, all geared towards the aims of unity, peace and brotherhood. Blessings must be shared and a conscious effort made to see that no one is left lonely or depressed. The rich must share what they have (any animals sacrificed for Eid must be shared, with at least a third going to the less fortunate) and the poor must be welcomed. The lonely must not be left alone, but invited to join in either with a family or at the mosque. (Muslims have a particular responsibility to look after orphans and see that they are being loved and cared for.)

People who are not usually particularly zealous in their religion make new resolutions and put in extra effort. Those who are involved in quarrels or feuds must settle them if they are to keep the spirit of Eid.

EID UL-FITR

Although Eid ul-Fitr is known as the minor festival, many young Muslims enjoy it more than the 'major' one, coming as it does at the end of the month-long fast of Ramadan. It is also known as *Sheker Bairam* (Turkish for 'sweet festival'), *Eid Ramadan* and *Eid ul-Sagheer* (the 'little festival'). It is little because it lasts for three days, whereas Eid ul-Adha lasts for four.

Preparations for the feast begin well in advance, as the amount of food required to feed many guests turning up for meals requires much shopping and advance cooking, usually in gargantuan quantities. Sometimes Muslim shops are so busy that they stay open all night for a few days beforehand.

Non-Muslims sometimes call Eid ul-Fitr the 'Muslim Christmas', because it is a favourite with the children – it includes presents, cards, parties, special pretty dresses and traditional outfits, special food, decorations, etc. Many Muslims are worried that it will become too commercialized and disapprove of too much non-religious celebration.

Many families make decorations and hang them up, or use the trimmings Christians use at Christmas (including tinsel decorations, trees, lights and Santas, but not the cribs commemorating the birth of Jesus). These can now be purchased at any time, all over the Muslim world. The Muslim use has nothing to do with Christmas at all – they are just glittering signs of joy. Sometimes families take the opportunity to spruce up the entire house with a fresh coat of paint, or new curtains or cushion covers.

Gifts or sweets are prepared, and cards made or bought and sent out to relatives and friends. These cards usually show famous mosques, or flowers, or designs, and carry the message Eid Mubarak ('Happy, or blessed, Feast-time').

Special contributions are collected for the poor, the *zakat ul-fitr*. This is not the same as the annual *zakah*, but is charity bestowed as an act of purification for the giver. Zakat ul-fitr is the equivalent of a good meal from each adult member of the family, and should be paid well before the Eid day to ensure that the poor are able to take part in the celebrations, and perhaps to buy some new clothes.

Non-Muslims may notice that post offices and banks are rather more full than usual; this is because so many Muslims whose roots lie elsewhere send money to the country of their origin, to help known poor people, or to add to a particular fund. Many use the opportunity to send their annual *zakah* at the same time.

The announcement

The Eid depends on the sighting of the new moon, and this has caused some confusion in countries where the night sky is not always clear. If the new moon is sighted during the evening of the 29th day of the month, that night becomes the first of the new month, but if the moon is not sighted some Muslims fast an extra day to be on the safe side. In the United Kingdom, it has not been uncommon for Eid to be celebrated on three different days, as various communities decide their date of Eid from different sources – a source of irritation to those involved in planning such things as school diaries in advance. Many Muslims have also become irritated by these differences, and feel that scientific calculations should be used to make the whole matter beyond dispute.

Traditionally, the fast is broken by the call to prayer from the mosque, or by the firing of cannons and guns, or the beating of a drum. In Indonesia, for example, the drummers are known as *al-musaharati* and they also wake the faithful before every dawn during Ramadan. The time is also announced on radio and TV in Islamic societies, and mosques get the news by radio, telex and telephone (if one can get through, the switchboards are so jammed at this time!).

Breaking the fast

As soon as the signal comes, there is a release of emotion and much hugging and greeting, handshaking and kissing. The fast is traditionally broken with something very simple, as was the practice of the Prophet ﷺ – usually dates or other fruit, and fruit drinks or milk. After this simple food and drink, the family leaves the table to make the maghrib prayer. The big meal comes later.

In Muslim societies people are so excited and full of the urge to congratulate each other on completing a successful fast that they go out into the streets in party mood to wish each other 'Eid Mubarak'. Visitors go round to call on friends and family, trying to make sure that no one is forgotten.

THE EID DAY

In Muslim countries there is no work or school on Eid days – everybody has a three-day holiday. In the United Kingdom, Muslim children are granted a day off school, and sympathy from employers towards their Muslim employees is increasing. Others have to content themselves with making the early *salat ul-fitr* prayer, an hour after sunrise, and then getting on with their jobs as usual, looking forward to a good feast in the evening. Salat ul-fitr consists of two rakat with extra *takbirs* (saying of 'Allahu Akbar') and a sermon, usually about giving in charity. There is no call to prayer. Other Eid prayers take place in congregation between sunrise and noon.

Insight

Getting everyone bathed properly can need some organizing in a large family – some will take their bath at night after the prayer, so that they are ready in the morning and can leave the bathroom for others.

Each person going to Eid prayer must first take a full bath or shower, and then dress in new or best clothes. They take a quick breakfast, and hurry to the Eid congregation, which might be at the local mosque, or could be a huge gathering in the largest mosque in the area, or the principal mosque of the city, known as the *Jami'a Mosque*. Sometimes the congregation can be so large it overflows on to the street outside.

It is preferred if the congregations from all the mosques in the region can come together for Eid prayers to make as large an *ummah* as possible, so sometimes they arrange for the use of a large open space, such as a large car-park, or a local park or playing field. A very big crowd can gather. The congregation may consist of thousands of people, because women and children are also encouraged to attend. In Muslim countries there are sometimes open fields called *Eid gahs* which are used for the festival prayers. Care must also be taken to arrange where cars will be parked, and not irritate neighbours by blocking their entrances. Streets can become so crowded that police often supervise or clear surrounding roads.

Insight

Muslims need to know the prayer times in advance, and get there early. Human nature often results in endless

(Contd)

disturbances after the prayer has started – phones ringing to check times, and men arriving after the place is full and finding no place in the lines in front of the ladies.

After the prayer, everyone greets each other with 'Eid Mubarak' and hugs and kisses, and then the round of visits to friends and family begins. Children get lots of presents and pocket money.

At midday there is a large dinner – the first meal eaten during the day for over a month! It may have to be in several sittings if large numbers of guests arrive. Needless to say, the female members of the family will have put a great deal of effort into preparation of these huge meals. Luckily, the Middle Eastern style of cookery lends itself to these large feasts, and it is fairly easy to expand the food to fit the numbers that turn up.

During the afternoon, families often visit the cemetery to remember all their loved ones who have passed away. They pray for them, and sit by their graves for a while.

The day ends with more visiting and entertaining, going on late into the night.

Figure 3.12 Enjoying a feast.

EID UL-ADHA

This is the major festival, lasting four days, and is celebrated at the end of the Hajj. It commemorates the obedience of the Prophet Ibrahim 🕮 when he was called upon to sacrifice his son Isma'il 🕮, and his triumph over the temptations of the devil.

Every Muslim takes part in this feast, not only the ones on Hajj. Everyone thinks about the pilgrims who have gone on Hajj, and joins with them in spirit, particularly any who have gone from their own family or community. In Muslim countries, the Hajj is reported on TV for everyone to see.

Eid ul-Adha is a serious occasion, symbolizing the submission of each individual Muslim, and the renewal of total commitment to Allah. The mind is concentrated on the idea of sacrifice and self-sacrifice, symbolized by the actual sacrificing of a sheep, goat, cow or camel.

The animal sacrifice

In Muslim countries this does not usually present a problem as many Muslim men will have been trained in how to slaughter an animal according to the principles of Islam. People in the West are often horrified at the thought of animal slaughter, and regard it as cruelty and a barbaric practice. They are confusing Islamic slaughter with the ancient worshippers of idols who used to consider that their gods needed the ritual sacrifice of blood to give them strength, and so on. This has nothing to do with Islam.

Neither the flesh of the animals of your sacrifice nor their blood reaches Allah – it is your righteousness that reaches him.
(Surah 22:37)

The creature is not slain in any way as a propitiatory sacrifice to God, but as meat for a communal feast. Any person who eats meat should be aware that the meat was once a living animal that was slaughtered specifically so that they could eat. In fact, the Islamic principles of slaughter are to slay the creature in the kindest possible way, with the least amount of pain, and without putting the animal to fear or distress. There is sometimes controversy among non-Muslims over whether or not *halal* (or 'permitted') killing is cruel or kind; Muslims maintain that it is the kindest possible method, ordained by God Himself, and that is why they do it. They do not regard killing an animal by electrocution, or by firing a bolt into its brain (normal United Kingdom slaughterhouse practices) to be kind methods at all.

> ## Insight
> Animals for sacrifice have to meet certain standards of age and quality – generally at least a year old, and in good health. One is expected only to offer the best to God – and, of course, the meat is cooked and enjoyed at the feast.

Muslim slaying should be done with a very sharp knife across the jugular vein, so that the animal loses consciousness immediately. Prayers are said throughout the proceedings. Killing the animal in this way causes the least pain or distress, and the blood drains away easily.

In the United Kingdom, people must have a special licence to slaughter animals, and it is not permitted for Muslims to slaughter their own on their own premises. Licence-holders have to go to the slaughterhouse to sacrifice there on behalf of the community. When newspapers sometimes print 'horror stories' of Muslims slaughtering sheep or goats in their backyards, it is usually newcomers who are unaware of the rules or facilities provided.

DATES

Months in the Islamic calendar are calculated according to a lunar year, therefore each month has 29 days, 12 hours and 44 minutes; the Islamic year is shorter than the solar year by 11 days. The odd 44 minutes of the lunar month means that some years will have 355 days instead of 354. (In a stretch of 30 years, there would be 11 of these 'leap' years.) Therefore, the Islamic festival days are not seasonal, like Christian festivals, and cannot have fixed dates. Each festival comes 11 days earlier each year.

Islamic months and their special days

The Islamic months are *Muharram, Safar, Rabi'ul-Awwal (al Ula),
Rabi ath-Thani (al-Akhir), Jumada al Awwad (al Ula), Jumada
ath-Thani (al-Akhir), Rajab, Shaban,* Ramadan, *Shawwal, Dhu'l
Qidah,* and Dhu'l Hijjah. There are no special days in Safar, Rabi
al-Akhir, Jumada al-Ula, Jumada al-Akhir or Dhu'l Qidah.

MUHARRAM

Muharram is the first month of the Muslim calendar. New Year's
Day is declared after the sighting of the new moon. The Muslim
year commemorates the Hijrah, the departure of the Prophet ﷺ to
Madinah, the moment that marked the turning point for Islam and
the beginning of the spread of Islam which took place in the month
Rabi'ul Awwal, but Caliph Umar took the start of year 1 AH back
to Muharram. Muslims date all their years from this year, and call
them AH – after the Hijrah.

On New Year's Day (Muharram 1) Muslims have to 'migrate'
from their past to their future, putting old sins and failings
behind them and making a fresh start with new year resolutions.

Ashura

The tenth of Muharram, known as *Ashura*, was already a time
of fasting before Islam, according to the Jewish tradition. It was
originally the Jewish Day of Atonement, when the High Priest of
that faith made sacrifices for the sins of the nation.

In Sunni Muslim tradition, this day celebrates a number of major
events: the creation of the seven heavens, the land and sea; the birth
of Adam ﷺ; the day when Nuh (Noah) ﷺ left the Ark after the
flood to begin a new life on Earth; the birth of the Prophet Ibrahim
ﷺ and the day on which he was supposed to sacrifice Isma'il ﷺ;
the day on which the Prophet Ayyub (Job) ﷺ was released from
his suffering; the day on which Allah saved Musa (Moses) ﷺ from
the cruel Pharaoh; the day on which the Prophet Isa (Jesus) ﷺ was
born, and the Day on which the Day of Judgement is expected.
Fasting is not obligatory for Muslims on this day, but most do keep

a day's fast. The Prophet ﷺ praised the excellence of fasting on this day.

Ashura is an extremely important and special day for Shi'ite Muslims (see page 30) for it marks the day when the Prophet's ﷺ heroic grandson, Husayn, was martyred at Karbala in the year 61 AH. Shi'ites mourn for the first ten days of Muharram, wearing black clothes, refraining from music (considered impolite when death has occurred) and pleasant pastimes, and listen to moving poems and sermons. On the tenth day, they perform dramatic processions led by a white horse, with floats called *tazias* depicting scenes of the events, and plays portraying the events of the suffering and death of Husayn. Some of the more fervent even beat themselves with chains and cut their heads with swords, to share in a small way the sufferings of Husayn.

Insight

The weeping is as heartfelt and distressing as if Husayn had died yesterday. The practice of beating one's chest with the palm represents plunging a knife into one's heart.

The Shi'ite ritual marches, flagellating themselves with a *zanjeer* (chain) or cutting their flesh with sharp blades, are highly emotional and bloody. They are not approved of in Sunni Islam, and even some Shi'ite societies are now trying – not very successfully – to ban or limit them.

Milad an-Nabi

12 Rabi'ul-Awwal is traditionally celebrated as the birthday of the Prophet ﷺ (probably originally 20 August 570 CE). There is some controversy among Muslims as to whether this day should be celebrated or not; some purists feeling it wrong to celebrate a human being, no matter how much loved and respected. Others feel it is wrong not to commemorate the birth of such a great Prophet ﷺ.

God and His angels send blessings on the Prophet. O ye that believe! Send blessings on him, and salute him with all respect.

(Surah 33:57)

The Prophet's ﷺ birthday was not observed in the early years of Islam, but was introduced by the Abbasid caliphs of Baghdad and made popular by the Sufis in the tenth century CE. There has always been opposition to it, because it is an innovation, and it is forbidden by strict sects such as the Wahhabi Muslims of Arabia and the Deobandis of India.

Insight

Muhammad ﷺ did not observe the birth or death anniversaries of any of his family or loved ones, nor did he advise his followers to observe his birthday; therefore, many Muslims do not celebrate any birthdays.

However, it now has an important socio-religious function in many communities as an opportunity to remind young and old Muslims alike of what the Prophet ﷺ taught and what lessons can be learnt from his life and sunnah. It is an occasion to generate love and reverence in Muslim hearts, and to send blessings on the soul of the Prophet ﷺ. Celebrations might include a procession in places with strong Sufic influence, and there are marches and meetings in Malaya. It is a public holiday in Pakistan. However, *Milad an-Nabi* is usually only celebrated with special meetings at the mosque to hear sermons about the Prophet's ﷺ life, mission, character, sufferings and successes.

Laylat ul-Miraj

27 Rajab is traditionally recognized as *Laylat ul-Miraj*, the commemoration of the Prophet's ﷺ night journey and ascent to Heaven (see page 7), three years before the migration to Madinah. The Prophet ﷺ travelled with the Angel Jibril on a winged animal known as a *buraq* from Makkah to Jerusalem, and was then allowed to see both Paradise and Hell before passing on through various heavens to the final heaven where there was the Presence of God. At that point, where he had attained the highest spiritual state attainable by humans, neither he nor the angel could go any further.

The main feature of this experience was the institution of the five daily prayers, as opposed to the 50 the Prophet ﷺ suggested.

Many Muslims will spend the entire night reading the Qur'an and praying. In some countries the mosques are illuminated for this night. Others reject this as innovation.

Laylat ul-Bara'at
Laylat ul-Bara'at is the 'Night of Blessing', also known as the 'Night of the Decree' and the 'Night of Destiny'. It is celebrated on 14 Shaban. It is the night of the full moon before the start of Ramadan, and it was at this time that the Prophet ﷺ used to begin his preparations for Ramadan by passing whole nights in prayer. Many Muslims also celebrate this night by staying awake in prayer all night. Muslims believe that every year on this night God makes His order known to the angels as to who will live and who will die, what will be the means of livelihood for each individual for that year, and whose sins will be forgiven and who will be condemned.

Muslims often visit the graves of their relatives on 15 Shaban, and pray for the good of the departed souls.

Insight
Spending the whole night in prayer for mercy and salvation is a practice known as *ehyaa*, or revival. Some Muslims regard this sort of prayer as unnecessary, and disapprove of it as lacking in trust in God's justice and mercy.

Sometimes a special meal is eaten, and candles are lit. Sweets are made, and sweets and loaves distributed among the poor. Many Muslims fast for two days. Others reject all this as innovation.

Laylat ul-Qadr
27 Ramadan is traditionally recognized as *Laylat ul-Qadr*, the Night of Power, on which the Prophet ﷺ received his first revelation of the Qur'an.

We have indeed revealed this (message) in the Night of Power. Who will tell you what the Night of Power is? The Night of Power is better than a thousand months. Therein came down the angels

*and the Spirit (meaning Jibril) by God's permission, on every
errand: Peace! This until the rise of the morning!* (Surah 97:1–5)

In fact, the date is not known for certain, and Muslims may celebrate
this night on any of the odd nights during the last ten days of
Ramadan. Most keep the night of the 27th as an all-night of prayer
at the mosque.

Figure 3.13 Kurdish Muslims celebrating Laylat ul-Bara'at.

**When the Night of Power comes, Jibril descends with a
company of angels who grant blessings to everyone who is
standing or sitting and remembering the Most Gracious and
Glorious Allah.** (Tirmidhi)

Some Muslims make a religious 'retreat' (*i'tikaf*) for the whole of
the last ten days of Ramadan.

10 THINGS TO REMEMBER

1 For Muslims, submission to God and service of Him involves the whole of one's life in all its aspects. Worship, therefore, is not limited to matters of prayer and fasting.

2 The compulsory Muslim prayers are known as the salat (sing. salah). There are five salat per day – before sunrise (fajr), at mid-day (zuhr), when the shadows lengthen in the evening light (asr), just after sunset (maghrib) and during the hours of darkness (isha).

3 The person who calls Muslims to prayer is the mu'adhin (or muezzin). The imam is the person who leads the prayer.

4 Before performing salat, Muslims ritually wash so as to be in a state of ritual purity. The qiblah is the direction Muslims face when they pray – the direction of the Ka'bah in Makkah.

5 Muslims are expected to give away a fortieth of their wealth for the sake of Allah. This 'tax' on saved wealth is called zakah (meaning 'to purify').

6 The Ramadan fast lasts from new moon to new moon, from first light of dawn each day until sunset.

7 The Muslim word for a regularly recurring festival is Eid. Ramadan ends with the Eid ul-Fitr.

8 The Hajj pilgrimage to Makkah in Saudi Arabia is compulsory for every Muslim who is able to achieve it, once in a lifetime. The pilgrimage takes places two months and ten days after Ramadan and involves a number of stages.

9 Pilgrims usually complete their Hajj with a visit to the Prophet's ﷺ grave in Madinah. His tomb (under the green dome) is where his bones lie undisturbed, awaiting the Last Day and the Resurrection, just like the rest of us.

10 The word jihad means to struggle, to make an effort. A Muslim's real jihad is to struggle for the sake of Allah against injustice, corruption and oppression. Jihad can only be declared by a religious leader in a religious cause.

4

....

Places of worship

In this chapter you will learn about:
- *places where Muslims pray*
- *the functions of a community mosque*
- *the major features outside and inside a mosque*
- *how to behave in a mosque.*

Figure 4.1 Dar al-Islam mosque, Abiquiu, New Mexico, USA.

The Muslim place of prayer is known as a *masjid* or mosque.
Masjid means literally a 'place of sujud or prostration. in other
words, it is any place where someone bows down before God.
Muslims kneel and place their foreheads on the ground in the
humblest parts of their prostration. This place of prayer does not

have to be a special building – any clean place will do. Indeed, the Prophet said:

The whole world has been made a place of prayer, pure and clean.
(Muslim)

Wherever the hour of prayer overtakes you, you shall perform it. That place is a mosque.
(Bukhari)

Mosques

SIMPLE MOSQUES

In Muslim countries it is quite normal to see people praying by the roadside when it is time for prayer. It is also normal for little areas to be set aside for prayer at places like railway stations, often just a rectangular area facing the direction of Makkah, marked out by a few stones, perhaps under a tree, sometimes with a wooden board or a mat to kneel on. You might also see an arrow erected somewhere like a weather-vane, showing the direction of Makkah to the stranger. If possible, there will be a water supply near at hand, for the ritual washing, although *tayammum* (dry washing) is acceptable for the traveller.

Insight

I have often prayed out of doors, either on my own, or with a small group. There is something very special about praying under a tree, in a garden, or at some beautiful viewpoint. One feels very close to the Creator at such times.

GREAT OR HISTORIC MOSQUES

The two most important mosques in Islam are the Great Mosque in Makkah and the Prophet's ﷺ Mosque in Madinah. The al-Aqsa Mosque in Jerusalem is usually accepted as the third most revered mosque in Islam, but many countries have a chief mosque, or a special place, which is often spoken of as 'the third most holy site in Islam'. This is because Muslims who cannot go on Hajj often go to their country's special mosque at Hajj time.

THE FUNCTIONS OF A COMMUNITY MOSQUE

Communal prayer

The mosque serves several functions. First and foremost, it is the place where Muslims gather to pray together. Mosques in the West began with groups of Muslims gathering together in somebody's house; then using properties bought specifically so that they could function as mosques. Nowadays, most Muslim communities in the West are wealthy enough to afford purpose-built centres with prayer halls, and increasing numbers of major beautiful buildings are appearing in most big cities.

Insight

If a building has been converted into a mosque, the people praying might sometimes seem to be at a very odd angle. This is because they always find out the direction of Makkah, and pray facing it – even if it is the corner of the room.

The mosque is a very important part of the social life of the Muslim community, and its size and facilities depend on the wealth of its communities or sponsors. Modern mosques run homework clubs, women's activities and youth clubs, and may have IT facilities, crêches and kitchens. Once the prayers are over, Muslims often stay on, chatting to their friends, and using facilities provided for activities such as table tennis and snooker.

Women's facilities

Initially, lack of funds and space has often meant that mosques have concentrated on facilities for men, but this is gradually being remedied. The sunnah is for women and small children to pray in lines behind the men in the same prayer space, but in many mosques they have a segregated space such as a balcony or a separate room. (See Islamic feminism, and women imams on pages 365–70).

Relaxation and company

Sometimes Muslims feel quite lonely in a non-Muslim community, so the mosque gives them a chance to meet and relax with people who speak their native language.

The imam can use the premises if he wishes to meet people, discuss problems in the community, or help people with problems concerning their families (or, perhaps, immigration queries).

Education

Most mosques have a collection of books for study, sometimes sufficient to qualify being called a library. Muslims often invite visiting speakers and use the mosque for lectures and talks, or to discuss problems of Muslim law. The mosque also fulfils an important function as the school (or *madrassah*) where people can study the Arabic language, the Qur'an and various Islamic subjects.

THE MADRASSAH

All Muslims are expected to learn as much of the Qur'an as they are able, and for many this is a difficult business as Arabic is not their natural language. Boys and girls usually start these Islamic studies at the age of five, and continue until they are 15 or so. It is quite possible to go on being a student for the rest of your life. Some madrassahs are famous universities staffed by the top Muslim intellectuals.

Classes to learn Arabic, and to study the meaning of the Qur'an (known as *tafsir*) are held every day, children usually going to a local madrassah after school and studying for around two hours, sometimes five nights per week. Some schools even demand weekend work, too. Adults study at later times.

Insight

Teachers in local madrassahs are usually amateur volunteers, and their skills vary, as do the interest and skills of the students. Non-Muslims often do not realize that the youngsters normally attend madrassah after their normal school day, and still have school homework to do as well. It certainly cuts down play and TV time.

There are mosque exams every year, and few children fail them. Many youngsters and new converts are also urged to study for the GCSE in Religious Studies when there is an Islamic option. Teachers are not usually specially trained, but are willing and knowledgeable volunteers. Discipline is considered important, the duty of an adult towards a child, and adults are allowed to use corporal punishment; however, it is virtually never needed because Muslim children are respectful to their elders and behave politely.

Social functions

The mosque can be hired out for all sorts of functions – meetings, parties for weddings and festival days, birthdays, circumcision parties, or welcome home parties, celebrating the passing of an important exam. These are all joyful functions, and usually involve huge meals. Most mosques will have a good kitchen area as part of the complex, and perhaps a special function room. Some even run a café for the public.

Hospital and hospitality

Sometimes people sleep overnight in a mosque, either on the carpeted floor of the prayer hall or in specially provided facilities. The oldest traditions reveal that many mosques also did service as primitive hospitals, feeding centres, and 'rest-room' facilities. Many still do.

Farewells to the dead

Less happy gatherings are those to mourn the dead and pay the last respects to friends and relatives before burial. The mosque may have an ablutions room where it is possible to administer the last washing to the deceased before shrouding them.

IMAMS

The *imam* is the leader of the mosque, but there is no suggestion of priesthood; every Muslim stands before God responsible for himself or herself. However, whenever two or more Muslims come together to pray, the one with the most knowledge, or the eldest, leads the prayer.

The imam also usually has the job of *khatib*, that is, he delivers the *khutbah* or double sermon at the Friday congregation, and probably organizes Islamic studies for the young people. After the first sermon, the imam will sit down for a few moments, and then give the second. Then the Friday prayer of two rakat follows, and after this people pray individually.

Any person respected by the mosque members, who has studied Qur'an and hadith, has good knowledge of the faith, and is known for his piety and common-sense can be elected imam for the community. In the United Kingdom, each mosque elects its own imam. Some imams have become famous teachers, and have rallied the faithful in times of persecution and war.

In 2005, the UK Government proposed a 'Britishness test' for foreign-born imams, after concern was expressed that some could speak little English and had hardly any knowledge of Western societies. The idea has been welcomed by many mosques, since community members frequently did not understand the sermons in either Arabic or the ethnic languages of the original immigrants. This has now been diluted to a test on life in Britain, including its constitution, legal system, customs and religious life, if they apply to settle after four years or seek citizenship after being in the country for five years.

It is hoped that future imams will be chosen who have good
understanding of Muslims brought up in the West, and will
perhaps be encouraged to take part in the civic life of the
community, including mixing with other faiths, as part of a drive
to improve community cohesion and end ghettoization. There are
now several training courses for imams, with certification.

THE MAJOR FEATURES OUTSIDE A MOSQUE

Muslims can convert any sort of building into a mosque – many
old churches and houses, warehouses and even a fire station have
been put to this use by the growing communities. Mosques do
not always look like mosques. None of the traditional features is
compulsory.

It is advisable to have good car-parking facilities and, where
possible, toilet facilities that are quite separate from the carpeted
prayer hall, for reasons of hygiene and to prevent wetness – from
the Muslim practice of washing after visiting the toilet.

Dome and Minaret

Where the mosque is purpose-built, the two most typical features
are the dome and the minaret. The dome is an architectural device
giving the impression of space and calm when one goes inside; it
also helps acoustically. It is also a feature that reminds Muslims of
their origins in the Middle East.

The minaret is a tall tower where the *mu'adhin* gives the call to
prayer known as the *adhan*. Throughout the Muslim world this
stirring cry is given five times per day, but in non-Muslim societies
it is frequently not sounded, so as not to upset and disturb those
who would not be sympathetic.

Symbol of Islam

Atop the dome and/or the minaret one can usually see the symbol of Islam, a crescent moon. Sometimes there is also a five-pointed star which reminds Muslims of the five 'pillars' or obligatory duties of their faith; the moon reminds them of God the Creator, and the lunar calendar which governs Islamic festivals and special days.

THE MAJOR FEATURES INSIDE THE MOSQUE

Clocks

A series of clocks usually shows the prayer times each day – prayer times are flexible when praying on your own, but have to keep to a strict timetable for a congregation to come together. The clocks will show the five *salat* and the Friday prayer.

Insight

None of the typical features of a mosque are compulsory. If the mosque did not have a minaret, dome or qiblah niche, it would not matter at all. Some mosques are very simple with very basic facilities – others are vast and full of wonderful architecture and decoration.

Washing facilities

It is not necessary to perform *wudu* at the mosque, and many Muslims prefer to do it at home before going. In the mosque, men and women usually have separate facilities for toilet and ablutions, where there is running water.

The toilets frequently have both the flushing style and the hole in the ground type, for people who are most used to this sort of design. There will be several pairs of slip-on shoes lying around for people with bare feet to borrow. There is always water available for washing in a Muslim toilet, but there might not be toilet paper. There will either be a pipe that will automatically wash you if you are in the right position, or it is traditional to use a *loti*, rather like a jug with a curved spout. (Use the left hand. The right hand is used for eating, and all 'honourable' purposes.) Outside the actual toilet there will be wash-basins and towels.

The most common arrangement for wudu ablutions is for a row of taps to be set in the wall over a drain, with stools arranged for people to sit on while they wash their feet. People coming to pray often leave the water to dry by itself and do not use towels.

Decoration in the mosque

The most noticeable thing straightaway is the lack of furniture or decoration in the prayer room. There are no chairs or pews for people to sit on. Everyone sits on the floor. There are no pictorial decorations or statues, because representation of this sort is forbidden in Islam as it encourages idolatry. You will never see any representation of God, angels, or the Prophets. However, this does not mean that mosques are dull places. Many are extremely beautiful, with richly coloured carpets, different marbles for columns and surfaces, intricately patterned and colourful tiles, carved woodwork, stained glass, beautiful chandeliers, gold-painted ceilings, ornamental calligraphy on texts from the Qur'an, and so forth.

Insight

Many Muslims feel that simple is best, and money is best spent on helping the needy and not on buildings. Others feel that it is right to offer nothing but the best to Allah.

The carpet in the prayer hall is generally marked out with lines or regular patterns, so that when the prayer lines form, people know where to stand and how much space to occupy. Some massive carpets such as the one at Regent's Park Mosque in London have patterns like individual prayer mats. However, when a large congregation comes together for prayer, they move very close together, shoulder to shoulder, and often literally toe to toe, with their toes touching those of the next person.

The qiblah and mihrab

The wall facing Makkah is known as the *qiblah* wall, and set in this wall is a specially decorated niche or alcove known as the mihrab. This is not in any way an altar, although it looks to a Christian rather like an altar area with the altar table taken away. It simply points the direction of the Ka'bah, and concentrates the Muslim's mind upon Allah.

The prayer leader stands in front of the *mihrab*, which is sometimes known as the 'niche of lights', the symbol for the Divine Presence in the heart. Some mihrabs incorporate a shell-shape; the shell symbolizes the 'ear of the heart', and the pearl within is the 'Divine Word'.

When Muslims have taken over existing buildings and converted them into mosques, the qiblah may seem to be in a very odd place, not at all a focal point – but it always indicates the direction of Makkah.

The minbar

On the right side of the mihrab is the *minbar*, the platform from which the imam gives the *khutbah* sermons. These can be very simple, or highly ornate. The simplest ones are usually just a couple of carpeted steps with a small platform at the top. Ornate minbars can consist of a high flight of stairs, beautifully carved and decorated.

Figure 4.2 The minbar.

WHAT TO DO WHEN ENTERING A MOSQUE

When visiting a mosque, one should be suitably dressed. For men, this involves being clean, smart and tidy. Muslim men would not go into a mosque with shirt hanging open, or wearing shorts. For women, it is polite if they are sensitive to Muslim custom and cover the arms and legs, and wear a scarf or veil over their hair. Muslim women's dress is always modest – transparent, over-tight or too short clothing would be out of place, as would too much make-up and any perfume.

Both men and women should bear in mind that they will have to take off their shoes, and will probably be asked to sit down on the floor, difficult and embarrassing with dirty feet/socks and short, tight skirts.

Insight

Personal cleanliness is a key feature of Islam. The Prophet ﷺ particularly stressed washing private parts, hands, mouths, ears, armpits and feet. Whatever a Muslim woman's normal dress, she will always cover everything for her prayers except her face and hands.

There will probably be two entrances at the mosque, one for men and one for women. In many mosques men and women pray in separate areas, and how this is arranged depends on the design. Sometimes the women have a balcony, or they might pray behind a curtain at the back.

On entering the mosque, both men and women take off their shoes and place them in the rack or on the shelves provided. (If it is a very big meeting, it is sensible to keep your shoes with you in a carrier bag to avoid an irritating scramble after the prayer.) In mosques where there are a lot of tourists, there may be someone employed to look after the shoes, but they are normally quite safe.

It is not necessary to take off socks, stockings or tights, but polite visitors will make sure their socks are clean and not smelly or full of holes. Muslims, who may wash their feet five times per day, are often somewhat shocked by the state of non-Muslim feet! It is impolite to soil carpets with dirt trodden in from outside, or with sticky, smelly feet.

How to behave in the mosque

Quiet, respectful behaviour is expected at all times. It is considered very bad manners to talk loudly or shout to someone or call out, to smoke, or to interrupt the devotions of people who might be already praying or reading the Qur'an. It is also 'not good form' for an individual to perform personal recitations of the Qur'an too loudly, and thus disturb others, unless the others are happy with that.

Muslims should not continue any meetings or activities in the hall up to the last moment before prayer time, so that the hall is not ready, or people arriving for prayer feel they are disturbing them. It is good manners in Islam to pray two *rakat* before the *salah* prayer to 'greet the mosque'.

THE MOSQUE IN THE HOME

All Muslims pray at home sometimes; most Muslim women pray at home every time. Therefore many Muslims have a special place set aside, perhaps an entire room, which is kept clean and ready at all times, and is usually carpeted so that people can kneel in comfort. Many Muslims use little individual prayer mats to kneel on as well as the carpet, but this is not compulsory. The prayer mat is simply an aid to providing a clean place.

A non-Muslim visitor might find it strange that an almost empty room is regarded as the most important place in the home, but it is the heart of the Muslim home, the place of prayer.

Figure 4.3 Muslims set aside a special place to pray at home.

10 THINGS TO REMEMBER

1 *A mosque, or masjid, is any place used for sujud – i.e. bowing down before God in prayer.*

2 *The two most important mosques for all Muslims are those of the Ka'bah in Makkah, and the Prophet's ﷺ Mosque in Madinah.*

3 *Mosques usually have a large space for prayer – either a covered hall or a large courtyard.*

4 *Mosques usually have a water supply, for Muslims are required to perform a ritual wash before prayer if they are not in the state of wudu already.*

5 *Women pray separately from men, either in rows behind them (the Madinah practice), or in a room or balcony set aside, or behind a veil.*

6 *The minaret is the tall tower from which the faithful are called to prayer. It is not a compulsory part of a mosque.*

7 *The minbar is a raised platform from which the Imam may deliver his Friday sermon or* khutbah.

8 *The mihrab is something that indicates the qiblah or direction of Makkah. It is often a semi-circular shaped niche carved into the wall, or built jutting out from the wall facing Makkah.*

9 *The mosque also serves social functions – for funeral prayers, as a law court, for meetings, lectures, festivities, parties, weddings, charitable fundraising events, and so on.*

10 *The madrassah is the mosque school where training is given in Arabic, reading, learning and understanding the Qur'an, and other aspects of Islamic study. Students usually start at around 7 years old, and there is no upper age limit.*

5

Social Islam

In this chapter you will learn about:
- *Islamic rights and duties*
- *the equality of male and female in Islam*
- *rules regarding dress and diet (including alcohol)*
- *Islam and the workplace*
- *the importance of friendship and hospitality.*

Islamic human rights and ethics

Many people seem to spend a great deal of their time and effort demanding their rights, and are frequently discontented whatever they receive. In Islam, rights are not an end in themselves, but the means to fulfil the duties of life. The human being who is worthwhile contributes to life and shares in the service of humanity, alleviating human suffering and working hard to take care of those in his or her charge. The true Muslim is interested in the economic and scientific advancement of humanity, as well as moral and spiritual well-being.

Insight

There is a difference between human rights and human needs. Many things the human needs – such as to be loved, or respected – are not rights, but have to be earned.

MORAL AWARENESS

It is moral awareness and participation in the good of society that makes a human being different from an animal, and was the aim of Allah in ordaining humans as His *khalifahs* on the planet.

Humans are granted the right to life in order to use it in the production of good works and deeds. They have free-will to behave as they choose, but when they choose to submit to the will of God, they strive to pass their lives in the best way possible.

Consciousness of these duties drives the Muslim to strive to uphold the rights of the oppressed by strengthening the legal and social foundations of society and by countering those who trample on the rights and dignity of others. Any so-called Islamic government that has itself become a tyrant has departed from the principles of Islam, no matter how self-righteous it might claim to be.

He will not enter Paradise whose neighbour is not secure from his wrongful conduct.

(Muslim)

THE BASIC HUMAN RIGHTS

All human beings are the creations of God, and loved by Him. Therefore there are certain basic rights which should be shared by the whole of humanity, whether people are Muslim or not. All have the right to be fed, clothed, educated, cared for and buried by the society which governs their existence. Every society contains people whose disabilities prevent them from working, or who are too sick or too weak to earn sufficient wages to secure a decent life. There are children who have lost parents, wives who have lost husbands, old people who are no longer able to care for themselves. Any society with the least respect for human dignity would not allow such people to be left neglected and uncared for.

ISLAMIC OBLIGATIONS

Islam makes it obligatory for the wealthy and able-bodied to support the less fortunate. No society should victimize or terrorize its weak members, or deprive people of liberty for no reason. No society should try to 'brainwash' its members, or attempt to force them to believe things against their natural will, ability or awareness.

These human rights have all been granted by God Himself, and not by any ruler or government, and it is the duty of Muslims to protect these rights actively. Failure to do so results in the loss of these rights, and leads to *tughyan* – tyranny and suffering.

None of you is a true believer until you wish for your brother what you wish for yourself. (Bukhari and Muslim)

Specific human rights in Islam

Islam teaches that once new human beings have been conceived, they have a right to life. A mother is not allowed to abort her unborn child for the sake of social convenience, or because she is young or unmarried.

In Islam, human rights include the following specific areas:

- ▶ *The right to life.*
- ▶ *The right to equality.*
- ▶ *The right to freedom.*
- ▶ *The right to emigration and refuge, to remove oneself from oppression.*
- ▶ *The right to work to provide for oneself and one's family.*
- ▶ *The right to justice and equality before the Law.*
- ▶ *The right to protect one's honour.*
- ▶ *The right to social welfare and the basic necessities of life.*
- ▶ *The right to reject sexual intimacy without marriage.*
- ▶ *The right to privacy, and security of private life.*
- ▶ *The right to dignity, and not to be abused or ridiculed.*
- ▶ *The right to education.*
- ▶ *The right to freedom of expression and to protest against tyranny.*
- ▶ *The right to freedom of conscience and conviction.*
- ▶ *The right to protect religious sentiments.*
- ▶ *The right to participate in affairs of state.*
- ▶ *The right to rise above the level of animal life.*

Freedom of speech and opinion should be weighed against the offence given to others. Muslims would always object to books, media reporting, TV programmes that vilify the prophets – who are no longer here to speak for themselves. They protest vociferously against films that slur the character of Jesus ﷺ, for example.

People have the right to freedom. Nobody should be kept prisoner without trial and sentence, or enslaved (unless it is a voluntary arrangement to pay off debt), or kidnapped or hijacked. Moreover, people should not be kept in enforced marriages, or by employers from whom they wish to break free.

There are numerous passages in the Qur'an and hadith expressing people's rights.

Why should you not fight in the cause of Allah and of those who, being weak, are ill-treated and oppressed? Men, women and children, whose cry is: 'Our Lord, rescue us from this town whose people are oppressors, and raise for us one who will protect and help us!' (Surah 4:75)

The Prophet ﷺ said:

How are rights neglected? When sins are committed openly, and no one prevents the sinners from wrongdoing. (Targhib)

He who amongst you sees something abominable should modify it with the help of his hand; and if he has not the strength to do that, then he should do it by word of mouth; and if he has not the strength enough for that, then he should at least (abhor it) from his heart. (Muslim)

THE USEFUL GUIDE OF THE CONSCIENCE

The conscience is the guide to the Muslim, and should always be listened to, for it brings the stirrings of Allah's will. The Prophet ﷺ accounted a person a believer 'when your deed pleases you and your evil deed grieves you'. He was then asked what sin was, and replied: 'When a thing disturbs your heart, give it up.' (Ahmad).

Moreover, the Prophet ﷺ had no time for hypocrisy. He said:

Look at your own faults. This will prevent you from finding faults with others. Never be in search of the faults of others. It is sinful on your part to detect those faults in others which exist in you. (Abu Dawud)

Insight

Any behaviour that abuses human rights, whether done in public or in private, is forbidden to Muslims. Any person abused by a Muslim has the right to seek justice and retribution.

In Islam, the conscience is used to determine the huge range of actions that are not specifically ruled to be *halal* (allowed) or *haram* (forbidden). Sometimes a matter might fall into several categories, depending on the circumstances, and how your conscience feels about it. (See Chapter 7 on Islamic law.)

ISLAMIC ETHICS

God does not look upon your bodies and appearances; He looks upon your hearts and deeds. (Bayhaqi)

Insight

The Prophet ﷺ said: 'The people of the Fire are five – the weak who do not have the will to avoid evil, those who are merely copiers of others, the dishonest whose greed cannot be concealed even in trivial matters, those who betray you morning and evening, and those of uncouth manners and foul speech.'

The aim of Islam is to promote certain values specifically, and deliberately try to reduce or stamp out others.

The key values in Islam
The key values in Islam are:

Faith
You should worship God as if you are seeing Him, for He sees you even if you do not see Him. (Muslim)

Justice

O believers, be seekers after justice, witnesses for God, even though it be against yourselves or your parents and kinsmen.

(Surah 4:133)

Forgiveness

Be forgiving and control yourself in the face of provocation; give justice to the person who was unfair and unjust to you; give to someone even though he did not give to you when you were in need, and keep fellowship with the one who did not reciprocate your concern.

(Bukhari)

Compassion

He who has no compassion for our little ones ... is not one of us.

(Muslim)

Mercy

Hold tight to the rope of God, and never let it go. Remember that God showed mercy to you and blessed you while you were still enemies. Remember how He united your hearts together in love, so that by His grace you became brothers.

(Surah 3:103)

Sincerity

God does not accept belief if it is not expressed in deeds; and He does not accept your deeds unless they conform to your beliefs.

(Muslim)

Truth

Always speak the truth, even if it is bitter.

(Bayhaqi)

Generosity

The truly virtuous person ...gives food, for the love of Him, to the needy, the orphan, the captive, (saying): 'We feed you only for the sake of Allah; we desire no recompense from you and no thanks.'

(Surah 76:7–10)

An ignorant person who is generous is dearer to God than a worshipper who is miserly.

(Tirmidhi)

Humility

Those who are humble for the sake of Allah will be exalted by Allah, for though they consider themselves lowly they are great in the eyes of others; but those who are proud will be debased by Allah, for though they consider themselves great they are lowly in the eyes of others to such an extent that they might be of less value than a dog or a pig.

(Bayhaqi)

Tolerance

Let there be no coercion in religion. (Surah 2:256)

To you be your religion, and to me, mine. (Surah 109.6)

Modesty

Modesty and faith are joined closely together; if either of them is lost, the other goes also. (Muslim, Bayhaqi)

Chastity

The fornicators who fornicate are not believers so long as they commit it. (Ahmad)

Patience and fortitude

Nobody can be given a blessing better and greater than patience. (Bukhari)

Responsibility

Every one of you is a shepherd, and will be questioned about the well-being of their flock. (Muslim)

Courage

Fight in the cause of Allah those who fight you, but do not go beyond the limits ...for tyranny and oppression are worse than murder. (Surah 2:190)

The key things that are abhorred

The key things that are abhorred are:

Hypocrisy

Woe to those who pray but are unmindful of their prayer, or pray only to be seen by people. (Surah 107:6–7)

Insight

The Prophet ﷺ said: 'Three things are signs of the hypocrite – when they speak they tell lies, when they make promises they break them, and when trusted they are dishonest.'

Cheating

The truthful and trusty merchant is associated with the prophets, the upright and the martyrs. (Tirmidhi, Darimi)

Backbiting and suspicion

O believers, avoid suspicion, for suspicion is a sin. And do not spy or backbite one another. (Surah 49:12)

Lying

If you do not give up telling lies, God will have no need of you giving up food and drink (in fasting). (Abu Dawud)

Pride

Do not turn your face away from people in scorn, and do not walk about in the earth exultantly; God loves not the proud and boastful. Be modest in your walk and lower your voice; the most hideous of voices is that of the ass! (Surah 31:19)

Envy

In the worshipper's heart, faith and envy cannot dwell together. (Nisa'i)

Beware of envy, for it eats up goodness as fire eats up fuel. (Abu Dawud)

Anger

Truly, anger spoils faith just as bitter aloes spoil honey. (Ahmad)

Allah holds back His punishment from him who holds back his anger. (Bayhaqi)

Divisiveness

This is My straight path, so follow it, and do not follow other paths which will separate you from this path. (Surah 6:153)

Excess and extremism

O people of the Book! Do not exceed in your religion the bounds, trespassing beyond the truth. (Surah 5:77)

Insight

Muslims should not be involved in persecuting or harassing the people of other faiths or their places of worship. The Prophet's ﷺ charter at Madinah gave every faith the right to security under Islamic governance, and freedom of worship.

O believers, do not make unlawful those good things which Allah has made lawful for you, and commit no excess. God loves not those given to excess. (Surah 5:87)

SUMMARY

These ethical values are shared with all serious followers of many religions – they are universal values. Islamic ethics could be summarized by this one verse from the Qur'an and this one famous hadith:

> *Goodness and Evil cannot be equal. Repay evil with what is better, then he who was your enemy will become your intimate friend.*
>
> (Surah 41:34)

The Prophet ﷺ said:

> **You shall not enter Paradise until you have faith, and you cannot have faith until you love one another. Have compassion on those you can see, and He Whom you cannot see will have compassion on you.**
>
> (Muslim)

Women in Islam

> *For Muslim men and women, for believing men and women ... for men and women who are patient and constant, who humble themselves, who give in charity, who fast, who guard their chastity, who engage in the praise of Allah – for them Allah has prepared forgiveness and a great reward.*
>
> (Surah 33:35)

This particular verse was the answer from Allah given in direct response to the Prophet's ﷺ wife Umm Salamah, who asked him one day why the Qur'an revelations never specifically mentioned women.

In Arabic, the word *insan* (man) means 'a human being', 'person', or 'male and female' without a particular gender identification, and thus every instruction given to Muslims in the Qur'an refers to both male and female believers alike unless it clearly specifies otherwise. They have been given the same religious duties and will be judged according to exactly the same criteria. If a verse is intended for men only or women only, this is made clear.

Equally erroneous is the common translation of *Bani Adam* into 'sons of Adam' or 'men' instead of a more accurate term 'children of Adam' or 'people'.

FROM THE SAME SOUL

Muslim doctrine holds that women are not in any way inferior beings to men, but were created originally from the same single soul.

> *O humanity! Have reverence for your Lord, the One who created you from a single soul (nafs) and from that soul He created its mate, and through them He spread countless men and women.*

(Surah 4:1)

> **Insight**
>
> Although the Prophet ﷺ referred jokingly to women being easily broken as they were created from a bent rib which would snap if you forcefully tried to straighten it, the story of Eve being created from Adam's ﷺ rib is not part of the Qur'an.

WOMEN'S RIGHTS

Muslim women are granted equal, but different, rights in Islam as well as equal responsibilities. Allah gave them the burdens of menstruation and childbirth, and therefore certain privileges and allowances are made for them, such as being excused from salah prayers and fasting while menstruating.

A woman in Islamic law is equal to her male counterpart, just as liable for her actions as a male. Her testimony is demanded and valid in court, her opinions are sought and acted upon, just as the Prophet ﷺ consulted his wives. She has the same duty as a man to become educated and a useful member of the community. To seek knowledge is the duty of every Muslim.

> **Insight**
>
> The concessions granted to women because of menstruation and childbirth (i.e. excused prayers and deferred fasts) do not make their worship inferior, only a little different – these concessions were ordained by God in the Qur'an.

The Qur'an clearly shows Allah's intention to liberate women from injustice by giving them rights not previously enjoyed. Some examples include rights of ownership, decision-making in marriage, divorce and so on. Both Muslim men and women are expected by God to 'enjoin the doing of what is right and forbid the doing of what is wrong' (Surah 9:71) in all spheres of life, and to act as His vice-regents in ensuring justice, freedom and equality for all. Yet Muslim women have varying roles, rights and obligations depending on the particular society in which they live. In many Muslim countries women have fewer rights than men with regard to marriage, divorce, civil rights, legal status, dress code, professional lives and education (see Islamic feminism page 361).

Insight

Many men (including Muslims) find the Islamic teachings on women's rights and equality notoriously hard to accept.

WOMEN AND EDUCATION

Muslim women were/are commanded by Allah to seek education from cradle to grave and from any source available. When Muslim women and girls are refused education this is the very opposite of what the Prophet ﷺ taught. He appreciated forthright women who were not frightened to speak out, or discuss and debate matters. He appreciated women who were educated and had knowledge, who were also kind and compassionate, and hard-working and hospitable. Certainly some Muslim women live in societies that do not stretch to education for girls, but happily, many Muslim women are among the most highly qualified professionals in the world.

In some places Muslim females are not allowed to be taught by men, yet all the women of Madinah were taught by the Prophet ﷺ himself; and moreover, even before his demise, men were also being taught by intellectual women – such as Umm Waraqah, Umm Darda, Shifa bint Abdullah, and the Prophet's ﷺ beloved Aishah, despite her youth.

These days many homes cannot afford the luxury of a housewife. Parents may think of their male offspring as future breadwinners, but ignore the fact that all too often men are unemployed and the females are the breadwinners. Girls are persuading their parents that there is a desperate need for Muslim women to acquire a good education using modern methods and tomorrow's technology, and to achieve useful qualifications.

Educated Muslim women are a necessity. It is highly preferable in Islam for women to be treated by female nurses and doctors, dentists and midwives, and taught by female teachers, and counselled by female lawyers – therefore Muslim women need to train. Muslim women's services are needed – as tailors, bakers, librarians, chemists, engineers, nurses, secretaries, teachers, police, those who work with the mentally ill, marriage counsellors, ambulance drivers, doctors, dentists, midwives, lawyers and so on. One has only to think of the Indian Muslim women fleeing Idi Amin's Uganda who now staff the UK's National Health Service.

The right of access to the mosques

In the Prophet's ﷺ day, women went regularly to the mosque to pray with the men, despite the attempts of some of those men to keep them away. The Prophet's ﷺ wife Aishah reported: 'I used to set out towards the mosque and observe prayer along with Allah's Messenger; and I was in the row of women nearest the row of men.' (Muslim). The Prophet's ﷺ order to menfolk reluctant to encourage their wives to attend the mosque was: 'Do not forbid the mosques to the women of Allah.' (Bukhari 11.12) 'When a woman asks one of you to go to the mosque, grant this to her.' (Nisa'i 2.32)

Insight

When a mosque has no facilities for women, it is usually because it is still in the 'pioneering' stage in a community, and has probably been set up by a cultural group that keeps men and women largely separate. Women should not be prevented from praying at the mosque.

Some small mosques are men-only prayer clubs, even turning away travelling Muslim women who arrive looking for a place to pray – when they should function as useful community centres with all sorts of facilities, and not only allow womenfolk to pray there, but to utilize their talents in the general running of the place. These places drive up-and-coming Muslim women to despair, and will no doubt find more and more people voting with their feet, leaving them to head to a community of like-minded souls, and joining other more progressive communities.

WOMEN AND WORK

There is no Islamic injunction against women going out to work, so long as that work is compatible with Islamic principles, and does not threaten the security and well-being of the home. The Prophet's ﷺ first wife, Khadijah, was a highly successful business woman, who was the Prophet's ﷺ employer before she became his wife. Several of his later wives also earned their own incomes.

Having a wife who does not work is usually a luxury of the wealthy. All over the world Muslim women work, and may be the breadwinners. Muslim women can get just as bored at home as non-Muslim women, and are just as entitled to employ household staff so that they can take other employment themselves – but many Muslim women do not wish to do this, or to leave the raising of their children to others.

In fact, Islam puts a big burden of responsibility upon the husband, for Allah granted Muslim women the right to be provided for, and not to be obliged or forced to go out to earn money if they do not wish to. Even if the woman happens to be more wealthy than her husband, he has the duty to keep her, and should not rely on her for support.

Insight

It is true that some of the world's poorest women are Muslims, but so are some of the most wealthy.

INHERITANCE

At the time of the Prophet ﷺ, giving a woman any inheritance was a radical departure from Arab practice. (Indeed, it was a radical notion in much of the West as well until the twentieth century.) Prior to the Qur'anic injunction, women not only did not inherit from their relatives, but women themselves were bequeathed as if they were property to be distributed at the death of a husband, father, or brother.

By giving women the right to inherit, Islam changed the status of women in an unprecedented fashion. Moreover, this right was God-given and not acquired as a result of political pressure.

It is interesting that inheritance rights were not granted to women in England until the Married Women's Property Act in the mid-nineteenth century.

Strict laws govern the shares of property and money Muslims may leave to others. The Qur'an lays down that a son would inherit double the share of a daughter, which makes daughters sound inferior. Where the society is tribal and patriarchal, and where women generally have no financial security other than that provided by men, the reason men are granted larger shares is because they are expected to provide for their womenfolk and the entire household, whereas women's bequests are theirs to keep, and they are not obliged to share them.

Insight

In societies where women do not contribute much to the finances of a household, it is just for male providers to inherit more. But today, where women share the burden of employment, financing, etc., a Muslim lawyer might argue the spirit of equality against the letter of the law of inheritance.

The injunction that a male receives a share equal to that of two females applies only to the inheritance of children from their parents. Parents who inherit from a deceased offspring each inherit equally.

In matters of witness

In matters where their witness would be just as valid as a man's, the witness of one woman is quite sufficient and accepted as the same as a man's. All the Qur'an references except Surah 2:282 apply equally to women as to men – this verse is the exception to the general rule that the testimony of a woman is equal to that of a man.

In modern society, where both women and men are well versed in business and financial matters, there is no special danger of a woman forgetting or misunderstanding a transaction. The Shari'ah generally accepts that two female witnesses are advisable in cases where women have little knowledge and no expertise of the subject, and could be cheated.

Insight

Women are well advised to have two witnesses to any transactions involving their own relatives, especially husbands – and to make sure they have everything in writing, preserved securely. When circumstances change (e.g. divorce), it is all too easy for unscrupulous men to cheat their women.

SECLUSION OF WOMEN

Seclusion of women was originally nothing to do with Islam but an aspect of social class, both for security and snobbery. Wealthy people were able to afford privacy. These days it is largely Muslim societies where the practice still persists, but extreme seclusion for all women was never asked for by Allah or the Prophet ﷺ, and the hadiths are full of descriptions of active, courageous and hospitable women out and about, entertaining, nursing, or on the battlefield.

The urge for Muslims to seclude women arose from a narrow interpretation of the following verses addressed specifically to the Prophet's ﷺ wives:

> O wives of the Prophet! You are not like ordinary women. If you fear Allah, don't be too casual in your speech, lest someone with an unsteadfast heart should be moved with desire ... live quietly in your houses, and don't make a worldly display as in the times of ignorance; establish regular prayer and give regular charity, and obey Allah and His Apostle.
> (Surah 33:32–3)

If devout Muslim women choose to regard this as binding upon themselves from the desire to emulate the Prophet's ﷺ wives, all well and good, and they have the right to it, but if they are forced into it, this is an abuse of Islam.

In a village community, a woman can often have considerable freedom, since most of the villagers will be her own relatives, and therefore *mahrem*. The Prophet's ﷺ wives lived eyeball to eyeball with the public, and must have appreciated being able to retreat from it. This is obviously not the same thing as being *forced* to stay indoors. The privilege of seclusion indicates distinct and superior rank in societies where much of life was lived 'on the street'. If a wife wanted to be totally secluded, and to live inside the home, she would normally require servants to perform the numerous errands.

PURDAH

Many Muslim men from the Asian subcontinent and various Arab countries do not like their womenfolk to mix at all with males outside the family circle. This practice is declining as, all over the world, Muslim women are receiving education and taking up employment. Seclusion is generally not practised by Muslims of other nationalities.

Purdah implies complete segregation of men from women, and in some Muslim societies the women have a separate and private part of the house (or even tent), and may use separate entrances. Most mosques have separate entrances for men and women, because the women pray at the back, but they usually rejoin their menfolk afterwards.

There is no text requiring women to be hidden away at all times, although in many cultures Muslim women are very shy of strangers, and many accept seclusion as one form of piety. In today's world, you can see Muslim women in public in every country and culture, content that in their modest dress and behaviour they are fulfilling any requirement of Islam.

Insight

It is important to separate cultural customs from the requirements of Islam. I was personally irritated by a well-meaning Imam who expected me to give a lecture from behind a curtain so that the audience (90 per cent men) could not see me.

EXPLOITATION OF WOMEN

The Prophet ﷺ was alert to unfortunate women being exploited in work situations, and commented on the injustices done to women workers in this way:

Allah will definitely enforce the settlement of the dues of those entitled to receive them on the Day of Judgement; even the wrong done to the hornless goat (i.e. the female) by the horned goat (i.e. the male) will be redressed! (Muslim)

Any woman working to increase the financial income of her family should have the same rights as a male worker, and should not be taken advantage of, or subjected to any form of harassment (especially not sexual harassment). She also has the right to fair wages, and decent conditions of work. If a so-called Muslim employer is using women more or less as slave labour, it is an abuse and he or she is flying in the face of Islamic principles and will ultimately be called to account for it.

The right to be protected

Women's honour is highly regarded in Islam, and a woman of any age has the right to be treated according to her position; as a protected virgin, a respected wife and partner, an honoured mother or grandmother.

Islam takes note of the physical differences between the sexes; it does not assume that men and women are 'the same'. Thoughtful allowances should be made to protect women and make them comfortable. Men do not have to endure menstruation, pregnancy, childbirth and suckling children. A Muslim woman has the right to be cared for at times of physical pain and discomfort. Men are not usually harassed because of their attractiveness, or forced to accept sex in order to 'get on', or not lose a job.

In many cultures women have been and still are subjected to all sorts of abuses and restrictions from their menfolk. It is not Islam that causes abuse or oppression of women, but chauvinism and the mingling of Islamic teachings with tribal customs and traditions.

Feminists are calling for re-evaluation of attitudes and practices that, although done in the name of Islam, are actually the result of strong cultural influence, some even contrary to the basic messages found in Qur'an and *sunnah*. They seek to revive the equality bestowed on women in the religion's early years by re-reading the Qur'an, putting the verses in context, and disentangling them from tribal practices.

A woman forbidden from driving a car in Riyadh will cheerfully take the wheel when abroad, confident that her country's bizarre law has nothing to do with Islam. A woman forbidden education or the chance to work in Afghanistan might have been a high Court Judge in pre-Taliban days.

Forced marriages may still take place in certain Indian, Pakistani and Bangladeshi communities, but would be anathema to Muslim women from other backgrounds. Female genital mutilation is still practised in certain pockets of Africa and Egypt, but is viewed as an inconceivable horror by the vast majority of Muslims (see page 367).

Insight

If the rule or practice does not apply to every Muslim woman, then it is a matter of culture and not an Islamic requirement.

Islamic clothing

People who have travelled about the world will be very aware that there are all sorts of styles and garments that qualify as Islamic dress. Basically, the principles are modesty and cleanliness. What people actually wear is very much governed by the society in which they live, but Islamic garments are always modest and, if possible, clean.

The Prophet ﷺ said:

Every religion has a characteristic, and the characteristic of Islam is modesty. (Ibn Majah)

MEN'S CLOTHING

There are few particular rules for men's wear, except for pilgrims in *ihram*, and when it comes to the time of prayer. At prayer times, even in the most primitive conditions, men must be covered at least from navel to knee. In ihram male clothing consists of two unsewn sheets of white cloth and nothing else. Otherwise, the only rulings are that men should not wear garments made of silk, unless they have a skin disorder that requires it, and should not wear jewellery other than a wedding ring, which should be made of silver and not gold. Women are allowed to wear gold and other jewellery.

Some Muslims adopt particular styles that indicate affiliation to sects within Islam. Men of the Tablighi-Jama'at, for example, go for long beards, prayer caps, and short trousers that clear the ankles. *Sufis* often have distinctive turbans or robes. The Nation of Islam men wear Western-style suits and bow ties.

HIJAB

Hijab means veiling, covering or concealing, and indicates modesty both in dress and behaviour, an expression of piety for all Muslim women. Discussion only arises over the extent of the cover. Muslim women are not expected to wish to display their sexual attributes in public. That is something reserved for their husbands, for whom they should make themselves as beautiful and attractive as possible.

Some Western women may regard Muslim women's dress as dull, and restrictive – but this is not how Muslim women see it. They prefer to dress in beautiful clothing which is graceful but modest, and regard revealing and sexually provocative clothing as pandering to the lowest instinct of the male, and encouraging men to look on women as sex objects rather than equal and independent characters. Women going about in public dressed to stir up male lust are regarded as 'offering the goods' and 'asking for trouble'.

Islam does not require women to wear long black robes and black veils, nor to hide their faces, but travellers will have become familiar with Muslim women so covered in certain places. The requirement of Islam is for Muslim women to cover their bodies from the neck to the wrist and foot. They should not wear garments that show the outline of their private parts. This can be done with any long robes, dresses and skirts, long shirts and trousers, and so on. Various cultures have different standards

Malaysian and Dutch hijab

Arabic hijab

Iranian hijab

Figure 5.1 Different types of hijab.

of modesty; in some Muslim societies colours are more muted than others, head veils less decorative, and so on. The majority of Muslim women cover their heads, and the extreme extent is to cover faces, and to also wear socks and gloves.

Face veils have become an issue in some non-Muslim societies, where masks are traditionally seen as threatening, sinister, or a means of hiding the identity of a criminal or terrorist.

> ## Insight
> Fully covered Muslim women outside societies where full cover is traditional and cultural certainly confuse non-Muslims if their public behaviour does not seem to be recognizably pious.

What does the Qur'an say?
The Qur'an 'verse of the hijab' was sent specifically concerning the privacy of the Prophet's ﷺ wives, and did not actually refer to an item of clothing at all. It gave them the right for a dividing curtain to be put up that allowed them to gain some privacy in their small houses. Previously, such 'dividers' had been used to divide guests from family in Bedouin nomad tents, but not in houses.

> *Believers, do not go into the Prophet's house ... unless invited. And if you are invited ... do not linger. And when you ask something from the Prophet's wives, do so from behind a veil (hijab). This will assure the purity of your hearts as well as theirs.* (Surah 33.53)

> ## Insight
> The ayah was given on the occasion of the Prophet's ﷺ wedding to his cousin Zaynab, when guests stayed far too long and were intrusive. Most women regard the separating off of space private to their family (a harem) as a privilege.

The one Qur'anic verse that does give a command for women's clothing is as follows:
> *Believing women should lower their gaze and guard their modesty; they should not display their awrah (lit. ornaments)*

except as is normal (i.e. socially acceptable). They should draw their veils over their bosoms and not display their ornaments except to their close male relatives.

(Surah 24:30–1; the surah then lists these relatives)

Insight

The Qur'an emphasis is clearly on modesty, and on women covering their bosoms, not their heads – although the verse does imply that they were already wearing veils.

There is considerable disagreement over what is meant by the word *awrah* – the majority opinion is that it refers to a woman's private parts, the parts of a woman's body that cause sexual attraction; others argue that it could include her hair, her face, her expensive jewellery, and, in the most extreme view, even her voice.

What mattered was that Muslim women should cover their female curves and not flaunt them in order to attract male attention. Certainly they were no longer to show cleavage, nor should they breastfeed in public, as many pre-Muslim ladies did. Moreover, they were expected to cover any flimsy indoor garments with an outergarment (*jilbab*) when going outside the home.

Insight

Full cover does not always indicate modesty. I have known some covered ladies be very proud and arrogant, and in the United States I was amazed by one African Muslim male preacher whose voluminous robe was decorated with flashing lights!

COVERING THE HEAD

The one item of clothing that usually marks out a woman as a Muslim is the head veil, of any material and in any style, that hides her hair from public view. Head veiling really is not mentioned in the Qur'an, but those who are convinced that it is compulsory are basing their view on the *sunnah* of the Prophet's ﷺ wives, and the hadiths recording that the Prophet ﷺ himself said on one occasion that nothing of a female past the age of puberty should be seen except her face and hands. Muslim women usually do cover their heads with some kind of scarf or veil.

The fact that millions of Muslim women dress modestly but do not cover their heads does not alter the fact that it is a sunnah. Those who do wear some sort of head-cover regard this as part of their discipline of piety, and where there is a resurgence of Islamic faith, women are choosing to wear a scarf in increasing numbers.

Insight

A modern Western Muslim woman might be fully covered in what is recognized as modest clothing in her own society. She is not required to adopt a dress style in imitation of Arab or Pakistani women.

COVERING THE FACE

There is no text in the Qur'an requiring Muslim women to veil their faces. In desert situations, both men and women cover their mouths and noses automatically as a practical measure. Wearing a face veil without the inclement weather conditions was considered a status symbol in pre-Islamic Arabia and other countries, a form of social snobbery that prevented the common masses from looking at the faces of those of high rank, sometimes men as well as women. Slave women were certainly not allowed to veil their faces. This is not the Muslim attitude.

The face veil (*niqab* or *khimar*) apparently was worn by some Muslim women at the time of the Prophet, ﷺ but did not become widespread for several generations – until conservatives became ascendant.

Insight

In some parts of the world today, Muslim women veil their faces leaving only their eyes visible; in Algeria, they may cover all but one eye, and hold their veil in place with their teeth. The extreme Taliban sect prefers burkhas that even cover eyes. Elsewhere, devout Muslim women do not veil at all and regard face veiling as odd, or attention-seeking.

There are dozens of hadiths where it is obvious that Muslim women's faces could be seen. Aishah commented that she used to draw her veil across her face when she did not wish to talk to strangers.

Veiling the eyes

The verse in the Qur'an used to justify face-covering for women is preceded by one in virtually identical words applied to men – but neither verse mentions faces – rather, it is a euphemism for modest behaviour and self-control. It is never assumed that an honourable Muslim man is supposed to wear a face veil.

> *Instruct believing men to veil their eyes (i.e. lower their gaze) and guard their modesty; that is more chaste for them. Surely Allah is well aware of their actions.* (Surah 24.30)

It is what he does with his eyes that matters – he is supposed to turn away from female temptation, and not leer or flirt, and to control any feelings of arousal. The Prophet ﷺ excused the first such look, but not the second.

Insight

A Muslim man should behave with modesty and self-control even if a woman offers herself. Even if she appears naked, he should 'veil his eyes' or 'lower his gaze'. Muslim women for their part should not be brazen or attempt to raise sexual feelings by intimate eye contact.

DIFFERENT CULTURES, DIFFERENT EXPECTATIONS

Veiling for Muslim women today is complex and varies from place to place. In Saudi Arabia and Afghanistan state law obliges women to cover completely, but that is not the case in Egypt, Morocco or most other Middle Eastern countries. In Tunisia and Turkey the veil is prohibited in governmental buildings like courts, universities, schools, town halls, etc. In Turkey, it is a source of controversy, as it is banned in various places, but both secular feminists and pious Muslim women march for the right of freedom to wear it. In many Western minds the 'cover' is an indication of oppression – an assumption that possibly derives from the West's past experience of its own history of repressive religious states and societies. In the twentieth century many Islamic feminists demanded the right to cast aside even their head-coverings, but today Islamic feminists demand the right to not face discrimination if they choose to wear them.

NO COERCION

There is no stipulation in the Qur'an or hadiths that any particular styles of garment are in any way compulsory, and any strictly pious male feeling that it is right for him to try to force a woman in matters of religion is ironically going against the true spirit of Islam. Some Muslim women have resisted the traditional hijab of their cultural communities because it is hot and cumbersome, and the pugnacious attitude of their males has put them in revolt.

It is particularly important to emphasize these things in societies where groups of extremist sectarians have gained the upper hand over moderate Muslims, because there is a danger in those circumstances of men becoming so obsessive and overzealous about women's clothing that it could lead to repression and even cruelty.

Many non-Muslims see the face veil and even the head veil as symbols of subjugation and repression of women. In some circumstances it is true that they are – but this is not the spirit of Islam at all. Many women find wearing hijab liberating – from unwanted attention, pressure of fashion and concern with one's 'looks'.

Insight
In some places, local culture might make veiling virtually compulsory, but the vast majority choose to cover of their own free-will.

STYLE AND TACT

Muslim women may wear any type of clothing provided it is not attention-seeking by being either too revealing, transparent, too brash, too tight or too short, and so on. Some wear dark, plain clothes, and others prefer brilliant colours decorated with embroidery or beadwork. The clothing does not have to be dull – Aishah was particularly fond of red and yellow.

I am always delighted to see an amazing range of colours and styles whenever Muslim women of different nationalities and types get together. I resist the notion that there should be a sort of 'school uniform' for Muslim women.

Many forms of trousers are acceptable for women, Asian women in particular favouring the *shalwar-qameez* outfits of a long shirt, with baggy trousers beneath. These can be as colourful or decorative as individuals desire, but they should be modest. Tight trousers are not approved of. Many Muslim women wear Western-style trousers, with an over-shirt or blouse long enough to be acceptable.

Some clothing presents women as 'naked even though they are clothed', and their only object must be to stir the passions of men and tempt them, which is neither fair, nor kind, nor sensible.

Transparent blouses or sleeves are not approved of, and it is worth noting that many Western garments, even those with long sleeves,

Figure 5.2 Bosnian girls, modestly dressed.

are thin enough to reveal the underwear (or lack of it) beneath. This is not approved of in Islam.

Tourist women who wear shorts, bikinis, flimsy tops and tight T-shirts in Muslim areas are regarded as tactless, and possible temptresses. Some Muslims might forget their manners, and the tactless visitors find themselves being tutted, or hissed at or pinched as they pass, or they might be ignored in embarrassment.

Insight

My Pakistani husband had hopes of seeing me wear highly colourful and decorative shalwar-qameez suits, and a *dopatta* (a long flimsy scarf, always falling off). I felt extremely conspicuous in such clothing, and preferred long skirts (including denim) and long-sleeved shirts. I found the dopatta highly irritating, and preferred a scarf fastened with pins.

TRUE ISLAMIC MOTIVES

A woman's standards of behaviour and dress should never be from pressure of others, but simply because she herself has the desire to please Allah, and submit to Him, even in the matter of her clothing. In fact, in certain societies, some Muslim women have taken to wearing hijab in spite of opposition from their husbands, or secular governments.

It is important to remember that God does not judge people by their clothing, but for their characters and the quality of their lives. A fully-covered woman might be proud, hard-hearted, cruel or selfish. A less-covered woman might have more natural modesty. Allah knows best.

Islamic diet

In Islam, foods are either *halal* or *haram*. That which is halal is allowed, and that which is haram is forbidden. This is not a matter of likes and dislikes, but of discipline and submission to God's will. As in every other walk of life, Allah gave instructions to guide believers, and even the need to eat is under discipline. Allah created all the goodness of the earth and its produce for humanity to utilize, but requested certain restrictions.

O believers! Eat of the good things that We have provided for you, and be grateful to God if it is Him you worship. He has only forbidden you meat of an animal that dies of itself, and blood, and the flesh of pigs, and that on which any other name has been invoked besides that of God. (Surah 2:172)

Forbidden foods include:
The strangled, the beast beaten down, the beast that died by falling, the beast gored, and that devoured by beasts of prey ... and anything sacrificed to idols. (Surah 5:4)

How the food-animal died matters. Islamic slaughter involves *tazkiyah* or cleansing, by dedicating the animal in Allah's name, cutting its throat with a sharp blade and draining the blood. Causing the animal needless pain or slaughtering with a blunt blade is strictly forbidden.

Insight

Other forbidden meats are flesh-eaters with sharp canine teeth, prey-eating birds with talons, tame donkeys, and any meat cut from a living animal. Forbidden omnivores include bears, rats, foxes, monkeys, apes, dogs and humans.

PORK

First, no Muslim should ever eat the flesh of the pig, or any pork product. This does not mean a Muslim convert simply giving up sausages, bacon, ham and pork pies. It also means checking whether or not a product includes animal fat, for that fat might well have come from a pig.

In the East, the pig is regarded as a very unclean animal, with good reason, for it gobbles up excrement. In some places it is deliberately used for this purpose. Therefore, no Muslim would contemplate eating it, for it is simply regarded as disgusting. To put a piece of pork on a Muslim's plate would have the same effect as putting excrement on their plate; some Muslims would be physically sick.

> ### Insight
>
> Most Western non-Muslims would never think of cooking a cat or a dog and eating it – the very thought would sicken them. Muslims are not brought up to eat pork.

Many Muslims are quite frightened when they come to the West, because they know that the populace is fed on pork. They believe it is the cause of all sorts of ailments and allergies, and there is increasing medical evidence that this may very well be so. In the East, pork meat is certainly riddled with minute worms and eating it causes all sorts of horrible disorders.

> ### Insight
>
> My Pakistani husband found the very thought of putting a piece of bacon on the side of his plate sickening. I did ask why God forbade pork, as it was such a tasty meat. His reply was that 'other women were also tasty'.

OTHER MEATS

Other meats, such as chicken, beef, lamb, and goat, are all allowed for Muslims, provided they have been slaughtered by the halal method, which is to cut the jugular vein with a very sharp knife, accompanied by prayer. Pronouncing the name of God is a rite to call attention to the fact that they are not taking life thoughtlessly, but with the permission of God for food.

Muslims believe that to cut the throat is not only the kindest method of killing an animal, but also that it is beneficial for the person who will eat the meat. Blood congeals in animals that are stunned, electrocuted, shot, clubbed or gassed, whereas to cut the jugular vein allows the beast to lose consciousness immediately and the blood to rush out freely. Muslims leave the animal carcass to bleed completely.

Muslims are not allowed to eat the meat of any creature which has died of itself, or been strangled, or clubbed to death, or savaged or gored by other animals. By analogy, birds of prey, animals with claws and fangs, rodents, reptiles and insects, with the exception of locusts, are also haram.

Insight

'Dead animals' include animals that died by drowning, fire, electrocution, trauma (e.g. killed on the road), or by boiling while alive. The prohibition is not applicable to fish and locusts, which are collected, dried and salted by desert peoples, and eaten as a savoury, like a packet of crisps.

HALAL SHOPS

Muslims in the United Kingdom usually buy all their meat from halal butchers, or special Muslim shops, not regarding the meat in ordinary butchers' shops to be acceptable. In Muslim countries all meat would be slaughtered by the halal method, so there would not be any problem of finding a supplier. As the Jews follow the same rules of slaughter for their kosher meat, Muslims are allowed to eat meat from Jewish shops, if they wish.

Insight

Modern methods of slaughter, such as firing a metal bolt into the animal's brain or electrocution, are prohibited. These methods are regarded as more cruel than the halal method.

Some Muslims take the point of view that since one of the last revealed verses of the Qur'an says that both Jewish and Christian food was lawful for Muslims, then Muslims who live in Christian countries should be allowed to eat commercial meat (apart from pork), so long as they pronounce the name of God on it at the time of eating (Surah 5 16). However, many

Muslims would rather do without meat than do this; nowadays halal shops are becoming more common, so the problems are lessened.

OTHER FOODS

All fish, fruits and vegetables are halal, and all grains and seeds. However, Muslims should still check packets for ingredients, for many biscuits, cakes, ice creams and soups contain the fat of animals or animal gelatine. Unless it is kosher or of vegetable origin the gelatine found in many desserts, creams, cake fillings, sweets, commercial yoghurts and other foods is usually made from animal hide trimmings, including those of the pig.

Insight

Gelatine made from halal animals (e.g. fish) is acceptable. Kosher gelatine comes from certain fish to avoid the Jewish prohibition against mixing meat and dairy in the same meal – fish does not count as meat. Therefore, gelatine in food certified as kosher is halal.

WASTE

Muslims believe that food should never be wasted. If anything is left over, it should be given away to the needy, or fed to the birds or the animals that come into the garden.

WHEN NO HALAL FOOD IS AVAILABLE

If a person is forced because there is no other choice, neither craving nor transgressing, there is no sin committed. Indeed, Allah is forgiving, merciful. (Surah 2:173, 5:4)

In cases of absolute necessity, Muslims may eat what there is available, but no Muslim should eat the haram food eagerly, or become accustomed to it, or use this principle as an excuse to enjoy it under the pretext of necessity.

Work and wealth

The economic principles of Islam are to build up a just society in which people behave responsibly and honestly, and are enabled to find honourable employment that is not exploitative, corrupt, pornographic or based on cheating and swindling.

Earning for the family is still the responsibility of the Muslim man in most Islamic societies, although there is no ruling in Islam to prevent women from going out to honourable work, so long as they dress and behave modestly.

Insight

Several of the Prophet's ﷺ wives were working women who made their own money. He was an employee of his first wife, Khadijah, for some time. His wife Zaynab made leather goods. When his Jewish wife Safiyyah died, she left a fortune.

THE IMPORTANCE OF WORK

It is considered very important that a person does work, and does not stay idle or become a burden to others. It is considered very dishonourable to be a parasite on society, unless, of course, one is unable to work through illness or other handicap. Begging is strongly disapproved of, unless there is no other alternative and it is a case of extreme necessity. The Prophet ﷺ said:

Receiving charity is permissible for three sorts of people only; one who is in grinding poverty, one who is seriously in debt, or one who is responsible for a debt and finds it difficult to pay. (Abu Dawud)

Even people who have to be supported by others because of their devotion to religion are disapproved of:

Some people once brought a hermit (religious recluse) to meet the Prophet. 'Who is he?' he asked. They replied that he was a man who had devoted himself to worship. The Prophet then

said: 'Who feeds him?' 'We all do,' they said. 'Then all of you are better than he,' said the Prophet.   (Bukhari, Muslim)

On the other hand, any work one does for anybody else (providing it is acceptable in Islam) is counted as if it was done for Allah.

Lawful and unlawful work

Islam makes a difference between lawful and unlawful methods of earning a living.

No body which has been nourished with what is unlawful shall enter Paradise.   (Ahmad, Darmi and Bayhaqi)

Basically, if someone's means of earning a living hurts another, or results in another's loss, it is haram (forbidden). If it is fair and beneficial, then it is halal (allowed). Obviously, any form of making money that involves dishonesty, deceit or fraud, bribery, robbery, hoarding in order to take advantage of hardship, exploitation, artificial creation of shortages, or anything to do with alcohol, gambling or lotteries, sexual degradation or immoral practices, is forbidden to Muslims.

People make long prayers to Allah although their food and their clothes are unlawfully acquired. How can the prayer of such people be accepted?   (Muslim and Tirmidhi)

THE DIGNITY OF THE MENIAL WORKER

> **Insight**
> Muslims should never look down on those who have menial employment or humble tasks, so long as they are not haram occupations – i.e. exploitative, abusive, degrading or sexual.

The Prophet ﷺ taught that there was no room in Islam for snobbery. There was no disgrace or humiliation in doing menial work, or work that was 'looked down on' by those better off. The only shame was in depending on others for hand-outs when you were capable of helping yourself. Communities need rubbish collectors just as much as professors. Nobody need regard any useful employment as being beneath them, and Islam gave dignity to many professions previously considered lowly and degrading.

The toilet cleaner has as much dignity and worth in the eyes of Allah as the manager of a business empire. What counts is his or her faith, honesty, and attitude towards the work he or she is doing.

SLAVERY

Seizing people outside of warfare, kidnap, and forced bondage are all criminal offences in Islam, subject to *hadd* punishment (see page 294, hirabah). Slavery as such was not specifically prohibited in Islam as for many people it was a way of avoiding debt and penury, but the Prophet ﷺ set the *sunnah* of welfare for slaves, and helping them gain freedom.

- *Slaves were to be treated as family members, and fed and clothed well.*
- *Releasing or buying freedom for slaves was one of the best deeds a Muslim could do (many regarded their 'owners' as benefactors and refused to leave when freed).*
- *Children were not to be split up from their mothers.*
- *Slaves acquired as prisoners of war were to be treated kindly and ransomed if possible.*
- *Forced sexual intimacy with slaves was forbidden, and Muslims were encouraged to marry them and give them status.*

Insight

Islam made the enslavement of free persons a criminal offence – which included kidnapping and hijacking. As regards prisoners of war, the tradition at the time was to kill whole tribes en masse – the Prophet ﷺ encouraged keeping defeated enemies alive and well-treated, as household slaves, or better still, getting them ransomed safely.

The Prophet said, ﷺ 'He who has a slave-girl and teaches her good manners and improves her education and then manumits and marries her, will get a double reward.' (Bukhari).

Child labour

Throughout history children have always worked, and the Prophet ﷺ himself worked as a child, and was employed from the age of 12. The abolition of child labour is one key aim for today's reformers. In many Third World nations working children are deprived of education and a right to their youth. Often, the harsh truth is that when companies stop using children it does not change the economic conditions that had them working in the first place, or the local cultural standards that accept and expect child labour. Muslim reformers agree with human rights agencies that this is a problem to be urgently addressed.

COLLECTIVE RESPONSIBILITIES

Muslim economy regards certain crafts and industries as essential to the community, those known as *fard kifayah* or 'collective obligations'. Every Muslim community should try to include people to meet the needs of education, medicine, science and technology, politics and community welfare, and clothing, utensil and agricultural industries. All productive resources should be brought into use as far as possible, and not left idle or wasted, including unemployed manpower, unused land, and water or mineral resources.

The duty of employees and employers

Employed people have a duty to their employers, as well as to those they support, so they should not cheat on hours for which payment is claimed, or be lazy, or encourage any practice in the workplace which cheats the employer in some way. They should not waste money irresponsibly, or fritter it away on worthless and wasteful things. Extravagance and waste are strongly discouraged in Islam. Employers should treat their employees with justice and kindness, and should pay them fairly, without undue delay. The Prophet's ﷺ order was:

> **Give the worker his wages before his sweat dries.** (Ibn Majah)

> **Insight**
>
> Muslim employers should not exploit their workers, particularly females and children. They should have rest periods, a chance to eat and drink, use of a chair, fair wages, reasonable hours, application of health and safety regulations, and decent rates of pay, paid promptly.

Workers should be protected adequately from danger in the workplace and not exploited or made to work unreasonable hours, or worked to exhaustion in appalling conditions, with no opportunity to take rest or refreshment. Muhammad ﷺ insisted that:

An employer should not ask an employee to do anything beyond his capacity. If that which the master demands is necessary, the master himself should lend a helping hand to the servant. (Bukhari)

Insight

A Muslim boss who scrupulously 'pops out' to say his prayers, but obliges his staff to stand long hours and work to exhaustion for a pittance, has hardly understood the ethos of Islam.

RIBA – EXPLOITATION AND INTEREST ON LOANS

Making interest on loaned money (*riba*) is regarded as a despicable, capitalizing on another person's misfortune or need, and is totally forbidden by the Qur'an. Charging interest makes rich people richer and the poor poorer, since they are forced into more debt and dependency.

Insight

When people in debt turn to 'loan sharks', they can get ripped off with very high rates of interest. Muslims prefer to borrow from friends to pay cash for a house, and then pay back to these friends exactly the same amount they borrowed.

This is why Muslim societies establish their own Islamic Banks, which have worked out honourable ways of utilizing deposited money without the system of giving or taking interest on money, according to the complicated Shari'ah laws.

Allah has permitted trade but forbidden usury; those who cease the practice after hearing our Lord's command will be pardoned for their past sins ... but those who repeat the offence will be companions of the fire. (Surah 2:278)

Riba means any unjustified advantage in trade dealings, a much wider meaning than the simple notion of taking 'interest' on one's money in the bank. In Islam, in order to be honourable, money has to be used as a facility and not a commodity, or the owners of money gain an unfair advantage over the producers or traders. They could wait until the merchandise lost value (as in food crops and other perishables) and force merchants to sell at a low price; or they could buy up commodities and hoard them until they increase in value. These practices are forbidden in Islam; wealth should be in circulation and not hoarded away for the private benefit of a few. To regulate this, Islamic governments impose a tax on all money which is not spent in circulation.

ISLAMIC BANKS

The payment or receipt of interest is the cornerstone of modern conventional banking. Specifically Islamic banks keep separate so that they can maintain the principles of not mixing their funds in any way that would compromise Shari'ah Law.

Insight

Securities that comply with Islamic law and its investment principles, which prohibit the charging or paying of interest, are known as *sukuk*.

They are supervised by Islamic scholars who act as a Shari'ah supervisory committee, and have the responsibility of approving all services, activities and investments, and will undertake regular audits to ensure everything is *Shari'ah* compliant.

Islamic modes of financing are based strictly on the following principles:

▶ *transactions must be free of* riba *(interest, exploitation)*
▶ haram *(Islamically illegal) goods and services cannot be produced or consumed*
▶ *activities or transactions involving* gharar *(speculation, chance) must be avoided*
▶ zakat *(the compulsory Islamic tax) must be paid.*

So, if a person borrows funds in order to create a business and it makes a profit, the lender has a share in that profit. But if it makes a loss, the lender also shares the loss, and does not carry on making a profit by charging interest on the funds loaned, as in non-Muslim banking systems.

Insight

Shari'ah-compliant assets worldwide are worth billions and have grown at more than 10 per cent per year since 2000, placing Islamic finance in a global asset class all of its own.

Many mainstream banks are now considering how to make themselves 'Muslim-friendly'. In fact, customers are attracted by Islamic banking and in the next decade conventional banks may lose 30–40 per cent of their customers to Islamic banks or those that conform to Islamic regulations. Several top conventional banks have already designed commercial mortgage equivalents for use by Muslims. For example, Lloyds TSB already offers Islamic banking in many branches and the HSBC Amanah range of products includes the Home Tafakul policy, the first of its kind to be nationally available.

Sex

Sex is regarded in Islam as the gift of Allah that gives the human being, in a small way, the experience of the bliss of Paradise, in advance. It is a basic and fundamental urge in human beings, and in the search for sexual fulfilment people can give each other great joy and happiness, but it can also give enormous scope for great despair, hurt, and embarrassment.

Interest in sex starts early, and many youngsters become sexually active as they enter their teens. The youngest age for marriage in the UK is at present 16, but promiscuous unmarried sexual intimacy has now become commonplace, despite the dangers of disease, AIDS and unwanted pregnancies.

Youngsters usually discover they have a rampant urge for sex when their hormones get going at puberty. Muslim societies have traditionally preferred to see youngsters married at the onset of puberty, rather than risk illicit relationships and unwanted pregnancies. This way they can gratify their desires as much as they like, but within the marriage relationship.

> ## Insight
> The intention of marriage at a very young age was not to provide pretty virgins for old men, but to guard virginity until marriage, give a legitimate outlet for sexual urges once they had arisen, minimize abortions and the stresses and heartbreak of 'young love' going wrong.

CELIBACY

Since sex is a creation and gift of Allah, Muslims cannot regard it as evil and unclean, or that it should be resisted and suppressed. People who choose to be celibate for religious reasons are not approved of in Islam; celibacy is seen as a form of ingratitude towards Allah which might lead to a dangerously stressed, repressed or perverted personality. For example, when Uthman b. Mazun decided to live in celibacy, the Prophet ﷺ forbade him to do so. (Muslim).

However, a celibate person who is quite content, and perhaps channelling their energies into study or research, or concentrating on doing good to others, is in no way sinful.

> ## Insight
> Celibacy becomes sinful if a spouse refuses wilfully to grant sexual satisfaction to their partner, while at the same time expecting their fidelity. No married person has the right to force celibacy upon a partner – it is grounds for divorce.

PROMISCUITY

On the other hand, the gratification of sexual urges without moral considerations is also regarded as an abuse of Allah's intention; Islam seeks for sexual desires to be satisfied, but that the individual and the family are protected from dangerous consequences.

The practice of marriage is seen as the 'fortress' that protects people from being lured into immoral ways by their passionate urges. Sexual promiscuity is usually referred to in Islam as *zinah*, whether it refers to fornication (sex before marriage) or adultery (sex outside marriage after marriage).

THE DANGERS OF SEXUAL FREEDOM

Not only does Islam prohibit sexual activity before marriage, it does not approve any kind of privacy between unrelated people of the opposite sex past the age of puberty who are not married to each other, in order to avoid temptation.

Insight

Being alone in a situation where sexual intimacy becomes possible and a temptation (*khulwah*) is strongly discouraged in Islam. The horrors of so-called honour killing sometimes arise because a daughter has found herself in a compromising situation where her innocence can be doubted.

The Prophet ﷺ knew that it was natural for men to see women and be stirred physically; that is why Allah requested that men and women should not seek to be alone together in situations where sex could become possible, that they should not tempt each other by seductive clothing or ways or looks; and that if a man happened to feel a sexual urge for someone other than his wife while out, he should:

...go straight to his wife and have intercourse with her, for that would take care of what he had felt. (Muslim, Abu Dawud)

HOMOSEXUALITY

Of all the creatures in the world, will you (men) approach males and abandon those whom God created for you as mates? (Surah 26:165)

This topic presents a problem for Muslims living in places where homosexuality has become not only acceptable in law, but is increasingly socially acceptable. Recently non-Muslim homosexuals have even been permitted to marry and raise children.

There is a need to look into the possible genetic origin of homosexuality, as it makes a difference to Islamic logic if a person is born homosexual or simply decides to become one as a matter of personal preference, perhaps through distaste for or some psychological fear of the opposite sex. A homosexual might argue that they can hardly be held to blame if Allah created them that way; but a jurist would claim that Allah would not forbid anything He had created.

In Islam, if a person is born homosexual, this is not regarded as simply being just another version of 'normal' but as a disadvantage and a test, much the same as being born blind or deaf. Very likely the same percentage of Muslims are born homosexual as the rest of the population. The individual can hardly be blamed for it, and indeed has done nothing wrong, but has a physical difference that has to be coped with, a matter for sympathetic understanding and tolerance, and perhaps the attention of genetic research.

Persons of the same sex having sexual relations was forbidden by Allah in the Qur'an and in a revelation to the Prophet Moses ﷺ. (Leviticus 18:22, 20:13, the story of Lot and the people of Sodom):

> *You satisfy your lust with men (homosexual) instead of women. Indeed you are a nation that has transgressed beyond bounds.*
>
> (Surah 7:81)

The Prophet ﷺ even declared that women should not wear male clothing and vice versa; neither should people imitate the opposite sex in their ways of speaking, walking or moving.

Muslim attitudes towards homosexuals vary according to the behaviour of the individuals concerned. God's law requires all sexuality with another person to be within the marriage relationship. This is a very hard test for many people, of both sexes, for all sorts of reasons, homosexuality being only one of them. Those who can control themselves and live within Islamic law are greatly to be commended for the sacrifice and control. 'Sleeping around' is as forbidden to homosexuals as it is to heterosexuals.

Insight

In modern Western societies, people are urged to accept homosexuality as an equally acceptable form of sexuality as male/female relationships. Muslims can never agree, for it is against God's command.

Private sexual behaviour is a matter for individual consciences, and no person has the right to hound or victimize another for what is done in private between consenting adults. If a Muslim homosexual chooses to take a same-sex partner, it is a matter between his/her own conscience and the Almighty, and will be judged in the Life to Come. Allah knows best if this sin is worse than taking forbidden substances in private, or choosing to be spiteful or cruel. He is the Judge, and knows all the circumstances.

Any sexual behaviour in public, including heterosexual (even between married couples), is distasteful to Muslims, who are expected to behave with dignity and control their sexual urges. Illicit public sexual behaviour (*zinah*) is a punishable offence (see page 296). Enticing children into the practice is not only sinful, but criminal.

Modern alternatives to marriage

The modern notion that it is acceptable for single-sex couples to be 'married' is dismissed. Even less acceptable is the suggestion that they might deliberately arrange to have children by some means and bring them up. Whereas any person volunteering to take care of an orphan or a child in distress is highly recommended, the suggestion that homosexuals might deliberately engineer some way of having babies is regarded as an abuse of that child's human rights by:

▶ *depriving the child of its rights to a normal family upbringing*
▶ *affecting the child mentally and emotionally.*

SEX WITHIN MARRIAGE

The Prophet ﷺ said:

**When a husband and wife share intimacy it is rewarded, and
a blessing from Allah; just as it would be punished if they had
indulged in illicit sex.** (Muslim)

**Having sexual intercourse with one's wife is sadaqah
(loving charity).** (Abu Dawud)

Sexual intimacy becomes *sadaqah* if performed for the sake of
Allah – which means performed with skill, care and unselfishness,
placing the happiness and satisfaction of the spouse before one's
own gratification.

> **Insight**
> Islamic sex is notable for its physical cleanliness. Good
> Islamic manners include the regular removal (and careful
> disposal of) all pubic hair, nice clean feet, and a full bath
> (*ghusl*) taken between the sex act and the next prayer. Taking
> a shower before sexual activity is also usually appreciated.

Sex is encouraged and blessed between loving spouses so long
as what is done does not hurt, abuse, exploit or denigrate one's
partner. In an Islamic marriage, neither partner should ever try
to force the other one to do anything which is distasteful or
unpleasant or painful to them. Marital rape should never take
place, or abuse of the wife.

The Prophet ﷺ was a shy man who discouraged nudity, and Aishah
recorded that in ten years of marriage they had never seen each
other naked. Nudity between spouses was not forbidden in the

Qur'an, however, and although it may amaze the young, many people past their first flush of youth are actually quite grateful for a little cover, including the cover of darkness!

Sexual intimacy is not forbidden during menstruation, but many prefer to set aside full intercourse and use other ways of satisfying each other.

Many non-Muslims think the Prophet ﷺ was obsessed by sex because he had many wives. Muslims point out the reasons for these marriages, and stress his restraint and shyness, and a life of prayer that left little time for prolonged sexuality.

Insight

Even though the Prophet ﷺ visited all his wives every day it is highly unlikely that he had sex with them all. It is known that his wife Sawdah chose celibacy, and granted 'her' night to Aishah.

The duty to please

Since Muslims should only have sex with their marriage partner, both partners have a duty not only to be faithful, but to honour and satisfy the needs of their spouses as best they can. If either side neglects this duty for no good reason, it is bound to cause suffering, depression, and may lead to the breakdown of the relationship. It is considered grounds for divorce. The Prophet ﷺ said:

> *By Him in Whose hand is my life, when a man calls his wife to his bed and she does not respond, the One in Heaven is displeased with her until her husband is pleased with her.*

(Muslim – and vice versa applies!)

Obviously, there come times when there are good reasons for refraining from sexual intimacy, such causes as illness, menstruation, exhaustion, grief and so on. Only an extremely selfish person would try to insist at these times. Pleasant wooing is a different matter, of course.

The Prophet ﷺ was very concerned about male sexual selfishness,
which was as commonplace in his society as it frequently is in
many others. He urged his male followers to respect their wives
and cherish them. They were not to fling themselves upon their
women as if they were no more than animals, or just satisfying
their own urges and then leave their women disappointed and
frustrated, while they dropped off to sleep.

Discretion

Marital relationships should be discreet, and intimate details not
divulged to any outsiders which would be hurtful and embarrassing
to the partner concerned. However, the rule of necessity does allow
private discussion with medical personnel.

**The most wicked of people is the man who goes to his wife,
and she comes to him, and he then divulges her secret.**

(Muslim, Abu Dawud)

SEXUAL EDUCATION

Muslims do not feel that instruction from strangers (whose own
personal morals they do not know, or they do know and disapprove
of) is a good thing, hence there is much resistance to sexual
education programmes in schools. Also, it is not seen as good or
necessary to invade young minds with sexual knowledge before they
are mature enough for it. An innocent childhood is much preferred.

However, wives and husbands have a duty to make their marriages
as happy as possible and, therefore, although Muslim youngsters
are protected as much as possible from exposure to the sexual
experimentation now common in the West, it is their duty to know
how to please their partners, and to strive to do this with the same
Islamic dedication that they strive to do their best for Allah in any
other sphere of life.

Drugs, alcohol and other substances

Any substance which intoxicates is known in Arabic as *khamr*, and is forbidden to Muslims. The word '*khamara*' means 'veiled, covered or concealed'.

Drugged and drunk people have little control over their actions or words. Normally there is an inhibitory control in the brain which tells us not to engage in shameful or wrongful acts. Any suppressant drug, including alcohol, takes away this control, and along with it restraint and the ability to make a judgement. The inhibitory centre itself is inhibited, and inebriated people start to act irresponsibly, become belligerent or maudlin, use abusive and foul language, think they are safe to drive, urinate in public or even in their clothes, stagger about and are sick in the street, go home and upset or maltreat their relatives, and act carelessly and dangerously (e.g. falling asleep with a lighted cigarette, and setting fire to the house).

Insight

Haram is the Arabic word for that which is forbidden. It is a similar concept to immoral, and generally that which is immoral to a Jew or a Christian will be haram to a Muslim. Haram also has the meaning of unclean, that which will defile a person.

ALCOHOL

At the time of the Prophet ﷺ, alcohol was consumed in large quantities, and its antisocial effects were very well known. Allah's prohibition, interestingly enough, took human weakness into account, and was given in stages over quite a long period of time. First, it was pointed out that good and evil could come from the same thing; both nourishing and harmful products can actually come from the date palm or the vine. The harm of khamr far outweighed the good, but people were left to make their own decisions (Surah 2:219).

Next came the request that Muslims should not be intoxicated when they come to prayer:

O believers! Do not come to prayer with a befogged mind, but come when you can fully understand all that you are saying.

(Surah 4:43)

Finally came the order, the complete prohibition:

O believers! Intoxicants, gambling and trying to foretell the future are the lures of Satan; if you wish to prosper, you must keep away from these things. It is Satan's plan to stir up enmity and hatred in your midst with them. (Surah 5.90-91 – see also Surah 5.93)

Insight

When the verse prohibiting wine was announced, Muslims threw away what they were drinking, and tipped out their storage jars and wineskins into the streets. It was said that the streets of Madinah were flowing with wine.

The effect of the prohibition

As news of the revelation spread like wildfire, the Muslims poured away any alcohol they were drinking and got rid of their stores; no 100 per cent Muslim has touched alcohol ever since. Not only that, but Muslims should not sell it, buy it for others, give it as a gift, or work where it is served. The Prophet ﷺ commented that:

Allah has cursed khamr, those who produce it, those for whom it is produced, those who drink it, those who serve it, those who carry it, those it is carried to, those who sell it and those who buy it.

(Tirmidhi)

Why is alcohol haram?

There are many reasons why alcohol is haram. Heavy drinking is known to cause anxiety and depression, which may accelerate or uncover an underlying predisposition to a psychiatric disorder. Its effect on the brain can be acute (intoxication, delirium) or chronic (ataxia, memory loss, loss of co-ordination). In extreme cases, it may cause irreparable brain damage.

It damages all organs of the body in due course – from fatty livers and stomach bleeding (ulcers) to heart damage (cardiomyopathy).

It affects the sex hormones and the immune system. It is linked to breast cancer and foetal damage in women. The vital organ that bears the real brunt of long-term drinking is the liver. Although it has a powerful ability to regenerate itself, excess alcohol slowly destroys it; progressive deterioration leads to hepatitis and cirrhosis, which can lead to total liver failure and death.

But it is violence, homicide, suicide and drink-driving that take most lives.

Insight

Obviously, there are many Muslims who do drink. Some argue that drinking in moderation is not harmful, but this does not alter the ruling that it is haram.

There is no penalty laid down in the Qur'an for drinking alcohol, but the mildest punishment laid down for slander and abuse was a flogging, and since alcohol often makes people abusive and slanderous, flogging is sometimes ordered for publicly offensive drunk behaviour. It is not part of Shari'ah law to pry into private dwellings or spy on people, but any antisocial, threatening or dangerous behaviour caused by alcohol that is witnessed is always dealt with.

Alcohol in medicine

The Prophet ﷺ disapproved of the use of alcohol in medicine, even when it formed the base or preservative in the medicine. Muslims should consult the pharmacist before taking medicine. If there is no alternative, the alcohol base would be allowed.

DRUGS

The plant world is full of substances which affect the human body and mind, and nowadays the medical profession manufactures artificial substances also, to give similar effects. Their use to provide cures for illness is not forbidden in Islam. However, many drugs, such as marijuana, cocaine, opium and nicotine – powerful intoxicants which affect the human mind – are all classed as khamr. They are frequently misused in a harmful way, totally in opposition to the spirit of Islam.

> **Insight**
>
> The rate of growth of heroin addiction is now higher in Pakistan than in the USA. The first known case was recorded in Pakistan in 1980; by 1986 there were half a million cases, and now there are an estimated 1.5 million cases. In addition, there are about 1 million opium and hashish users.

Drugs are used to escape from the pains and distresses of life, or to indulge in exciting fantasy experience and artificially induced euphoria. Those who experiment often find themselves on the downward spiral to crime, physical decline, insensitivity and depravity. The Muslim general principle against drugs misuse is the same as for alcohol – Allah owns our bodies, and anything which harms or injures them is haram.

QAT

Qat (*Catha edulis*) is a plant which produces alkaloid stimulants with a similar effect to strong coffee or tea, and chewing qat is a habit of many Yemenis, Somalis, Ethiopians and other peoples. In the Yemen up to 75 per cent of adults do it each afternoon for a period lasting at least five hours, and spend a considerable amount of their cash income on it.

There is debate over whether it ought to be subject to stronger disapproval.

> **Insight**
>
> Complaints have been made in the UK of young Somali Muslims being in a 'permanent state of intoxication', and that qat can become an addiction.

Taken in moderation, the chief forms of abuse would probably be the length of time devoted to the chewing session, or chewing in an unhealthy environment (excessive smoking, limited aeration) or excessive expenditure on the substance.

SMOKING

Millions of Muslims smoke. However, it is obvious that if one extends the principle of not doing harm to oneself or others, then smoking can never be an approved exercise. Non-smokers have the right to breathe clean air, unpolluted by others. Muslims, if they must smoke, should do so with discretion and not damage other people's lungs, furnishings, or set a bad example to the young, or encourage those who have given up to start again. By analogy with the rules for other harmful substances, it is really haram even if not declared so.

ISTIHALAH – TRANSFORMATION FROM HARAM TO HALAL

The most conservative Muslims reject anything that originated in non-halal ingredients or sources. The Prophet ﷺ said: 'Whatever intoxicates in big quantity, a small amount of it is haram.' However, the majority of scholars agree that this refers to the 'intoxicating substance' in itself. For example, Muslims are not allowed to take even tiny drops of wine and drink them under the pretext that they won't get drunk.

But the rules of *istihalah* (transformation) state that if a minute amount of any haram substance is so mixed with an overriding halal substance, that its haram status is totally altered or becomes irrelevant, then it is forgiven. So, when alcohol is mixed with another substance to the effect that it is not an intoxicant at all but has become something else (e.g. as in ketchup, mustard or mayonnaise) then the majority of scholars would rule that the transformed substance was halal.

Insight
Vinegar is halal even if it is made from wine – because it has undergone transformation and chemical change (istihalah). So the ruling against wine does not apply to it any more, and Muslims are allowed to use it.

Friendship and hospitality

Muslims are not supposed to abstain from the world in order to find 'religious purity'. They are part of the world, and must live out their faith in their communities. They belong to an *ummah*, or community of believers. They serve Allah, who they cannot see, by their service and love to others, who they can see. The Prophet ﷺ set the example, living in the midst of his followers and showing them how to live by his personal example, his sunnah.

Insight

We are here to serve God by service to others – we serve Him whom we cannot see by serving those we can see.

THE UMMAH

The unity of believers was one of the Prophet's ﷺ top priorities; on accepting Islam one's 'brothers' and 'sisters' were no longer just members of one's own family, but all believers in the 'family' of Islam, one ummah or set of people (one community). Each individual was part of the whole, each person important and cherished. Believers were to love each other, and support each other, and take care of each other in times of need.

If any single part of the body aches, the whole body feels the effects of it and rushes to its relief.   (Muslim)

Believers are like parts of a building; each part supports the others.
(Muslim)

Non-Muslims often cannot understand why Muslims in one part of the world get so worked up over what they regard as injustices done to Muslims in other parts of the world; they do not understand the deep feelings of ummah Muslims have for each other, or the duty of support they feel towards each other. Muslims feel passionately about injustices done to other Muslims thousands of miles away.

NO MONASTICISM

Islam disapproves of monasticism, and encourages people to mix and co-operate. Withdrawal from the world (apart from temporary 'breaks' from it) is considered anti-social and not God's will.

Muslims who live in the midst of society and bear with patience the afflictions that come to them are better than those who shun society and cannot bear any wrong done to them. (Abu Dawud)

FRIENDSHIP

Do not nurse hatred or jealousy or enmity, but be friends of each other and servants of Allah. Believers should not go for more than three days without checking on their friends. (Muslim)
The better of the two is the one who is first to give greeting. (Muslim)

Friends are treasures to be cherished, respected, cared for, and loyally defended. Generosity, concern, and loyalty are expected – it is not unusual for Muslims to lend their cars, houses, or finances to each other.

Those to avoid

Friendships are a vital part of life, and highly influential in moulding the individual's mind and attitude. Muslims, therefore, consider it very important to choose their friends wisely. If friendship is based on love of Allah and commitment to the faith, Muslims believe it will be blessed. On the other hand, they are warned against becoming too friendly with people who may try to influence them away from Islam.

Believers should not take unbelievers for their patrons rather than believers; if you do that, there will be no help from Allah except to caution you, that you may guard yourselves from (their influence).

(Surah 3.28)

Insight

A friend is someone who will listen to you, care for you and help you, whatever your misfortune, and whether you deserve it or not.

Muslims are very serious about their religion, so they usually avoid people who take faith as a joke, belittle it, or deliberately agitate against it.

Leave alone those who take religion to be mere play and amusement, and are deceived by the life of this world; proclaim to them this truth – that every soul delivers itself to ruin by its own acts.

(Surah 6:70)

Is friendship with Jews and Christians forbidden to Muslims?

Not at all. All people are created by God and loved by Him. Moreover, people of any race are all separate individuals, and to think otherwise is racism.

Sometimes an unlearned Muslim might take a verse out of context and use as if it condoned racism:

O believers! Take neither Jews nor Christians as your protecting friends (awali): they are only protecting friends of one another. Whoever of you disobeys this commandment will be counted as one of them.

(Surah 5.15)

This verse was revealed to deal with specific problems that arose from the Treaty of Hudaybiyah when Muslims were allowed permission to fight such Jews and Christians as broke their sworn treaty of loyalty to the Islamic State of Madinah, as well as any other enemies who attacked them (Surah 9.29–31). It did not constitute an injunction against the normal friendly relations between Muslims and such Jews and Christians as were well-disposed towards Muslims. The term *wali* has several shades of meaning – ally, friend, helper, protector, etc. Later in the same surah, Allah revealed:

> **Rest assure that the believers (Muslims), the Jews, the Sabians and the Christians – whoever believes in Allah and the Last Day and does righteous deeds – will have nothing to fear or to regret.**
>
> (Surah 5.69, also 2.62)

No racial superiority

No race of people should ever consider itself better than any other; all people are of equal value, irrespective of faith, language, race, belief and so forth.

> **No Arab has superiority over a non-Arab; a white has no superiority over a black, nor a black over a white, except in piety and good deeds.** (from the Prophet's ﷺ Last Sermon)

Good friendship

Having a good friend is a wonderful gift of God, and a treasure worth protecting. Muslims should make a deliberate effort to be good and loyal friends themselves, friends who are worth having, unselfish and considerate. Muslims are encouraged to keep in close touch with their friends, not neglecting them for more than a few days, and to be aware of their needs and distresses. If people practise sympathy, tolerance, unselfishness and genuine concern for each other, they will be actively carrying out the will of God.

....

Insight

Muslims should try to help the weak (in any sense of the word) to improve, but should not embarrass others by pointing out faults, criticizing or backbiting.

....

Muslims are also expected to avoid gossip and backbiting, hurtful jokes, embarrassing remarks, snobbery or fault-finding.

The Prophet ﷺ said:

> Beware of suspicion, for suspicion is a great falsehood. Do not search for faults in each other, do not spy on each other, nor yearn after that which others possess, nor envy, nor entertain malice nor indifference; do not turn away from one another, but be servants of Allah, brothers (and sisters) to one another as you have been ordered.
>
> (Muslim)

> Whoever believes in Allah and the Last Day should speak good things or be silent.
>
> (Muwatta)

Figure 5.3 Islam extends across all places and ethnic groupings.

> Don't sever ties of kinship, don't bear enmity against one another, don't nurse aversion for one another, and don't feel envy against the other. Live as fellow brothers and sisters, as Allah has commanded you.
>
> (Muslim)

HOSPITALITY

Muslims are expected to view the guest as a gift from God, and to enjoy entertaining and giving food and gifts. Visitors to a Muslim house expect to be offered food and drink and, if necessary, facilities to wash, rest and pray. Many Muslims keep facilities ready at all times. If guests admire something, they will often find themselves urged to take it. Muslims expect to give for the sake of Allah, their only reward being to please Him, and to expect nothing in return.

....

Insight

If someone has taken the trouble to visit you, they should be welcomed even if their arrival is inconvenient. A guest is a blessing, and good Muslims always do their best to have something to give them.

....

For their part, guests are also expected to be considerate and bear in mind the circumstances and health of their host (or rather, hostesses). Their 'rule' is to expect to be treated as royalty the first day, then as a member of the family, and they should leave after three days at the most (unless invited to stay by invitation).

Green Islam

The whole Earth has been created a place of worship, pure and clean. (Muslim)

To be 'green' means to care for the environment, the world in which we live, both on the intimate and local level, and in the wider sense of caring for the well-being of the planet. Both aims are specifically a part of Islam, for God required His created humans to be His *khilafah* (sing. khalifah – ruler on His behalf), in looking after the planet and using it in the best possible way.

It is He who has made you custodians, inheritors of the Earth. (Surah 6:165)

After many centuries of neglect and exploitation by people who simply saw the planet's resources as a free gift to be plundered so that they could get rich quick, it has now become important to be green, and to worry about what has happened. Muslims are required to care for the planet, and not to waste, damage, pollute or destroy it. On the Day of Judgement, they will be asked about their responsibility towards the Earth and its creatures.

ANIMALS

Since Allah loves every creature He has made, the principles of mercy and compassion should be extended to every living creature.

All creatures are Allah's children, and those dearest to Allah are those who treat His children kindly.

(Bayhaqi)

It is forbidden for Muslims to be cruel or even inconsiderate to the animals that live and work among them. All domestic animals (whether pets or farm livestock) should be properly fed, housed and looked after.

Beasts of burden should not be made to carry or pull loads too heavy for them, or to labour until they are exhausted, or their flesh has raw patches and sores – a common enough sight in many so-called Islamic societies where Islam is not being carried out.

Hunting

Islam rejects hunting and killing just for sport and amusement; one may take the life of animals only for food or other genuinely useful purpose.

If someone kills (even) a sparrow for sport, the sparrow will cry out on the Day of Judgement: 'O Lord! That person killed me for nothing! He did not kill me for any useful purpose!'

(Nisa'i, Ibn Hibban)

Where animals have a natural hunting instinct (such as hawks or dogs) they cannot be blamed for doing what comes naturally to them – but deliberate cruelty is never encouraged. Animals used for hunting should be well-trained, under control, and not clumsy or savage.

If animals are hunted with weapons, they must not be blunt (like clubs for bludgeoning), but efficient and able to pierce the animal (such as spear, sword or bullet) and not such as would club it or throttle it.

Blood sports

Any sport which involves goading one animal to fight another is forbidden in Islam. This includes dog fights, cock fights or bear baiting. All sports involving hunting down and killing animals for fun are also forbidden, such as fox hunting and bullfighting. If a cull or control is necessary, it is not killing for fun and therefore allowed.

The luxury trade

Any destruction of animal life simply to satisfy the vanity of wealthy ladies is abhorrent to Islam. No Muslim could condone the clubbing of baby seals, for example, or hunting beautiful animals simply for their fur, horns or tusks. However, the Prophet ﷺ did not approve of waste, and if an animal died or was killed for food, Muslims were encouraged to use its skin, horns, bones, hair, fur or hide. Animals should never be flayed alive.

Factory farming

Unnatural or cruel methods of farming which deprive livestock of all enjoyment of life are forbidden in Islam, such as keeping them in cramped and dark conditions, force-feeding them unnatural foodstuffs in order to interfere with their natural flavour or fat content, and making them grow unnaturally quickly so that their natural life is unreasonably shortened.

Insight

Muslims should never be cruel or callous towards animals. They are most certainly responsible for all animals in their care. No life should ever be wasted for no good reason.

Animal experiments and vivisection

Any experimentation solely for reasons of luxury goods and vanity is forbidden in Islam. Muslims should enquire carefully whether the products they buy have been produced by halal methods – those which do not inflict suffering or cruelty. Any animals used for necessary medical research should be well cared for, and made to suffer as little as possible.

Slaughter

Animal slaughter should always be by the halal method, which Muslims maintain is the kindest possible way. It should be done with a very sharp knife and in an atmosphere that does not cause the animal panic or distress. Animals should not be killed in front of each other.

It is forbidden to deny food or drink or decent living quarters to an animal on the grounds that it is shortly to be killed.

OWNERSHIP OF LAND – MUKHABRA

Muslims believe that the whole Earth, including particular patches of land upon it with boundaries, belongs to God. Only the person who cultivates it has the right to it and its produce. The practice of renting land to others to cultivate against a fixed share in the harvest was known as *mukhabra*, and was forbidden.

Insight

Human beings are vital as caretakers of the planet – to bring order, production, good environment, and so on. A garden or field left to itself soon gets overgrown and covered with weeds.

All places liberated from the Byzantine and Persian Empires were followed by the liberation of the peasants and serfs. When Persia was liberated feudalism came to an end. Sadly, this ruling of Islam did not survive the rise of the Umayyad caliphs!

MULTINATIONAL CORPORATIONS

The twentieth century was characterized by an unprecedented transfer of power from people and their governments to global institutions and multinational corporations. It is corporate profits that poison our land, air and seas, determine if our rivers are swimmable or choked with toxic by-products and untreated sewage, or if genetically engineered food grown in warehouses will eliminate the small farmer throughout the developing world, just as corporate greed and agribusiness giants have virtually eliminated family farms.

Insight

Great care should be taken that our plant life does not become extinct – there is still so much to discover about its uses, especially in medicine. The Prophet ﷺ said that for every disease except old age, its antidote already existed, whether we had discovered it or not. (Abu Dawud) The human duty was to research and use wisely.

Profit is the primary impetus behind the provisions of GATT (General Agreement on Tariffs and Trade) and the associated World Trade Organization (WTO), which many Muslims feel allows massive transnational corporations to dump cheaply produced junk food, junk products and junk culture on any nation in the world, with the right to declare any opposition to that process as an impediment to free trade.

GREEN INDIVIDUALS

Muslims can follow green principles in all sorts of ways, mainly by being aware of what they are doing and by avoiding waste and pollution. Everyday products should be used and recycled as much as possible, energy use should be cut down, products such as fur or ivory (obtained from the killing of rare or endangered species of animals) should not be traded, nor should products tested on animals captured or bred for this purpose.

Muslims should use biodegradable products as far as possible and prefer unleaded petrol and detergents that do not pollute the water supply. The Prophet ﷺ said:

Whoever plants a tree and diligently looks after it until it matures and bears fruit, Allah will count as charity for him anything for which its fruits are used. (Ahmad)

10 THINGS TO REMEMBER

1 *Muslim life involves fulfilling God's rights, which are usually involved with the rights of His creation, animal, vegetable and mineral.*

2 *All animals and other life forms are precious, and should be carefully cared for. Slaughter should always be humane, and the halal method.*

3 *Islam teaches the equality of men and women, both created originally from the same single soul – but they usually fulfil different roles.*

4 *Sex should only be engaged in as part of a halal relationship.*

5 *Celibacy is disapproved of in Islam as an unnatural state which could lead to all sorts of problems. Fornication (sex before marriage), adultery (sex outside marriage) and homosexuality are forbidden.*

6 *The penalties for private sexual conduct between freely consenting adults is left to the judgement of Allah – public sexual acts (with four witnesses) may earn severe penalties.*

7 *Muslim women should never be forced to live in seclusion, but are allowed to earn a living, have careers, etc. – so long as they are halal. Some do not mix at all in male society.*

8 *Culture or Islam? An Islamic rule applies to every Muslim woman, no matter what their nationality, background and society (e.g. a chosen dress code is often cultural; modesty is an Islamic rule).*

9 *Muslims are expected to live in communities and be sociable, and not 'cut themselves off'. The ummah is the 'organic unity' of all believers – they become one 'family', or community.*

10 *The Prophet ﷺ emphasized friendship and neighbourliness as being vital aspects of Islam.*

6

Rites of passage

In this chapter you will learn about:
- *birth, marriage and death in Islam*
- *the Muslim attitude towards older people*
- *problems for Muslims living in the West.*

Birth

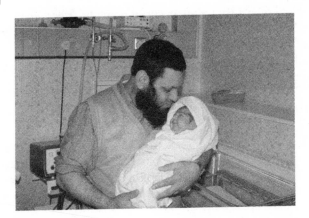

Figure 6.1 Babies are considered a gift from God.

A Muslim welcomes a new baby into the 'family of Islam' or *ummah* as soon as it is born, by whispering the call to prayer (the *adhan*) into the baby's right ear, and the command to rise and worship (the *iqamah*) in its left ear, sometimes using a hollow reed or tube. Thus the word 'God' is the first word the baby hears.

It is sometimes thought to be the case that boys are preferred to girls, but this is a cultural matter, and totally against the spirit of Islam. The Prophet ﷺ loved his four daughters and commended any Muslim men who raised fostered girls.

> **If anyone has a female child and does not ... slight her, or prefer his male children to her, that will bring him to Paradise. If anyone cares for three daughters, trains them, gets them married, and does good to them, he will go to Paradise.**
>
> (Abu Dawud)

TAHNIK

Tahnik is the ceremony of touching the lips or palate of the baby with honey, sweet juice or pressed dates, accompanied by prayers for the welfare of the child. This symbolizes making the child 'sweet', obedient and kind. Sweets are often sent to relatives and friends.

AQIQAH

The *aqiqah* ceremony occurs when the baby is seven days old. Its head is shaved and the equivalent of the weight of the hair in gold or silver is given to the poor and needy. Even if the baby is bald, a donation is usually still given.

SACRIFICE

The sacrifice of an animal is the ancient ritual of thanksgiving, and predates Islam. The usual tradition is to offer two animals for a boy and one for a girl. The meat is used in a celebratory feast – and some of the meat should be distributed among the poor and needy.

NAMING

The choice of name is important to a Muslim, and the Prophet ﷺ changed the names of some of his friends when he thought them unmerited, unfortunate, ugly or insulting. Muhammad has now become the most common boy's name in the world, and the second most common is Ali (even before the Christian names Peter and John).

The Prophet's ﷺ actual recommendation was: 'The most pleasing of names to Allah are Abdullah ("servant of Allah") and Abdul-Rahman ("servant of the Merciful One" – also frequently spelled Abdu'r Rahman).'

If a boy has the name Abdul, this means 'slave of', and should be followed by one of the 99 names of God – for example, Abdul Karim ('slave of the Generous One'), or Abdul-Rahman (see above). Muslim babies should not be named 'slave of' any human being, even Muhammad ﷺ. Many Muslim girls take the names of women in the Prophet's ﷺ family, such as Khadijah, Aishah, Fatimah, Ruqaiyyah and Zaynab.

The Prophet ﷺ disapproved of names that suggested in a rather snobbish and conceited manner that the child had certain qualities or attributes (e.g. 'the sweet-tempered one', 'the beautiful one'), when this might not turn out to be the case at all. He frequently changed people's names especially when they had become known by an unkind nickname, or a name that implied pagan worship.

Nicknames were common among Arabs, and usually picked out some notable physical feature or characteristic or activity – not always complimentary. You might not wish to be known as 'Mother of all Noses'.

The Prophet's ﷺ most intimate servant (a famous Muslim and great man) was known as Abu Istanja ('Father of the wash-pot') because he used to carry the water for the Prophet's ﷺ private ablutions. Ali got called Abu Ruqab ('Father of dust') because after rows with his wife he used to sleep on the ground.

Kunya names

When Muslims become parents they may rather confusingly drop their own names and take a *kunya* name; they become 'father of' (*Abu*) or 'mother of' (*Umm*) the child – for example, a couple named Abdullah and Fatimah, on having a son named Husayn become Abu Husayn and Umm Husayn. The offspring will become known as *Ibn* (or *Bin*) Abdullah, or *Bint* Abdullah, meaning 'son of' or 'daughter of'. This can be confusing, as they are also the son or daughter of the mother, and may use her name.

Insight

The Prophet Jesus ﷺ is always known in Islamic tradition as Ibn Maryam, Son of Mary. Bin Adam ﷺ means 'Son of Man' (i.e. a human being), Banu Isra'il ﷺ means 'The sons of Israel, or Israelites'.

They might also become known by the name of a famous grandparent or ancestor even further back, someone notable in the tribe. All members of a tribe are known as the *Banu* Somebody – the famous originator of the tribe or subsection of it.

Insight

It was common in the Prophet's ﷺ time to be named after the matriarch of a tribe – the Prophet ﷺ often used the epithet Ibn Awatik for himself – 'the son of the Atikahs' – he had 14 female relatives called Atikah!

214

CIRCUMCISION

Circumcision, or *khitan*, is the cutting of the foreskin at the end of the penis to enable greater male cleanliness, the practice of all those submitted to Allah, commanded in the revelation to the Prophet Ibrahim ﷺ (Genesis 17.11).

This is usually done at the same time as the *aqiqah*, if the baby is well. If the child is weak or ill it can be delayed, but should be done as soon as possible. If circumcision is left until the boy is more than ten years old, this is considered shameful, and the parents cruel and neglectful. It is far less traumatic for the child if done while a baby.

In some countries the culture of the land leaves it until the boy is seven to ten years old, and it becomes a serious ordeal for the child, although these days anaesthetics are available. In Turkey, the young boys are dressed up like glittering princes and are often circumcized at a public party.

Insight
Muslim males, like Jewish ones, are circumcized because it was God's command revealed to Abraham. (Genesis 17.9–12)

Some non-Muslims have recently campaigned to have the circumcision of boy babies questioned, because it is a form of mutilation and the infant has not been given any choice in the matter. However, Jews and Muslims regard it as one of God's key commands, and maintain that as adults circumcized men will find themselves more able to keep clean, and enjoy more pleasurable sexual intimacy. Some evidence (National Institute for Communicable Diseases, Johannesburg) has suggested it significantly protects men from contracting the HIV virus.

Adult male converts do make the choice themselves whether or not to have this operation. There is no ruling that it is compulsory for them.

Female genital mutilation

Female circumcision (better called female genital mutilation) has nothing to do with Islam but is a barbaric cultural practice that predates Islam. (See page 367.)

BISMILLAH

As soon as a child is able, he or she begins to learn the Qur'an. At the age of four or five a *Bismillah* ceremony sometimes takes place in which a devout senior relative, or perhaps the imam, invites the child to recite *surah* al-Fatihah and to write the alphabet in Arabic. The successful child feels very happy and proud. After this, the child learns how to perform *wudu*, and begins to have proper lessons in Islamic studies.

By the age of ten the child should know enough to perform the five daily prayers meaningfully on his or her own, should have started fasting, should be familiar with good Islamic manners and practices, and should have learned to be respectful, modest, clean and aware of haram and halal food.

Figure 6.2 Children study Islam from an early age.

Marriage

And among the signs of Allah is this, that He created for you mates, that you might live in tranquillity with them; and He has put love and mercy between your (hearts). Truly in that are signs (about the nature of Allah) for those who reflect.

(Surah 30:21)

Marriage is not thought of in Islam as a mystical sacrament 'made in heaven' between two perfectly attuned souls, or as a contract which will only necessarily end at death, but as a social contract which brings rights and obligations to ordinary men and women, and which can only be successful when these are mutually respected and cherished.

It is not Islamic to think of marriages just in terms of a sex life, although this obviously has its important role; Muslims think of wives as potential mothers, and it is in the role of mother that a Muslim woman is most important.

Do not marry for the sake of physical attraction; the beauty may be the cause of moral decline. Do not marry for the sake of wealth, for this may become the cause of disobedience. Marry rather on the grounds of religious devotion.

(Tirmidhi)

THE IMPORTANCE OF FAMILY IN ISLAM

Islam teaches that the family is irreplaceable by any other social form or structure. It is the way of life Allah intended for us. Since a good and devout home life is so essential to Islam, making a good marriage is of the utmost importance.

Whoever has married has completed half of his faith.   (Bayhaqi)

Muslims believe that the stability of any society or civilization hinges on healthy families. We see all too often the social phenomena of rampant divorce, cyclic family violence, partnership and producing children without marriage, and dramatic changes in gender roles, which pose problems for all of us – not just Muslims.

The idea that the pursuit of happiness is a panacea for modern ills, or that unlimited freedom leads to happiness, are two of the mass media's grand illusions. Discontent is fuelled by fairy tales (both Hollywood and Bollywood) of 'love' (what is usually meant is hormonally driven infatuation) that focuses on self-gratification – me first, my rights. The love-struck couple sail through difficulties and 'live happily ever after'; 'Love conquers everything', 'All you need is love'. You also need hard work, tolerance and unselfishness.

Freedom based on selfish needs, wishes and desires without mature responsibility is anti-family because it plays down the necessary components of self-discipline, duty and self-denial. Marriage is seen as something easily discarded if a better offer comes along. In Islam, a marriage is a *mithaq* – a firm contract between two consenting adults of sound body and mind, in which everyone is answerable for their own deeds and actions.

It is the mother who sees to the well-being of the family, and generally sets the standard for its morality, politeness, and the children's first learning about Islam. As only women are capable of bearing children, Islam assigns to the mother the primary responsibility for home and family. The father is nevertheless the head of the family, assigned the primary responsibility for life outside the home, and the income and economic support of the family.

The best of treasures is a good wife. She is pleasing to her husband's eyes, obedient to his word, and watchful over his possessions in his absence. And the best of you are those who treat your wives best. (Abu Dawud, Ibn Majah)

Despite this ideal, men have the duty to share household burdens, and women are not debarred from roles outside the home.

Bringing a new husband or wife into the family is therefore a very serious business and never to be taken lightly. It is intended to be a bonding for life.

ARRANGED MARRIAGES

First marriages are frequently arranged by caring parents of Muslim young people, following the matchmaking traditions of centuries, since Muslim girls often live pretty sheltered lives. They seek to find good, compatible partners for their children.

Arranged marriage is not an Islamic requirement, but a cultural practice – of other cultures as well as Muslims. Young Muslims do not usually have the opportunities of Western youngsters to meet and 'fall in love', and in any case, to be under the influence of love is considered to be a state of intoxication that clouds sensible judgement.

In Islam, youngsters have the right to refuse to be married off to proposed mates without giving their consent freely. Some young people trust their parents' judgement so completely, or are so devout they would accept their parents' judgement without quibble. Some see their spouses for the first time at the wedding; but all have the right to say 'yes' or 'no' without pressure, even if the proposed spouse is a relative and harder to reject without embarrassment.

On the other hand, Muslim youngsters should not arrange marriages for themselves without consulting their fathers or legal guardians, to protect them from rushing into something foolish. If they have no parent or guardian, they are entitled to have access to a protecting adviser (*wali*), in some places even the ruler of the land (Abu Dawud).

Insight

Arranged marriages should never be forced on Muslim youngsters. In the West, laws are now being formulated to help persuade parents of certain cultures that coercion or duping youngsters into marriage is not just morally wrong but a criminal offence.

FORCED MARRIAGES

Islam forbids parents to force their youngsters into marriage with someone they do not like. Aishah recorded that she asked the Prophet ﷺ about the marriages of young girls whose guardians arranged matches for them and whether it was necessary to consult the girl involved, or not. He said: 'Yes, she must be consulted.' (Muslim)

Islam gave women the right to reject spouses they did not want, especially in cases where family money was involved, or where female orphans had guardians who wished to engineer matches to keep their wealth within the family. This background no longer applies for the vast majority of Muslim women, and in many cases has never applied.

Any Muslim parents who force or trick their offspring into marriages they do not want are committing *haram*. Moreover, if either spouse is tricked or forced into marriage, that marriage is actually invalid in Shari'ah law, and may be declared null and void in Western law. In the West, some parents have coerced their offspring into unwanted marriages:

▶ *to bring another relative over to the West*
▶ *to get a visa for someone to whom a debt of money or honour is owed*
▶ *to keep family money or property in the family.*

Several previously accepted marriage traditions were forbidden to Muslims as being cultural practices abusive to women:

▶ *Temporary marriages (see below –* mutah, sigheh, urfi*).*
▶ *Arranging the legally binding future marriage of an unborn daughter to someone's son (obviously without their free consent – Abu Dawud 2098).*
▶ Shighar *or exchange marriages (see below).*
▶ Istibda – *in which a man who failed to make his wife pregnant or who wished his wife to carry a child of a particular noble blood-line could arrange for her to sleep with another man until she did become pregnant. In Islam, married couples should accept Allah's will for them as regards pregnancy, with the proviso that a man could marry a second wife if his wife was barren (so long as this did not cause hurt to the first wife).*
▶ *Guardians pressuring orphan girls into adoption or marriage in order to take over any inheritance they might have. (Bukhari 7.2, 71)*
▶ *Men were limited to a maximum of four wives at any one time. Women were limited to marrying only one husband at a time, as opposed to the pre-Islamic tradition of having up to ten (nomadic) husbands.*

Insight

Of course, sometimes it is the man in the marriage who cannot produce children. Today's artificial methods of becoming pregnant are matters currently being addressed in Islamic law.

SHIGHAR MARRIAGE

These are exchange arrangements, where one bride and her dowry are exchanged for another bride and her dowry. For example, a man might marry the daughter of an acquaintance and the acquaintance will marry his daughter, without either of them paying either bride her *mahr* (Muwatta 28.24, Abu Dawud 843). These transactions are often a barter of children rather than being real marriages between consenting adults.

TEMPORARY MARRIAGE (MUTAH OR SIGHEH – 'MARRIAGE FOR PLEASURE')

A *nikah mutah* is a marital agreement which has a set time limit – this could be for a few years or as short as a few minutes. Both parties agree on the period of the relationship and the amount of compensation to be paid to the woman, and the 'marriage' is automatically dissolved upon completion of its term. This arrangement requires no witnesses, and no registration. The point of it is to give some sort of legitimacy and payment to a woman who is being 'used' as a wife for that agreed time, and it may lead to permanent marriage afterwards. Thus students, workers and scholars find a way to fulfil their sexual and emotional needs if they are temporarily in another country.

Unmarried Muslims may see it as a permissible alternative to *zina*; in practice they are engaging in something very similar to western relationships without marriage, although a *mutah* differs in that there is a specified time for which the relationship is supposed to last, with the possibility of prolonging that period.

Mutah is now forbidden to Sunni Muslims (who believe the practice was disallowed by the Prophet ﷺ), while Shi'ites believe it was forbidden by Umar and hence the ban may be ignored since Umar had no authority to ban it.

URFI MARRIAGE

Nikah urfi (from *urf* – custom or convention) is another form of arrangement of temporary marriage for which the girl is paid. This is also forbidden to Muslims. There is no official contract. Couples simply repeat the words, 'We got married' and pledge commitment before God. Usually a paper, stating that the two are married, is written and two witnesses sign it. Most Islamic countries do not recognize these arrangements. There is no 'legal' divorce since the legality of the marriage is not recognized in the first place.

Insight

Urfi is similar to a common-law marriage in the West, while in some countries, such as Egypt, it could mean a marriage that has taken place without the public approval of the bride's guardians, even though the contract is officiated by a religious cleric and sometimes by a state representative.

MAKING USE OF A WALI

Someone needing a spouse is advised to take the assistance of a *wali*, a supervising guardian. The best supervisor is not necessarily one's parent – parents have all sorts of axes to grind. The more unbiased the 'expert' the better. A wali is expected to find out all the necessary details about the proposed spouses, and make recommendations.

The normal procedure is to arrange a few meetings in a chaperoned situation (usually at other people's weddings or family gatherings), where they can meet and observe the prospective partner. If either side rejects the suggested partner, it can be done discreetly, without hurt feelings.

Many Arab and Asian Muslims marry their own relatives, and so their character and background will be well known. These days, Muslims are being alerted to the dangers of first-cousin marriages, especially if this has been the practice for several (or many) generations, as it can increase the chances of inherited defects.

CHILD MARRIAGES

When Muhammad reached the age of 52 he married a motherly woman to help raise his daughters; he also contracted marriage with a child, Abu Bakr's daughter Aishah, who was said to have been only six years old. This action had far-reaching consequences in that it:

▶ *established a precedent and, since his followers are commended for following his example, to this day in rural villages some very young girls find themselves being made to marry men old enough to be their grandfathers*
▶ *led to accusations that the Prophet ﷺ was a paedophile*
▶ *led to accusations that Muhammad ﷺ could not have been a genuine prophet, for God would not have allowed him to do such a thing.*

There is actually dispute over the dates for Aishah's birth, marriage and death. Most Muslims accept that she was born in the fourth year of the Prophethood, i.e. 614 CE, and that she was therefore contracted to the Prophet ﷺ when she was only six years old. Others point out that various dates given in the traditions do not 'add up', and if she was born four years **before** the Prophethood, i.e. 606, she would have been 13 at her *nikah*, probably the average age for this ceremony in Arabia.

That the Prophet ﷺ had no depraved urge to have sex with a child was proved by the fact that he could have done anything he liked to her, yet there was no physical intimacy between them for several years, and she continued to live in her father's household.

To be married without consummation was not an unusual thing, and to this day it is still accepted that some couples who have been officially married by nikah (even adults) will not consummate their relationship for varying lengths of time, for all sorts of reasons.

In the West today sex is illegal for girls under the age of 16, but this is an arbitrary choice of age,[5] and many girls are sexually active much younger. Muslim culture prefers honourable marriage as soon as pregnancy becomes a possibility to dishonourable sex before marriage with its attendant tragedies and abortions.

Suitable age for marriage

Before the coming of Islam, marriage arrangements could be made from birth (or even from before birth – see previous page), and sexual intimacy was considered acceptable once a girl had become technically capable of childbirth with the onset of menstruation – which could be as early as nine or as late as 18. The usual age for a girl to marry was between 11 and 15.

Insight

If very young girls are married to much older men, it is only Islamic if done with their free consent. Many would argue that even that is not acceptable, since they are not able to judge the possible consequences and ramifications properly.

Islamic feminists point out that there is no Qur'anic text requiring or encouraging men to marry very young girls. If physical intimacy is allowed to take place with the onset of menstruation, it must be primarily dependent upon the Islamic general ruling that no Muslim should ever force any other person to do something that would

[5]Child marriage was also considered acceptable in the West in the past. Chaucer's 'Wife of Bath' married at 12, and Richard II married Isabel of France when she was seven, a cause for celebration! In 1721 at the age of 11, King Louis XV of France was betrothed to his first cousin, Marie-Anne-Victoire, the three-year-old Spanish Infanta, daughter of Philip V of Spain.

cause them hurt or abuse, and the specific ruling that men were forbidden to force or coerce women into unwanted sexual intimacy.

Insight

Many of the Prophet's ﷺ Companions were teenagers or young men who married much older women. His own wife Khadijah was 15 years older than him; his fostered 'son' Zayd married Umm Ayman, 20 years his senior. It was not uncommon.

This would in itself rule out young girls being forced to marry any person they did not wish to, let alone much older men. The Prophet's ﷺ marriage to Aishah was in no way forced, but she had seen him every day of her life and loved him dearly.

THE MAHR (MARRIAGE PAYMENT)

Islam makes it obligatory for men to pay a *mahr* (an agreed settlement) to each of their wives, which remains the property of the wives. If a wife later wishes to divorce a husband who had done nothing wrong and is unwilling to let her go, she could be obliged to return his mahr. However, if a husband divorced his wife, or if the wife had normal grounds for divorce against him, she is allowed to keep it. Many women, therefore, are glad when a large mahr is negotiated.

Insight

The mahr is often referred to as a dowry – but a dowry is usually taken to mean the amount of money provided to a girl by her father which will go to her husband upon marriage – the very opposite of mahr.

The mahr system was not intended as a burden. The sum varies and some women may ask very little or forego it altogether.

> *And give the women (on marriage) their dower as a free gift; but if they of their own good pleasure remit any part of it to you take it and enjoy it with right good cheer.* (Surah 4.4)

Others expect a huge sum. Some unfortunate men find themselves obliged to save for years and marry quite late as a result!

A Muslim bride's family should never be asked for money by the husband or his family. On the contrary, the rule is for the husband to pay his new wife a negotiated sum which is hers to keep, so that even if she previously owned nothing, she can start her married life with money or property of her own. The only exception should be if the new wife specifically agrees to forgo any settlement.

THE WEDDING

An Islamic wedding or *nikah* may be a very simple affair, and the bride does not have to dress up or even attend if she does not wish to. If she chooses, she can send two witnesses of her agreement. Normally, the ceremony consists of readings from the Qur'an and the exchange of vows in front of witnesses for both partners. No special religious official is necessary, but often the imam is present.

Many wedding customs, such as the bride's dress, are matters of culture. Many brides these days wear a white wedding dress; Asian brides often wear a *shalwar-qameez* outfit (long shirt with baggy trousers beneath) in scarlet, embroidered with gold thread, their hands and feet patterned with henna. This is a cultural practice and nothing to do with Islam.

Muslims living in non-Muslim societies should be aware that to be legal their marriages must also be in accordance with the laws of the land. In the United Kingdom, all marriages have to be registered. A nikah on its own is not a lawful marriage in the UK, and must be registered at the registry office as well. Polygamous marriages are illegal in the West. The marriages of Muslims who married before coming to the West are legal.

Figure 6.3 A newly married Muslim couple. The bride is wearing a traditional scarlet dress.

WALIMAH

Islamic marriage is never to be done secretly. If secrecy is attempted, it usually means that some principle of Islam is being broken.

The *walimah* is the wedding party given for friends and family, which makes the marriage public. It usually takes place either at the wedding or within three days of it. In some cultures there is a sumptuous meal, and sometimes families go to enormous expense and invite hundreds of guests. The expense is in part defrayed by the system of the guests giving presents of money, the value of which is carefully recorded; presents of similar value are expected to be given when their relatives get married in turn.

Insight

Ostentation and expense are directly opposed to the spirit of Islam, and many families struggle to foot the enormous bill quite needlessly. The Prophet's ﷺ arrangements for all his wives except one and all his daughters were very simple, involving little expense.

The main reason for the walimah is to make public the fact that the bride and groom are now legally married and entitled to live together. In cultures where the bride is very young, sexual intimacy may be deferred for a considerable time – as for example with the Prophet ﷺ and his young wife Aishah, or with the Virgin Mary (mother of Jesus ﷺ) and her husband Joseph.

MIXED MARRIAGES

Muslims may marry any other Muslims, no matter what their race. Muslim boys are also permitted to marry Christian and Jewish girls, but not vice versa. Muslims may only marry Hindus, Buddhists, etc. if the other party agrees to convert to Islam. This might sound harsh for societies used to young people meeting and falling in love at random, but in Islamic societies it would be extremely rare for a Muslim girl to request marriage to a non-Muslim boy.

This is a matter for concern to some Muslim parents who now live in non-Muslim societies, where their teenage daughters attend state schools and mingle freely with boys with whom they might fall in love. This is one main reason why Muslims seek single-sex schools for their children.

Insight

A growing worry in the West is that Muslim girls and boys make friends with non-Muslims, but avoid Muslim boys and girls – who have been taught that they must not mix freely in case tempted into sex before marriage.

A non-Muslim converting simply to marry a practising Muslim would be acceptable, but without genuine religious commitment they would probably find it too demanding to live the Islamic way. However, vast numbers have started on the path to Islam through falling in love with Muslims, and have thereby changed their entire lives.

SHOULD HUSBANDS BE OBEYED?

The husband is always the head of the household in an Islamic marriage, but this does not mean that the woman is inferior in any way.

A man is ruler of his family, and he will be questioned on the Day of Judgement about those under his care. A woman is ruler in the house of her husband, and she will be questioned about those under her care.   (Bukhari)

Insight

I often jokingly tell girls not to marry an idiot! Muslim wives need to respect their husbands, and respect does not come automatically – it has to be earned. A wife cannot respect a husband who is not worthy of respect, for one reason or another.

A woman might be more intelligent, more educated, or more spiritually and morally gifted than her man. That's fine – it is only to safeguard the smooth running of the home that a Muslim woman accepts a man as her leader. Therefore, a Muslim woman should take great care to marry a man whom she really does respect and who is worthy of her.

Qawwam

Men are the protectors and maintainers (qawwam) of women, (only) because God has given the one more than the other, and because they support them from their means. Therefore righteous women are devoutly obedient, and guard in (the husband's) absence what God would have them guard.   (Surah 4.34)

The word *qawwam* (guardian) does not imply a domineering boss or master, but rather 'one who stands firm in taking care of the business of others, protecting their interests, and looking after their affairs'. If a man orders his wife to do anything contrary to the will of God, or to condone his doing anything contrary to the will of God – in other words, any nasty, selfish, dishonest or cruel action – then as a Muslim woman she actually has the right and command of Allah to refuse to obey him. Her husband is not her master; a Muslim woman has only one Master, and that is Allah.

Feminist scholars point out that this verse is often translated as 'Men have authority over women because God has given the one more than the other…' They suggest that this is a poor translation, and not an unconditional statement of male authority and superiority over all women for all time. Rather, it conveys the notion of responsibly providing for women in the context of child-bearing and rearing. It does not necessarily mean that women cannot provide for themselves.

Insight

Qawwam does not mean 'boss' but 'protector'. Surah 9.71 states: '*Believers, male and female, are protectors of one another.*'

POLYGAMY

In pre-Muslim Arabia, polygamy was unrestricted and quite normal for wealthy men. There is even evidence that it was also practised by wealthy women. Islam forbade polygamy for women and limited a man to four concurrent wives, but only on the condition that:

▶ *the first wife is not to be hurt by it*
▶ *later wives must not be a cause of distress to earlier ones*
▶ *equal physical intimacy (or loving passion) is not something that is required (or possible), but the giving of equal time is*
▶ *all wives must be treated fairly and equally as regards homes, food, clothing, gifts, and so on. Nights have to be spent with each in turn, unless a wife forgoes her turn.*

A wife may have it written into her marriage contract that she should be allowed divorce if her husband seeks another wife.

Insight

The Qur'an does seem to discourage polygamy, even though it was allowed, by pointing out that all wives had to be treated with absolute justice and equality, and this was an impossible task.

Two verses from the Qur'an have led many Muslims to argue that God really intended all marriages to be monogamous:

> *Marry such women as may seem good to you, two, three or four. But if you fear that you will not be able to act justly, then marry one woman (only).* (Surah 4:3)
> *You will never be able to deal equitably with your wives, no matter how eager you may be to do so.* (Surah 4:129)

However, it is a fact of history that the Prophet ﷺ and all his Companions did have more than one wife, and this would not have been possible had they thought it was counter to the will of Allah.

Reasons for polygamy

Polygamy is considered a kindness if a large number of women are left without male protectors and companions, as for example, after a war. Strict monogamy in these circumstances (as after the First World War) would mean that many women would have no chance of marriage at all, and could more easily be tempted into immoral relationships. Many women without menfolk would rather share a husband than face long years of widowhood and loneliness, but it is a very generous, tolerant and understanding already-married woman who would agree to share her husband with another wife.

Insight

With the coming of Islam, polygamy was forbidden for women and limited to four wives for men. There is no verse requiring a man to ask the permission of an existing wife or wives – but a key underlying rule of Islam is that no Muslim should ever deliberately seek to hurt another.

However, the spirit of Islam is to defend the weak, and not to leave women to fend for themselves if they do not wish to do so. (Of course, if they choose not to marry, that is up to them.)

Polygamy is also allowed if a man's wife becomes so physically ill that she is no longer able to look after him or the family, or if she becomes mentally ill. It is considered more acceptable than the man living the rest of his life without any sexual comfort, or divorcing the unfortunate wife to marry another.

If a man did fall in love with someone other than his wife, it is considered more honourable to marry the second woman rather than take her as a mistress, and to carry on maintaining the first wife honourably rather than throw her out. However, although as always one can easily find situations where abuses have taken place, Islamic polygamy should always be with the consent of the wife.

The rights of a woman are sacred; ensure that women are maintained in the rights assigned to them.

(From the Prophet's Last Sermon)

Insight

Although it is not an obligation for a Muslim man to consult an existing wife when wishing to take another, he would be a complete fool not to do so!

Muslim men are expected to be able to provide for wives and children at their own expense. A man who takes on several wives with no income or resources should not expect a state system of benefits to finance them, so polygamy is far from the norm, and Muslim men who marry polygamously in the UK and have children on state benefits are committing haram acts and taking advantage of the UK system.

Divorce

In Islam, marriages are not regarded as being 'made in heaven' or 'till death do us part'. They are contracts, with conditions. If either side breaks the conditions, divorce is not only allowed, but usually expected. Nevertheless, the Qur'an makes it clear that of all the things God has allowed, divorce (*talaq*) is the most disliked.

> **Allah has created nothing on the face of the earth more hateful to Him than divorce.**
> (Surah 66.10)

A Muslim has a genuine reason for divorce only if a spouse's behaviour goes against the *sunnah* of Islam. This does not just mean that a spouse is refusing to pray or fast, but includes matters of behaviour, morality and ethics.

Insight

Behaviour that breaks the Islamic marital contract includes becoming cruel, vindictive, abusive, unfaithful, neglectful, selfish, sexually abusive, tyrannical and perverted.

It is the duty of families and friends to do everything in their power to negotiate and heal the rift that has come between husband and wife. Divorce is considered as a very serious matter as it affects entire families. However, if the marriage contract has been broken and the relationship has failed, Islam does not force people to remain together in misery.

> **Either keep your wife honestly, or put her away from you with kindness. Do not force a woman to stay with you who wishes to leave. The man who does that only injures himself.**
>
> (Surah 2:231)

The actual procedure for an uncontested divorce is reasonable, and is less of a strain than the Western legal system.

Muslims living in non-Muslim societies should be aware that to be legal their divorces must also be in accordance with the laws of the land, and legally registered. It is very important to keep legal papers safe.

GROUNDS FOR DIVORCE

The normal grounds for divorce are usually irretrievable breakdown of marriage, adultery, desertion, cruelty and abuse. Both spouses have grounds for a divorce if one partner deceived the other when they were drawing up their marriage contract or concealed important information concerning the marriage; if the husband is sterile or impotent; if he refuses to maintain his wife, abuses or ill-treats her; if he becomes insane; if he deserts her or has gone away and not communicated with her for an unreasonable time (usually taken to be four months); or if he has been sent to prison for a very long period.

Khul divorce

If the wife has none of these grounds but still wishes for divorce, or if she presses for divorce when the husband does not wish it, it is known as *khul*, or divorce by settlement or negotiation. She may approach an *imam* to act on her behalf. The husband is entitled to ask for a return of the *mahr* he had settled on his wife when they married, although she would not be obliged to give it if she no longer had it, or if the husband was at fault for the failure of the marriage.

CULTURAL DIFFICULTIES

Some societies make it almost impossible for a woman to survive after divorce; others make it very easy for a man to repudiate a wife unjustly. Both of these things are the opposite of Islam.

Similarly, it is against the spirit of Islam to condemn a divorced woman to a life of loneliness and unhappiness, either struggling to survive on her own, or to return to her parents' home.

The Prophet's ﷺ sunnah was to choose divorced and widowed women as his wives, and also take their existing children into his household with them. He also approved his Companions who considered the welfare of divorced women, and did their best to see them safely settled in new relationships.

> **Insight**
>
> Of the Prophet's ﷺ own wives, Zaynbab bint Khuzaymah, Zaynab bint Jahsh, Safiyyah, Juwayriyyah and Umm Habibah were all divorcees. Three of his four daughters also experienced divorce.

THE 'WIFE-BEATING' VERSE

Sometimes Muslim men feel that they have the right to hit or beat their wives because one verse in the Qur'an seems to sanction it. In fact, the only verse in which striking a wife was mentioned was specifically in connection with divorce proceedings in cases of a wife's *nushuz* (refusal to listen to reason).

> *As to those women on whose part you fear nushuz (disloyalty and ill-conduct), rebuke them, refuse to share their beds, beat (or overcome) them; if they return to obedience, seek not against them means (of annoyance).*
> (Surah 4.34)

These are probably the most controversial words in the Qur'an, and a perfect example of how important it is to refer to the sunnah of the Prophet ﷺ to make meanings clear:

- ▸ *the Prophet ﷺ himself never used this sanction*
- ▸ *he never once struck any woman (or child, or slave or old person)*

236

- *he pointed out that a man could hardly hit his wife and then expect her to calmly share his bed later that night*
- *Aishah reported that 'he never struck anything unless it was in struggling for the sake of Allah' (Ibn Sa'd 1.431-2)*
- *he regarded those who did so as being far from 'the best' of his followers. In fact, he despised any sort of abuse of those who were weak.*

Insight

The Prophet ﷺ was asked: 'What do you say (command) about our wives?' He replied: 'Feed them with the same that you feed yourself, and clothe them to the same standard that you clothe yourself, and do not beat them, and do not revile them.' (Abu Dawud)

However, if a husband who had not been at fault found that his wife was conducting herself to his shame, then as protector of his household he should not just ignore it, but it was his duty to do something about it. *Nushuz* (rebellion) meant ill-will, every kind of deliberate bad behaviour of a wife (and vice versa) towards a husband and family (including the children of the family, old people or dependent household staff). With luck, it would be enough for the husband to merely draw attention to it verbally. Communication is everything in a relationship, especially in marriage.

The next verse advised that if the marriage really was breaking up, then the couple should call in the help of two supporters, one for each spouse, who could listen to everything that needed saying and help calm things down. If the couple really wished for peace, God would show a way of reconciliation.

Insight

The Prophet ﷺ never once struck a woman, child, old person, slave or animal, and thought very badly of his companions who did.

There was never any suggestion that one spouse should ever hit the other out of anger, frustration, irritation, annoyance or disappointment. People would ultimately be held to account for that kind of behaviour on the Day of Judgement even if they got away with it on Earth. Furthermore, if a husband bruised his wife he could be sued according to Islamic law.

> ## Insight
>
> I debated once with a man who thought he had the right to hit his wife. I pointed out that if she could prove it, she had the right and the grounds to divorce him, or she could accuse him of physical assault in a criminal court.

A wife has no religious obligation to take a beating. She can ask for and get divorce any time. She can take him to court and if it rules in her favour has the right to apply the law of retaliation and may have the husband beaten as he beat her.

TALAQ

Either spouse can declare that they wish for a divorce (*talaq*). The best way is to divorce with no bitterness or rancour. Either spouse may make the declaration that they no longer wish to remain married, and they then completely abstain from sexual intimacy for three menstrual cycles (*iddah*). If, at any time in those three months, they are reconciled and resume a marital relationship, the divorce is cancelled. However, if, at the end of three months marital relations have not resumed, the divorce is considered valid, and if the couple wish to 'make it up' after that, they would have to be remarried. Muslim men are expected to behave decently during the iddah and do nothing that would prevent the cancellation of the divorce (Surah 2.226–32).

If marital intimacy was resumed, but they then decide to separate a second time, a second divorce declaration has to be made, and they go through another month of separation during which time they could reconcile. If it happens a third time, the divorce becomes irrevocable and if they wish to reconcile yet again after that, the Islamic ruling is that they may not do so until the wife has legally married another man, and been divorced by him. Only then would she be free to remarry the original husband (Surah 2.229–30). Fake marriage arrangements to expedite procedure may happen, but are illegal.

> ## Insight
> The iddah is a period after a statement of divorce during which a woman may not marry another man. It is calculated on the number of menses that a woman has, usually three, and was intended to ensure that the male parent of any offspring produced after the divorce would be known.

Sometimes men make the three pronouncements of divorce in one sitting, and there is no waiting. There is no provision for this procedure in either Qur'an or sunnah although this abuse has managed to embed itself and is considered valid today in some cultures (notably India/Pakistan).

TAFRIQ

Divorce by way of *tafriq* (a judicial divorce) involves the intervention of the court if the continuation of the marriage would be harmful to the wife's interests or health.

LI'AN

If there were no witnesses but an accusing spouse claimed to have caught his partner in the act of adultery, the *li'an* procedure was that the accuser would be allowed to swear four times that the adultery really had been committed, and then the accused would have to swear four times that the accuser was lying and they were innocent. The fifth oath would bring the curse of God upon whoever was not speaking the truth. The couple would then be divorced – and any *hadd* punishment for adultery would be avoided in this world and left over to the next (Surah 24.6–9). (See Chapter 7 for more detail about hadd punishments.)

LONGER OR SHORTER IDDAH

If a marriage had not been consummated no iddah or waiting period is necessary before remarriage; there has been no sexual intimacy, the wife cannot be pregnant, the unconsummated marriage may simply be dissolved.

If a woman is pregnant, her iddah continues until after the birth of the child, which could be longer or shorter than three months. During this time the wife is entitled to continue living at the house even if she has been divorced, and is also entitled to full maintenance and to receive good treatment. She should not be forced out. After the birth the father has to provide or pay for her food and clothing while she is suckling, for a period of up to two years unless she agrees to make it shorter, or provide the baby a wet-nurse (Surah 2.233; 65.6).

WHEN DIVORCE IS FORBIDDEN

For the declaration of divorce to be counted as valid, the declarers must be sane, fully conscious and not under pressure from some outside party, or under the influence of alcohol or drugs, or so angry that they do not fully appreciate what they are saying.

Divorce is forbidden when the woman is menstruating, or is postnatal, when perhaps the husband's lack of sexual fulfilment might have made him tense, or led him to a hasty, ill-judged decision.

Also forbidden is *zihar* (or 'back') divorce, a cruel practice that long predated Islam. It involved a husband ending his sexual relationship with his wife, declaring that she was to him 'like the back of his mother' (Abu Dawud). It kept the woman in a kind of limbo, divorced but not allowed to remarry, remaining forever in her husband's custody. This practice was forbidden in Islam (Surah 33.4, 58.1–4).

CUSTODY OF CHILDREN

Normally, custody of children is given to the mother, but the responsibility of providing for them remains with the father.

All settlements concerning children should be done amicably and with the best interests of the children at heart. Sometimes, it was even considered best for the child to choose with which parent he or she would live with.

The Prophet said to one child: 'This is your father and this is your mother, so take whichever of them you wish by the hand.' The child took his mother's hand, and she went away with him. (Abu Dawud)

In some circumstances, however, women keeping custody is not considered wise. Muslim men who have married British women will often seek to keep custody of the children, or may take the children to their mother's household. This is considered better than the common single parent situation in the United Kingdom, with women sometimes struggling to raise children in poor housing on very meagre finances.

It is very wrong, however, for a Muslim man to cause terrible grief and anxiety to the mother of his children by kidnapping them. All arrangements should be negotiated openly, legally and as amicably as possible and, if possible, both parents should maintain contact with their children. Divorced parents must make sure they love their children more than they hate each other.

Senior citizens

> *Your Lord orders that you ... be kind to parents. If one or both of them attain old age with you, do not say one word of contempt to them, or repel them, but speak to them in terms of honour ... and say, 'My Lord, bestow Your Mercy on them, as they cherished me when I was a child.'*
>
> (Surah 17:23-4)

Many old people experience fear, helplessness and loneliness as they grow older and become less capable of caring for themselves. As their friends and companions begin to die, and they become more frail and less able to get about, and their illnesses and wounds hang around longer, it is inevitable for them to turn their thoughts to 'When will it be my turn?' and 'What will become of me?' Loving care of parents is a Muslim's prime duty.

It is particularly frightening for aged Muslims who are obliged to end their days in an environment very different from that of their normal culture.

So, when does old age begin? It used to be thought that the age of 70 was as much as any person had a 'right' to expect; in some places and times humans were not really likely to live much past the age of 40. But statistics play games, and there have always been those who made it to 90 and over. The Roman Empress Livia died at 93, and some of the Prophet's ﷺ Companions topped 100.

There is nothing worse than getting to the 'top of the tree' as regards experience, skill and expertise in employment, then suddenly reaching an age regarded as 'too old', and either being retired, made redundant or replaced by a younger model (with less expertise and knowledge), and suddenly becoming a nonentity instead of a figure of some authority.

> **Insight**
> Older women suddenly discover they have become invisible on the streets; but they may find polite people giving them seats on buses or helping them with heavy baggage.

As people become old as opposed to middle-aged or elderly, they often become confused, impatient or bad-tempered, or suffer the torment of constant pain that gives them no respite. They may lack energy and become incontinent and increasingly housebound, or even bedridden. Their hearing or sight becomes weaker and more care needs to be taken with their diets so that they do not become malnourished. It may become difficult for them to travel or even make the journey to the shops independently.

Insight

People who have been used to independence and/or some authority may well dislike being 'taken over' by carers, no matter how well-meaning. Losing control of one's own life is a highly stressful experience, and may also involve grieving for the control/life/career/ability that has been lost.

It is quite distressing, too, when the religious duties of prayer and fasting become increasingly difficult, and eventually not possible. People with conditions such as diabetes and arthritis may need gentle reminders that it is perfectly all right to pray seated or even lying down, and that fasting is not required of those who would be made ill by it, or whose illness would become worse.

Insight

I recall the last time I prayed 'normally' at the mosque; I suffered cramp and was dizzy as I stood up, and nearly plunged into the row in front. Thankfully, somebody grabbed me, or everyone would have fallen like dominoes! Since then, I have either stood to pray, or used the chair provided.

They may live alone, and become very depressed, moody and unsociable towards any who try to help them. It is important for them not to be ignored or dismissed as beyond help, but to be checked up on with thorough medical examinations, and be reminded often that Allah is always near to the broken-hearted.

Do not be like the unbelievers who ... (have) regret and anguish in their hearts. It is Allah who gives life and death. Allah watches over everything you do. If you should die or be slain whilst in the service of Allah, His forgiveness and mercy will be far better than all the riches you could have saved up.

(Surah 3.156–7)

THE DUTY TO CARE

Muslim families have a duty to be aware of the problems faced by old people and not to turn their backs on them or regard them as a nuisance. An increase of patience, kindness and real physical help is what is required to cope with these problems.

Muslims do not regard it as kind to relegate the care of their old folk to strangers, unless there is absolutely no alternative. Just as the mother expects to care for and nurse her own child until it reaches independence, so the Muslim 'child' is expected to care for parents who are approaching the end of life and to nurse them safely through into the next life.

Insight

The care of aged parents generally falls to the son rather than the daughter in Asian culture; sons' wives are expected to be unselfish and loving towards them.

May his nose be rubbed in dust who found his parents approaching old age and lost his right to enter Paradise because he did not look after them.

(Tirmidhi)

In fact, the Prophet ﷺ thought care of parents so important that not even personal religious zeal should be used as an excuse for neglecting them.

A person came seeking permission to participate in jihad, but the Prophet found he had parents living, and sent him away saying: 'Go back to your parents and look after them.'

(Muslim – and it is worth noting that these parents were not themselves Muslims at that time)

Old people often feel they are inadequate, a burden on others, and lose their feeling of self-worth and usefulness. Everyday activities can become a real struggle, and it is all too easy to lose the incentive to keep going.

On the other hand, many senior citizens work out all sorts of ways of overcoming problems – mobility scooters, new bathing arrangements, and so on. Some remain extremely useful and active. Many do all sorts of voluntary work, not to mention relieving tired and stressed mothers and enabling them to go out to work, study or socialize, by looking after babies and caring for grandchildren as they grow up. Muslims should encourage their elders to continue growing as far as possible through learning, participating in social activities, interacting with a variety of people, and finding meaning and fulfilment in helping others.

Insight

Many retired people take up new studies and hobbies – the internet has provided a wonderful new link with life for millions. Some volunteer to help out at local schools, especially with reading and providing one-to-one assistance for those with learning problems. Others staff charity shops.

Old people also have the knowledge, the experience and the time to pass moral and spiritual values to the next generations. The young so often need the counsel, the love and the prayers of the elderly – especially those who have spent their lifetimes building up their close relationship with Allah.

RESPECT

One of the Prophet's ﷺ most famous hadiths concerned the respect a Muslim should show to his or her mother. When he was asked:

'Who of all people is the most deserving of the best treatment from my hand?' He said: 'Your mother.' The man said again: 'Then, who is next?' He said: 'Again, it is your mother.'

He said: 'Then who?' He said: 'Again, it is your mother.' He said: 'Then who?' Thereupon, he said: 'Then it is your father.' (Muslim)

Muslims feel it is disgraceful to see children ordering their parents about and being rude to them, or treating them as if they were imbeciles. Muslim old folk expect to be treated as wise guides, with a lifetime of experience behind them. No Muslim should ever regard it as being beneath his or her dignity to be kind to old folk. It is considered beneath contempt to hurt or abuse an old person.

He who has no compassion for our little ones, and does not acknowledge the honour due to our elders, is not one of us.
(Tirmidhi)

SOME PRACTICAL DETAILS

Muslims consider it impolite for a young person to call an adult by his or her first name, or to do in front of them anything of which they might disapprove, such as smoking.

Young people should not walk in front of old people, or sit down before they do. They should not interrupt them, or hurry them in their speech, or argue with them – even if they do not agree with them. They should try to help before they are asked, and avoid doing anything that irritates them.

Insight

Many senior citizens feel guilty of being a nuisance if they have to ask for help. They have been used to coping for themselves, and it is hard to accept growing weakness and incapacity.

They should never draw attention to the care and support they are giving them, or point out what they are spending on them, to make them feel a burden, or feel guilty or embarrassed.

Parents are usually much more sensitive to any act of discourtesy towards them from their own children than from any other people.

Muslims strive to see to it that their dignity is preserved, and that they should never suffer from hurtful behaviour or speech.

> **Allah defers the punishment of all your sins until the Day of Judgement except one – disobedience to parents. For that, Allah punishes in this life, before death.** (Bayhaqi)

Culture shock for the aged

When living in non-Muslim societies, aged Muslims – particularly those who have migrated to the West – might be terrified of their children abandoning them to non-Muslim care-homes for old people, or to places where they would have great difficulty with language (some old people who have become fluent in English lose it and revert to their original language), lack of halal food, free mixing of the sexes (as in many hospital wards), men and women using the same toilets, women being nursed by men, and so on.

Insight

Many elderly Muslims have passed their lives without mixing with strangers of the opposite sex, and are therefore very embarrassed and uncomfortable in mixed-sex wards in hospitals and in gowns that come open at the back.

Peer pressure and shame make some aged Muslims highly reluctant to use facilities provided by the State, even when they need to. They expect to be cared for by their families, even though they may barely be able to cope and may be suffering under enormous stress.

Senior Muslims should try to fill their hearts with patience, love and confidence, remembering that no matter how many the sorrows and discomforts of age, if they have done their best to serve Him in this life, in the end Allah will draw out their souls gently and peacefully, and reward them with all the joys of spiritual vigour and youth and beauty beyond our powers to comprehend.

Death and burial

For a devout Muslim, death is a sobering thought, but should not be something to be feared. Muslims know that the time of their death will not be of their choosing, but when God wishes to call their souls back to Him. No one knows when, or how, or where they will die. Life is God's gift, and the length of one's life is His grant. The true Muslim accepts this as part of the submission to Allah, and greets the possibility of death with the attitude of '*Amr Allah*' – 'At Your Command, O Lord'.

Other people, of course, are very distressed by their sufferings and pray earnestly to have their lives ended, but God knows best and people who are required to live on, despite their hurts and pains, must be patient and try to find the faith to make the best of their circumstances and not concentrate on the worst side of it.

Insight

The Muslim faith that Allah knows, even before their birth, the number of breaths He has allotted to each person brings with it courage, patience and resignation. When the time comes to die, there is nothing any person can do to prevent it.

DEATH IS INEVITABLE

It is good for a Muslim to be reminded that no person was more righteous or more loved by Allah than the Prophet ﷺ – and yet there was no miraculous cure when he was sick, and he died, as all humans must die. His friend Umar could not bring himself to accept his death, and Abu Bakr reminded all Muslims of the verse:

> **Muhammad is but a messenger; there have been prophets before him, and they all died. Will you now turn back?** (Surah 3:144)

The Prophet ﷺ accepted nursing and medical help, and so other Muslims should not refuse it, or try to rely on prayer and faith alone. Medicine (painkillers, etc.) functions by God's will.

A Muslim will always acknowledge that the final outcome is in God's hands. If personal prayers are made for the sick, dying and bereaved, they are never wasted; God always hears us, and something always 'happens', even if it not what the person has prayed for. Euthanasia is forbidden (see page 282).

AT THE DEATHBED

Muslims hope to die surrounded by their loved ones, family and friends. However, even if they have to die alone, they should not feel alone, for they know angels will help them.

For those tending the dying, a tactful, respectful and sympathetic atmosphere is recommended as the best way; not becoming so 'holy' that the dying person is irritated, or feels they are being 'hurried' out of this life, and not being so casual that the dying one feels they are not important, or not loved.

Insight
Muslims should not feel distressed or hurt if the dying person's attention seems more on what lies beyond than what is taking place at the bedside. Those who tend the dying bear witness that this is often the case and normal. It should, rather, console them and ease their grief.

If possible, the bed should be turned so that they can be facing Makkah, with the face in the direction of the Ka'bah. Prayers should not be intrusive, but as the dying one finds comfortable. Many relatives will pray using words from Surah Ya-Sin (Surah 36 – 'Surely We will give life to the dead' ...), though the reciter should pray inaudibly so as not to disturb the dying person. It is always considered the best thing if a believer dies with prayer, or thoughts of Allah.

This is not a matter of fanaticism, however, and the dying should not fear that God will be disappointed if these are not their last words; He knows best. What is important is that one dies in the state of belief.

The Prophet's ﷺ sunnah was to settle everything before he died, so that his mind was at rest. Any debts should be paid (or settled by relatives as soon as possible after the death of the loved one), and forgiveness requested for any sins committed against anyone, either sins committed, or sins of omission. Then, the dying one may feel at peace, and may relax and prepare for the next stage of life.

DUTIES AFTER DEATH

When the loved one has died, the eyes should be gently closed and a prayer said, such as the Prophet's ﷺ own prayer (over his cousin Abu Salamah):

> **O Allah, forgive Your servant, raise him to high rank among those who are rightly guided; make him as a guardian of his descendants who survive him. Forgive us and him, O Lord of the Universe; make his grave spacious and grant him light in it.**
>
> (Muslim)

Although Muslims believe that the soul departs at the moment of death, and the body left behind is nothing but an empty shell, nevertheless the mortal remains of a Muslim should be treated with dignity and respect, and the last services done to them in a prayerful and loving atmosphere.

The deceased should then be given the final ritual wash as soon as possible. This duty should not be performed by strangers, but by members of the family, preferably male relatives for men, and female relatives for women – but a husband is allowed to perform this duty for his wife, and a wife for her husband.

Insight

Those who wash the dead are not expected to look at them naked, but to preserve their modesty. A cloth is usually laid over the body, and the body washed beneath it. Anything unseemly should be covered and not mentioned.

If there is no relative available, the washing is a duty that falls on any member of the community, to see it is done as decently as possible. If males are washing females, or vice versa, their hands should be covered so that they do not touch the naked bodies. If clean water cannot be found (as in some circumstances), sand will suffice as in *tayammum*. The ritual wash is not given to non-Muslims, aborted foetuses or dead bodies that have been bomb-blasted. Martyrs are traditionally buried 'with their blood'. In these cases, they are usually shrouded in their clothes. If pilgrims die in *ihram*, they should be buried as pilgrims, with heads uncovered (for men) and faces unveiled (for women).

Insight

Muslims strive to bury the deceased as soon as possible after death, avoiding the need for embalming or otherwise disturbing the body of the deceased. An autopsy may be performed, if necessary, but should be done with the utmost respect.

For these reasons, Muslims always appreciate hospitals that are aware of their beliefs and customs, and allow the relatives to take their dead away, to do the washing and shrouding, or provide facilities for them to do it themselves in the hospital. If hospital staff wash a body it does not count as *wudu*.

SHROUDING

It is not commendable to use expensive materials, but traditionally three white winding sheets are used for a man, and five for a woman. The shrouding could, however, be two sheets, or even one, provided it covers the whole of the body. A woman's shrouding consists of a cloth to bind her upper legs, waist wrapper to tie it in place, a shift, a head veil (after her hair is plaited, if it is long) and the final winding sheet.

The sheets are spread out, the deceased lifted and laid on top of them and perfumed with incense. Then the edge of the top winding sheet is folded over the deceased's right side, and the other edge over the left side. The second and third sheets are treated in the same way. These are all fastened in place around the deceased and only unfastened when laid in the grave.

> ## Insight
>
> I visited Bosnia just after the war there, and attended the washing and preparation of one deceased lady. As much tender care was taken as if she was still living, and when the family came in she was lying at peace, wrapped in fresh linens, her face calm as if in sleep.

The face may be left visible until last farewells have been said.

If no sheet can be found big enough to cover the entire body, then the head should be covered with it, and grass or paper placed over the legs. If the dead are many, two or three may be shrouded together and buried in one grave.

FUNERAL PRAYER – SALAT UL-JANAZA

This has to be performed by at least one Muslim. The best person to perform it is whoever the deceased chose personally, providing that person is not immoral or an unbeliever. After that, preference goes to the imam or his deputy, the deceased's father, or grandfather, then son, grandson, or closest male relative.

These prayers are commonly held outdoors, in a courtyard or public square, not inside the mosque. The community gathers, and the imam stands in front of the deceased, facing away from the worshippers. The whole prayer is made standing; there is no prostration as in the normal prayer, and the entire prayer is said silently but for a few words.

> ## Insight
>
> It is hard, sometimes, to realize that our family relationships here on this Earth will not necessarily be the same in the Life to Come. At death, we are no longer somebody's wife or son

or parent, but just our own selves – our forms and future relationships lie beyond our knowledge.

THE FUNERAL

Cremation is not approved in Islam but not from any fear it would affect the state of the soul. Allah can resurrect persons as He pleases, whether destroyed by burning, explosion, being dissolved in acid, or eaten by birds, animals or worms.

People should always stand in respect when a funeral passes whether the deceased is Muslim or not. The Prophet ﷺ recommended that it was more respectful to walk than to ride. (Hiring funeral cars is almost universal in the West. The principle is to be respectful without being ostentatious.) He allowed women to accompany processions, but did not recommend it. The tradition is for processions to move at a brisk pace rather than slowly – to hurry a good person along their road to Paradise, or be rid swiftly of a bad one. Many people may share in carrying the corpse, or may touch it out of respect. Coffins, if they are used, should be simple and not expensive. Muslims prefer bodies to be laid in the earth, rather than in a coffin.

Insight

Grief at the death of a beloved person is normal, as is weeping for the dead. However, Muslims should not wail in a loud voice, shriek, beat their chest and cheeks, tear their hair or clothes, break objects, or scratch their faces.

The grave

Graves should also be simple and not ostentatious. At the graveside, people should remain standing until the person has been buried (although they may sit to wait if they have arrived before the cortege).

The grave should reach the depth of a man's chest, and preferably have a *qiblah* niche in it. It is preferable if the cemetery is a Muslim one, or at least a part of it made over to Muslims, so that the graves may be orientated towards Makkah.

> ## Insight
>
> Extravagance is always distasteful in Islam; there is no class
> system for the dead. It is preferred for a Muslim to be buried
> where he or she died, and not be transported to another
> location or country (which may cause delays or require
> embalming the body).

A woman's body should be lowered in by men within her family,
and all bodies are placed in the grave feet first. The deceased are
placed on their right sides, with their faces in the direction of the
Ka'bah, and supported so that they do not roll over on to their
backs. The fastening of the shroud is undone, and bricks, canes, or
leaves set in place so that no earth falls on the body. A little earth is
then sprinkled into the grave, saying:

> **We created you from it, and return you into it, and from it We will
> raise you a second time.**
>
> (Surah 20:55)

Then the earth is heaped over, while the people pray. The surface
of the grave should be raised a hand's breadth so that it will be
recognized as a grave and not trodden on. It is also considered very
disrespectful to sit on graves, or lean against them.

The grave may be marked with a headstone, but Muslims should
not spend money on elaborate tombstones or memorials.

Figure 6.4 A simple Muslim headstone.

Instead, donations may be given to the poor. Making structures over the grave or plastering them is considered a pre-Islamic practice and is, therefore, disapproved of. Mosques should not be erected over graves.

MAKING GRAVES INTO SHRINES

It was, and is, the culture of many places to go to the graves of saintly persons for superstitious motives, to pray to the holy soul to help them or grant them offspring, and so on. This is actually forbidden in Islam. Prayers should be addressed to none but Allah. Prayers for the dead are loving remembrances, and will not affect God's judgement or mercy.

> *Intercession with Him will be in vain, unless it coincides with His will.*
> (Surah 34:23)

Insight

Prayers may be said at the graveside **for** the deceased, but **not** to them, which is a form of *shirk*, and the reason for the Wahhabi sect demolishing many much-loved historic graves in and around Makkah and Madinah.

Figure 6.5 Praying at the grave of a saint.

Death tosses the human being into spiritual turmoil. One of the biggest problems for devout believers is the attitude of so many friends who, because of their sincere faith in the Afterlife, simply do not seem to see that people are grieving; or refuse to admit it. They feel that a committed Muslim should accept there is nothing to fear about death, and therefore should be expected to cope wonderfully.

In reality, the mourner may not be coping very well, but because of the attitude of these pious 'comforters', cannot speak up or make it known that help is needed. In fact, religious people who speak like this are quite possibly trying to escape their own emotional involvement, which they find embarrassing or are unable to handle. Everyone feels inadequate, and lacks confidence in what to say for the best to a bereaved person. In fact, a companionable silence is often preferable to false platitudes.

Condolences

Too much mourning implies lack of acceptance of Allah's will and lack of faith in the Life to Come. Muslims are allowed to mourn a husband or wife for four months and ten days (Surah 2.234), and must wait that length of time before contracting a new marriage. For other deceased, the period is three days and nights. Although one is naturally very sad at a death, the Muslim faith is that people will go to their reward, and the only ones really to be mourned are those who rejected belief in God and lived in such a way that would earn punishment.

Insight

The widow's *iddah* (or waiting period) of four lunar months and ten days is a balance between mourning her husband's death for too long and protecting her from criticism that she wants to re-marry too quickly. During this time, the widow should not move from her home.

Condolences may be offered in any words so long as they lighten the distress, induce patience, and bring solace to the bereaved. Visitors are expected to pay their respects, but it is important that they should not put burdens on the bereaved. Polite visitors bring contributions of refreshments and keep their stays short – unless it is seen that it is helpful to the grieving to plunge into work and conversation.

Many of the practices carried out by grieving Muslims for their dead may console them but are of no benefit to the deceased. For example, a Hajj undertaken on their behalf, or fasting, or giving zakat may be noble deeds, but the deceased will not get the credit of it since they have not done it themselves.

Insight

The moment human beings die, their records are sealed and nothing can change them one way or another. Any plea imploring God to amend, alter or improve His judgement means that we are trying to persuade or bribe Him to be more favourable – suggesting we are more merciful than Him.

Qur'an readings

Some Muslims gather for a recitation of the entire Qur'an on behalf of the deceased, either doing it personally or asking someone on their behalf. This is a tradition, and no sin has been committed if it is not done. Rather, it is not allowed to ask someone to recite the Qur'an on behalf of the dead and pay them money for doing so.

URS AND RAWDAHS

The custom of holding *urs* or rawdahs (commemoration services) on the third day, the fortieth day or the hundredth day, or on the anniversary of someone's death, has no basis in Qur'an or sunnah, but is a matter of tradition. They are respectful occasions, but not compulsory. In Iran, the *cheleh* (the 40th day after the death) is the significant day of remembrance for the dead person.

Problems for Muslims living in the West

Islam is the fastest-growing religion in the West at the present time, and the number of Muslims in the UK, for example, has now reached around the 2 million mark.

Balancing the converts and number of Muslims born into already Muslim families are the Muslim-born men and women who find the Islamic life too much for them and, in the freedom of Western society, choose to abandon it. It is too early to guess how many of these will come back to their roots in later life.

SCHOOLS

Segregated-gender schools

There are lots of issues to do with education. First comes the question of the segregation of the genders at puberty. Muslims prefer their girls to be taught in an all-female environment, and vice versa, and even when they are sent to single-gender schools, if these are available, there is still the question of the gender of the teacher. Muslims would prefer female teachers for girls, and male teachers for boys. They would also prefer at least some of the teachers on the staff to be Muslim by faith as well.

For these reasons, many Muslims are now attempting to set up their own schools, and encouraging intelligent girls to take up further education so that there will be a good supply of qualified female Muslim teachers.

Insight

Many of my friends prefer to educate their children at home rather than send them to a mixed or state school. The main problems are the inadequacy of the education given, the lack of 'mixing' and social experience, and interaction with non-Muslims.

School dress

Muslims prefer their girls to cover their arms and legs and wear *hijab* if possible. Some schools do not allow this, but generally the situation has eased in the West, and most schools will now allow Muslim girls to wear trousers or long skirts as part of their school uniform. Some schools need to grasp that 'Muslim' does not equal 'Asian', and should make the same allowances for Muslim girls of other ethnic backgrounds, including white girls.

Varieties of Islamic clothing have caused confusion; in 2005, for example, when one girl at a school that already allowed *shalwar-qameez* and hijab claimed that her faith required her to wear a *jilbab*, it drew attention to the fact that female Muslims define Islamic clothing differently. Her case, defended by the Prime Minister's wife, was successful, despite the fact that a jilbab is an outdoor covering garment, more typical of Somali ladies than Pakistani ones.

Insight
Many Muslims long for their young to be educated in a Muslim ethos, where their codes of diet, clothing and conduct, and prayer routines are catered for, and the students grow up in an atmosphere and acceptance of belief in God.

Some countries (notably France) insist upon state schools being secular, and wearing hijab has become an issue. In Turkey hijab was banned from all state-run institutions including schools and universities in 1997, and in 1999 when the member of parliament Merve Kavakci attempted to take her parliamentary oath in a headscarf she was banned and has never been allowed to take her seat. In November 2005 the European Court of Human Rights upheld the hijab ban despite the hopes of Prime Minister Tayyip Erdogan whose party (JDP) had been working to relax the ruling.

Sports
Mixed sports lessons, especially mixed-gender swimming, are not approved of, and Muslim girls are not encouraged to wear revealing swimsuits. For most sports, a track suit is approved,

or some modest covering such as a bodysuit with shorts worn over it to 'veil' the private parts. A recent invention has been the 'burkini'. Many swimming baths now make special arrangements for females only, or even Muslim ladies only, and it would be tactful if schools took note of this.

> **Insight**
> Showers after PE are another issue if there are not separated cubicles – Muslims do not show themselves naked even to friends of the same sex.

Sex education

Muslims are very wary of their young being taught sexual matters by people whose own morals they are not sure of.

Muslims are also wary of sex education being carried out when pupils are too young or where boys and girls are being taught together. They feel this is something better left to the parents. However, Muslims are not against sex education as such, so long as it is taught in a Muslim moral context.

State school religious education

Since religious education is still compulsory in many schools, this can be another problem area. If the school presents a wholly Christian syllabus, the Muslim child may suffer from the notion that Islam is 'wrong' or that everyone else thinks it is 'wrong', which is depressing. Even where a multi-faith syllabus is taught, there is still the danger of faiths other than Christianity being 'talked down'.

Another problem is that, with the best will in the world, different faiths are sometimes taught by people who know hardly anything about them and, in fact, teach them wrongly. This used to be very common, but with today's highly researched textbooks the situation is improving. On the good side, Muslims should appreciate that since most state schools do include something on the major world faiths, virtually every youngster in the UK will get at least an introduction to Islam.

History syllabus

History lessons in the West often omit all mention of the Islamic input in world history, and/or depend on books presenting a very biased and colonialist point of view. The peak period of Islamic culture is 'the Dark Ages'.

There is virtually no syllabus coverage of the role of the West in India, Pakistan, Afghanistan, Palestine and Jordan, Iran, Iraq or African countries. If children from diverse backgrounds are to understand each other and feel included, the history syllabus needs to reflect the nature of British society today and validate the historical experiences of minority communities. It is hoped that a new history module might be created to give pupils the choice to study the background of immigrant citizens, and the politics and other causes of their coming to the West.

Special faith schools

Many Muslims now realize that they must establish proper academic Muslim schools in the West, but it is an uphill struggle; there is no tradition of them, and there is active resistance to them from fear they will become breeding grounds for extremism.

The school would be expected to deliver the full state curriculum, plus the Islamic studies, in a calm and devout caring atmosphere. New schools have struggled to produce the required standards of staffing, building or curriculum, and some have languished at the bottom of league tables – but there has been a huge surge of commitment, skills and finances, and now many Islamic schools head the league tables. The Leicester Islamic Academy, for example, has achieved a 100 per cent success rate in A* to C passes at GCSE.

So far in the UK, some 33 per cent of Christian, 39 per cent of Jewish but only 0.4 per cent of Muslim children have a choice of good academic schools for their own faith. According to OFSTED, there were 118 Islamic schools in January 2005, many with excellent academic success.

Insight

Notable Islamic schools include Manchester Islamic High School for Girls and the Islamia Girls Secondary School in Brent, London (opened in 1989 and financed by Yusuf Islam, the former pop star Cat Stevens), which topped the exam league in Brent two years running, and many more.

Rather than create special new schools, one idea is to utilize existing schools where the vast majority of children on the school roll are already Muslims. All that is needed then is an influx of good Muslim teachers.

Madrassah problems

Most mosques try to impart some Islamic knowledge to their young by lessons at the mosque after school or at the weekend. This has potential, but is frequently not really satisfactory. It is acknowledged that some *madrassahs* bore and stress children without providing any significant degree of knowledge or understanding of the faith.

Non-Muslims do not usually realize that Muslim children are studying at madrassahs, sometimes every night, over and above their normal school studies and homework.

CHRISTMAS AND EASTER

When it comes to celebrating special days, Muslims sometimes feel very awkward because of the emphasis placed on Christmas and Easter. No Muslims would celebrate Easter, for doctrinal reasons.

Insight

Although Muslims do accept the virgin birth of Jesus ﷺ, they do not believe that this made him 'Son of God', or that he was 'born to save us from our sins', making Christmas carols and nativity plays inappropriate.

Many Muslims can accept the notion of honouring the birth of the Prophet Jesus ﷺ, although others feel it is wrong to celebrate any birthdays, including that of the Prophet Muhammad ﷺ. Others point out that Jesus ﷺ was almost certainly not born on 25 December anyway, but this was a pagan sun festival, and they should not join in (a view shared by Oliver Cromwell). Yet others feel it is harmless and polite to share the celebrations and see nothing wrong in non-doctrinal 'Season's greetings' cards, or giving gifts (even if some families put aside the gifts given to their children until Eid days).

Time off for Friday prayers and Muslim Feast Days
Many Muslim males would like to attend the compulsory Friday prayers at the mosque, but are not able to leave school or their workplace. Some employers are more sympathetic than others about the hour or so an employee would be missing from work depending on travelling time. The actual gathering is usually about 30 minutes. At school, it is sometimes possible for Muslim youngsters to gather together to pray, but there are not always facilities for this, or for the washing that comes before prayer.

Insight
It is ironic that pupils trying to wash their feet before prayer in a high sink can be regarded as 'dirty' – perhaps due to the visible naked feet, or a bit of splashed water. Many youngsters find performing their prayers where non-Muslims can see them (and often laugh at them) very embarrassing.

Many Muslims have to do their best to enjoy their Feast Days without being excused from work or school.

Halal food
When Muslims are new in an area they often cannot get *halal* meat unless they are allowed to do the slaughter themselves, which would generally horrify the neighbours. Some give in and eat non-halal meat after praying over it, others become vegetarian. These

days halal food is widely available, although there are fears of fake labelling and scams.

MUSIC

Some Muslims believe that all music is disapproved of or even forbidden in Islam, and some ban all instruments except drums, but will accept songs (*nashid*) for the unaccompanied voice.

Certain types of music are certainly disapproved of as they lead towards the *haram*:

▶ *Pop music with sexual lyrics or sexually provocative rhythms.*
▶ *Nationalistic and jingoistic music ('God save the Queen' is acceptable, 'Rule Britannia' is not).*
▶ *Music which is intended to stir up tolerance for haram substances or behaviour.*

Yet there is no ban mentioned in the Qur'an and it therefore falls into the category of that left to the conscience of the individual. Indeed, the Qur'an tells of Allah bestowing the gift of song upon the Prophet-king Dawud (David) ﷺ, and the mountains echoing him and the birds praising God along with him (Surah 28.79, 34.10).

Islam has a long tradition of music and song used as a medium to express joy in the faith. There is no 'typical' Muslim music, for there are different styles from Africa, Uzbekistan, Bosnia, Turkey, Spain and India.

MEDICAL TREATMENT

Muslims prefer women to be treated by women, and men by men, and this is not always possible in hospital situations. However, it is usually possible to choose one's general practitioner (GP). Hospitals are not always very sympathetic to mass visiting from large families, or relatives bringing in (and eating together) familiar spicy food, and there is sometimes a language problem, with very frightened patients unable to understand what is going on, although nowadays people can usually be found who can speak the Asian language of most local Muslims.

When a Muslim dies in hospital, the family is grateful for sympathetic authorities that allow relatives to take the dead away quickly for washing and burial.

BURIAL

Muslims seek burial grounds that permit bodies to be laid with their heads facing Makkah, and to be buried without coffins. Many cemeteries now do provide a special area for Muslim alignment.

DOGS

Muslims do not dislike dogs, but if their saliva touches clothing, it is considered unclean for prayer, and the Muslim would have to go home and change.

Sniffer dogs are increasingly used to find hidden drugs and explosives. Planes going to the Middle East often use sniffer dogs. This annoys many Muslims who like their aircraft to be ritually clean so that they can pray in them when it comes to the appropriate times.

RACISM, ISLAMOPHOBIA AND INTOLERANCE

Sadly, this can always be found in any country. Muslims have to be tolerant themselves, and understand that if some individuals make life unpleasant for them, there are countless others who are ashamed of the racism and intolerance these ignorant people show.

Insight

In his lifetime the Prophet ﷺ was vilified, insulted and abused countless times, yet did not retaliate against personal insults, and prevented followers who sought recriminations. His generous and forgiving attitude converted many of his enemies.

Distortion of the image of Islam by the media

Since the end of the Cold War and the collapse of Communism, many Muslims feel they are now being demonized as the world's major enemy of peace and stability and that many equate Islam with terrorism. Muslims are naturally distressed that the nature of Islam as a religion of reason, tolerance and justice does not reach people as it should.

Unexamined assumptions are made about Islam – 'they' threaten 'our' freedom', 'they' want to destroy 'our' values. Who are 'they'? The 2005 UK suicide bombers enjoyed British freedoms and way of life as much as anyone else. Is such propaganda constantly peddled because it allows politicians and commentators to focus on 'Muslim beliefs' as the cause of violence rather than the real circumstances and injustices that lie behind it? Incorrect statements about Islam convince the Muslim world that the West is an implacable enemy.

Insight

Muslims are often criticized for not criticizing their own 'baddies' – in fact, many do speak out but it is frequently a case of not being able to get media space. More 'soundbite' skills are needed.

Muslim fears and conspiracy theories

Many feel there is a deliberate conspiracy against Islam, and suggest that the media distorts its image and presents Islam as an evil leading to oppression and violence in order to mobilize public opinion against it.

The distortion of the image of Islam and Muslims takes a variety of forms. Occasionally, it genuinely results from reporters' ignorance of Islam. Very often, however, it does seem to represent a deliberate effort by certain news agencies and reporters who use their free speech to discredit Islam and defame Muslims. They:

▶ *deliberately distort Islamic world views and practices with half-truths and downright lies*

- associate the views and practices of fanatical groups and individuals with Islam itself
- give out subtle messages and tactics by the use of such phrases as 'Muslim bomb' or 'Islamic terrorism', whereas violence by Christian individuals and groups is virtually never referred to as 'Christian terrorism' or a 'Christian army'
- ignore the huge contribution of Muslims to Western society and simply present Islam as a source of threat and menace
- justify imposition on, and aggression against, Muslims
- give media accounts that refer to Muslims as 'believers in Allah' as if they are referring to some false god and not simply the Arabic word for God.

Shooting oneself in the foot

Western media have a long tradition of seeking out sensation, corruption, hypocrisy, evil and catastrophe as the content of the news. Muslim fanatics seem quite unconcerned that their activities, statements and even clothing only serve to make all Muslims look irrational, hateful, oppressive, abusive and downright odd.

Insight

Westerners, who are on the whole tolerant, sometimes feel irritated that Muslims seem to make a big fuss over what they may consider to be unimportant matters, such as newspaper cartoons and disrespectful adverts, instead of important issues like world poverty and human rights.

The vast majority of criticisms of Islam made in the media are not actually criticisms of Islam at all, but of that weird type of Islam promoted by sectarian and bigoted people. It is the responsibility of the Muslim community itself to present Islam accurately, so that the small minority of those who seem to enjoy embarrassing all other Muslims with their narrowness of vision may be seen in perspective.

10 THINGS TO REMEMBER

1 *All Muslim babies should be wanted, and conceived within marriage.*

2 *The Prophet ﷺ did not regard boys as superior or more wanted than girls. He specially praised those who cherished and brought up girl children, and did their best to educate them and help them make good marriages.*

3 *Schooling in the West can present problems. For example: Muslims prefer girls and boys to be educated separately after puberty, access to halal food and correct prayer facilites may be difficult, school celebrations of Christmas and Easter may marginalise Muslim children, etc.*

4 *Marriages in Islam are not considered to be 'made in heaven' or necessarily to last 'until death do us part'. The nikah is a contract, and if broken, spouses are entitled to divorce.*

5 *Islamic weddings may simply be prayers and blessings, and the signing of the nikah contract with two witnesses of the free consent of each partner.*

6 *The mahr is a sum of money or a gift settled on the bride by her husband, so that if she previously owned nothing, she commences married life with money and property of her own.*

7 *Loving care of parents is a prime Islamic duty. It is not expected for Muslims to relegate their old people to strangers, care homes, etc. It is preferred for them to end their days within the family, as far as possible.*

8 *Muslims do not regard death as the end of human life – it pre-exists birth and continues after death of the body in soul state.*

9 *Those facing death, although accepting God's will, are nevertheless encouraged to take medical and other help. At death, they will be assisted by angels.*

10 *The dead should be buried as quickly as possible, the same day if possible. Bodies are buried in simple graves with heads towards Makkah, without coffins, and a small mound raised over them with a simple marker.*

7

Legal Islam

In this chapter you will learn about:
- *the Muslim 'way' – Shari'ah*
- *the principles of Islamic justice*
- *the importance of judges*
- *categories of crime and punishment.*

The Shari'ah

DIN AND SHARI'AH

The *din* (pronounced 'deen') is the sum total of Muslim faith and the complete dedication of one's life to Islam – recognizing God as one's sovereign and committing oneself to obey Him. The *Shari'ah* is Islamic law, the detailed code of conduct or the canons comprising ways and modes of worship, standards of morals and life, and laws that allow and prescribe and that judge between right and wrong, accepting as binding the guidance communicated through the prophets.

Shari'ah means literally the 'way to water' – the source of life; the way to God as given by God. Its supreme purpose and ruling spirit is justice. It is intended to manifest God's infinite mercy – correctly applied, it is the true embodiment of and the best way to justice.

The five categories of Shari'ah

The Shari'ah does not limit behaviour to just two categories – right and wrong – but five:

1 Fard *or* wajib – *things which are compulsory and must be done, such as keeping the five pillars.*
2 Mandub *or* mustahab – *actions which are recommended but not compulsory, such as making extra voluntary prayers.*
3 Mubah – *actions which have to be decided by conscience because there is no clear guidance.*
4 Makruh – *actions which are not actually forbidden, but are disliked or disapproved of, such as divorce.*
5 Haram – *things which are forbidden and should never be done, such as committing adultery or eating pork.*

Anything which Allah made compulsory or forbidden is clearly and specifically stated in the Qur'an, and there is no ambiguity. Whatever is not actually forbidden is permitted, under the guidance of Islamic principles and conscience. Most problems pertaining to modern life fall in the mubah section.

> **Insight**
>
> A person trained in fiqh is known as a *faqih* (pl. *fuqaha*). An Islamic jurist or scholar is an *alim* (pl. *ulema* – from the Arabic *ilm*, meaning knowledge).

Fiqh

If the Qur'an and sunnah are silent concerning a particular topic, jurists try to arrive at conclusions using analogy (*qiyas*) and the historical consensus of the community (*ijma*). The technique for working out Shari'ah law is called *fiqh* from the word for 'intelligence' or 'knowledge'. Fiqh is 'unrevealed', detailed law derived by the scholars from the 'revealed' – the Qur'an and sunnah – covering the myriad of problems that arise in normal everyday life, in order to establish a much wider array of laws.

Insight

Since scholars are human beings, there will be division of interpretation and differing views on details. This has resulted in different schools of thought, and thus fiqh is not regarded as sacred.

IJTIHAD, QIYAS AND IJMA

How can a law laid down 14 centuries ago in the Middle East meet all the complex demands and pressures of modern technological civilization? How can anyone know whether it is right or wrong to watch TV, play pop music, use birth control, etc?

But what has really changed? Technology has certainly advanced and some ways of looking at the world have altered, but the definitions of concepts like 'cruelty', 'civilized', 'justice', 'equality' have remained much the same. Our lusts and fears, hopes and anxieties, loves and hates, aspirations, yearnings and longings remain what they have always been.

When Muslims claim that Islam has a satisfactory solution for every problem in every situation for all times to come, this does not mean that the Qur'an, sunnah and rulings of Islamic scholars provide a specific answer to each and every minute detail of our lives. Rather, they lay down the broad principles in the light of which scholars of every time can deduce specific answers to the new situations arising in their age.

The working out of Muslim principles, the process of making a legal decision by independent interpretation of the Qur'an and sunnah, is known as *ijtihad*, from the root *jahada* – to struggle (the same root as *jihad*). Individuals use reason and judgement to decide on the course of action most in keeping with the spirit of Qur'an and sunnah. A scholar competent to apply ijtihad (known as a *mujtahid*) has the equivalent of a doctorate in divinity is, and status similar to a high court judge.

Insight

Muslims debate whether ijtihad or 'struggling with oneself', as in deep thought, should be a method of logical reasoning limited just to the traditional schools of jurisprudence, or if it should it be open to any intelligent thinker with knowledge of the subject.

Qiyas means analogical reasoning, using past analogies with their decisions as precedents in each new situation. Decisions made in this manner are called *ijma*, or consensus. In making decisions, account must always be taken of the opinions of respected people present and past; previous decisions and the reasons for them; the general sense of justice; concern for the public good; and a most practical consideration that is sometimes overlooked by ambitious leaders and politicians – the acceptance of the masses.

However, consensus does not mean the opinion of the masses, or even the majority or collective opinion of learned Muslim scholars – the *ulema*. Even if hundreds of scholars passed a law unanimously, if it contradicted the principles of Qur'an and sunnah, it would be anti-Shari'ah and rejected by Muslims. The principles behind Shari'ah deter any pressure groups – even highly religious ones – from imposing burdens and duties on people which go beyond the spirit of Islam, and become tyrannical.

Insight

Ijma are not regarded as totally binding like a Qur'anic command, since they are based on human opinions. The only ijma accepted as binding are the ancient ones made by the first caliphs, who had been the Prophet's ﷺ closest Companions.

Shi'ites differ – they strongly reject analogy (qiyas) as an easy way to fall into innovations (*bida*), and also reject consensus (ijma) as having any particular value of its own, but they regard

the teachings of their Twelve Imams – who were alive during
the period that the Sunni scholars developed their methods – as
extensions of the sunnah, and laws deriving from them are seen
as actually being part of the sunnah. A recurring theme in Shi'ite
jurisprudence is logic (*mantiq*) or intellect (*aql*), faculties employed
and valued to a higher degree than in Sunni Islam, as a way of
seeing if derived rulings are compatible with Qur'an and sunnah.

Closing the 'doors' of ijtihad

After the death of the Prophet ﷺ, the Shari'ah was quite flexible:
any qualified legal scholars could study a question, apply
independent reasoning (*ijtihad*), and issue a nonbinding *fatwa*.
In the eleventh century, however, when the legal judgments of
the *ulema* were crystallized into schools of Islamic jurisprudence,
progress stopped. The classical rulings of the jurists were recorded
and validated, making it far easier to regard them as immutable
and therefore be obliged to accept or imitate them, rather than
challenge in new contexts. Independent interpretation was
effectively banned. With the 'doors of ijtihad closed', the
traditionalists imposed their own conservative positions on
mainstream Islamic jurisprudence, which remained largely
frozen for almost a millennium.

Insight

The real danger of taqlid – pious imitation, or the
maintenance of existing rulings in an exclusive way – is that
the rulings come to reflect a culture that no longer exists.

The spirit rather than the letter – Istihsan

Modernist Islamic scholars place their emphasis on the concept
of *istihsan*. This means that justice can only prevail when legal
scholars are able to take a broad approach to the law by keeping
its 'spirit', rather than sticking to its letter, so that it does not
become burdensome or seem outrageous. Justice must be seen to be
just, the law should not 'be an ass'. This is the concept of istihsan,
the practice of using legal reasoning to interpret the law based
on the Qur'an and hadith literature in different ways, in the light
of the general principle of serving the public good (*maslahah*).

Muslims who insist on strict adherence to the 'letter' of the law
as opposed to the spirit certainly desire to maintain its purity, but
risk the danger of the Shari'ah seeming archaic and inadequate for
dealing with developing issues (see Chapter 9).

MADHHABS

A *madhhab* represents the entire school of thought of a particular
mujtahid, together with many first-rank scholars that came after
them in their respective schools.

Following the death of the Prophet ﷺ hundreds of scholars
(including female ones) had followers or 'schools'. By the third
century after the life of the Prophet ﷺ four major schools (known
as *madhhabs*) had emerged in Sunni Islam, and still remain – the
Hanifi, Maliki, Hanbali and **Shafi'i**, named after the most eminent
jurists of that early period. Their students attended particular
colleges, received training in a particular methodology of juristic
inquiry, and developed a specialized technical language. The main
Shi'ite schools of thought are the **Ja'fari** and the **Zaydi**. Two other
schools were significant – the **Ibadi** and **Thahiri**. Thus, on each
point of law, there can be at least ten different opinions (*ikhtilaf*)
and considerable debate.

Shi'ites also believe that there was a time when the spiritual
leadership of the world depended on the descendants of the

274

Prophet's ﷺ daughter Fatimah, and these imams had the right to exercise ijtihad freely. Esteemed religious scholars earned the title *ayatollah* or 'sign of God', and the most famous modern one was undoubtedly Ayatollah Khomeini of Iran, who led the people's revolt against the Shah of Iran.

WHAT ARE FATWAS?

A *fatwa* is a new legal opinion or verdict, which is issued by a qualified jurist, theologian or legal pragmatist. The word has become notorious in Western media when taken to mean a death-threat, but it is really a clarification whenever new and unprecedented cases arise – cases for which there is no clear directive either in Qur'an or sunnah. A fatwa is not required when Islam's position is already clear and unequivocal.

Insight

The word fatwa comes from *fata* meaning a 'young boy' or 'new boy'. It is used in Arabic as a metaphor for anything young, new, unfamiliar and unprecedented.

TASAWWUF

Whereas *fiqh* deals with the apparent and observable conduct of Muslims, or the actual fulfilling of duties, *tasawwuf* is concerned with the spirit behind them. For example, the performing of correct ablution, facing Makkah, the times the prayers are said and the number of rakat performed are all matters of fiqh; whereas the intention, concentration, devotion, purification of soul, and effect of prayers on our morals and manners are matters of tasawwuf. Fiqh governs the carrying out of commands of the minutest detail; tasawwuf is the measure of the spirit of obedience and sincerity.

It has been said that a worshipper devoid of spirit, although correct in procedure, is like a handsome man lacking in character; and a worshipper full of spirit but defective in performance is like a noble man deformed in appearance.

Figure 7.1 Tasawwuf is concerned with the intention and spirit behind our prayers.

The sanctity of life

To Muslims, human life is sacred.

> *Whoever saves a life ... it shall be as if he had saved the life of all humanity, and whoever takes a life, it shall be as if he had taken the life of all humanity.*
>
> (Surah 5.32)

Muslims believe that no human has an automatic right to life – it is God's gift. If God wills otherwise, that person will cease to be, or will not be granted life in the first place.

THE TIME SPAN

> *Allah decrees the time span for all things. It is He Who causes both laughter and grief; it is He Who causes people to die and to be born; it is He Who causes male and female; it is He Who will recreate us anew.*
>
> (Surah 53:42–7)

The human body is part of the world of matter, but the individual soul is God's 'loan' to that body, for so long as He wishes; it is in a sense a visitor, a guest. Moreover, God knows the exact length of the individual's lifetime, even before his or her conception.

Insight

In Islam, it is believed that an individual's life commences long before birth. Before conception, each individual exists in soul state – and we have no idea of how long that state of being has existed.

Just as the decision to grant life is God's prerogative, so is the time span for that life, and the ending of the soul's occupation of the body. Muslims believe it is gross presumption for any human to try to interfere with that decision, no matter how well meaning, or even to try to find out when it will be. That is not a matter granted to human knowledge.

Muslims should be grateful to Allah for their life, whatever the circumstances in which they are born, or whatever hardships they may have to face. But they should never forget it is God's gift, and it is a Muslim's duty to live every day so that they are ready to hand their life back with easy conscience, should God demand it.

Insight

No soul has the right to demand to be born – whether it is born or not depends not only on the free-will and actions of its human parents, but above and beyond that, entirely upon the will of God – who can overrule any human intention.

It is when facing death that a believer has a great advantage over a non-believer, for the peace of mind and hope that it brings. The choice of whether or not to believe in life after death is one of the freedoms granted to humans during their Earthly life; that freedom no longer exists after the moment of death, because they are confronted with the new situation, whatever it is, and must cope with it as best they can. All humans must die, and it is pointless and futile to resent the inevitable end of the human body.

When your time expires, you will not be able to delay the reckoning for a single hour, just as you cannot bring it forward by a single hour. (Surah 16:61)

Muslims believe it is a foolish gamble to assume that there is no afterlife and that all God's messengers who have taught of the life to come have been misled.

Do you think that We shall not reassemble your bones? Yes, surely, yes – We are able to restore you even to your individual fingerprints. (Surah 75:3–4)

Many people desperately try to prevent their deaths and pray for Allah to grant them some miracle that will keep them alive, but Nature runs its course and miracles are not granted. On the other hand, many people long to die because they are so unhappy or in such pain, but Allah requires them to go on living. It is, however, important to realize that there is a difference between dying (over which you have no control) and killing yourself (which is an act of your own free-will).

CONTRACEPTION

Islam permits birth control, so long as both mother and father have consented to it, and provided the method is one which prevents a woman conceiving in the first place and not one that aborts a conceived child. Thus, a condom or a conception-preventing pill would be acceptable, but the morning-after pill would not. In all cases, Muslims believe that Allah's will would override whatever the parents did if He desired a particular child to be born.

ABORTION

Do not slay your children because of poverty – We will provide for you and for them. (Surah 6:151)

Muslims do not allow abortion of an unwanted foetus, except in the case where a mother's life would be put at risk.

Insight

If a mother's life is in danger through pregnancy, the ruling is to 'sacrifice the calf to save the cow'. The actual existing life of the mother takes precedence over the potential life of the unborn child.

There are two schools of thought regarding terminating pregnancy in its early stages. Some believe the soul enters the foetus after 40 days (six weeks), and others that the soul does not enter the foetus until it 'quickens' at around the sixteenth week, and therefore if an abortion was absolutely necessary, it could be performed before that time.

Others maintain that no one really knows what the soul or spirit is, and when the Prophet ﷺ was asked to define it he was instructed by Allah to say that knowledge of it belonged to God alone. Therefore, the foetus represents a potential life from the moment of conception, and should be protected and given all the rights of human life.

Insight

Once conceived, Islam teaches that a foetus has a 'right to life', and should be defended from all threats upon it. To kill it is a form of murder. The mother may not argue that her foetus is 'part of her body'.

Some women argue that it is a woman's right to decide what she does with her own body, ignoring the rights of her unborn child's body and the fact that she may suffer an enormous burden of guilt later. The Qur'an reminds these mothers that on Judgement Day these infants will need to know why they were killed.

When the souls are sorted out, when the female infant buried alive is asked for what crime she was killed ... when the World on High is unveiled ... then shall each soul know what it has sent ahead.

(Surah 81:7–9, 11, 14)

Figure 7.2 Islam teaches that all human beings are loved by God.

Infanticide

Many nomadic peoples controlled the size of their tribes through infanticide. The supply of food available is limited, and surplus tribal members cannot be supported. The usual practice of birth control among the Arabs before the time of the Prophet ﷺ was to let the woman give birth, then babies (usually females) were simply left to die, whether from exposure, starvation, or more likely, being eaten by the first predator to find them. Some Arabs used the quicker method of putting newborn babies face down into the sand before they drew breath. These practices were totally forbidden in the Qur'an.

Femicide

Today, modern technology such as ultrasound scanning has made it possible to determine the sex of a baby long before birth, and this has led in many countries to the aborting of females. This is the case in cultures where the cost of raising daughters is high, either due to the un-Islamic need to accumulate a large dowry which is paid to the husband upon marriage (as in India), or where males are more valued than females. In the long term, it will create a serious imbalance of the sexes. The practice is forbidden in Islam.

Insight

Determining the sex of foetuses in order to kill females is forbidden in Islam. In some places, so many female foetuses have been destroyed that a problem is growing of a preponderance of males, with the consequence of a future lack of spouses for them.

(For honour killing, refer to page 366.)

SUICIDE

To kill yourself is just as forbidden as to kill any other person unlawfully. In most cases, its effects and hurts are even worse for others than in cases of murder or tragic accident. People who commit suicide are presumably very depressed and beset by problems that seem to have no answer, but to kill oneself is no escape whatsoever, for the torments that person will suffer in increased awareness after death are much greater than those endured while still living. They will realize who really loved them, and experience the hurt of those left behind, while being able to do nothing to alleviate the awful pain they will be condemned to suffer for the rest of their lives.

He who kills himself with sword, or poison, or throws himself off a mountain will be tormented on the Day of Resurrection with that very thing. (Muslim)

Insight

Life may be full of hardships, sufferings and loneliness, but Muslims are taught to accept these as part of their test, and to face them with patience and humility, and not lose faith. Suicide inflicts devastating and long-term suffering on families.

> **None of you should wish for death for any calamity that befalls you, but should say: 'O Allah! Cause me to live so long as my life is better for me, and cause me to die when death is better for me.'**
>
> (Abu Dawud)

Deliberate and calculated suicide is considered a total lack of faith in God and a terrible sin. It is a rare occurrence in Islam, for Muslims should not even consider it. Even 'honourable' suicide, done out of shame for crimes committed, is not acceptable. It would be better for the 'sinner' to live on, accept responsibility, and put right the wrongs committed. To commit suicide to escape punishment would be futile, and would merely postpone it to God's justice in the Life to Come.

Of course, nearly all people who commit suicide do not do it of their own free-will but as the result of mental illness, or when the balance of their mind is disturbed. It is important to realize that such people are in a different category, and are not counted as responsible for their actions, and are always forgiven by God, in His compassion.

(For 'suicide bombers', refer to page 353.)

EUTHANASIA

Sometimes a person's life seems such a burden or so painful that well-meaning people consider it would be better to end it. Just as one would not stand by and see an animal suffering, but would put it out of its misery, so they consider euthanasia (a 'good death') for humans, to end their sufferings. Euthanasia is usually thought of as being 'put to sleep' painlessly, perhaps by drug overdose.

Many hospital cases are considered hopeless, and doctors may decide that to keep on trying more and more drastic measures to keep the patient alive is pointless, and will only prolong their suffering. In these cases, the notice 'NTBR' ('Not to be resuscitated') appears on their medical sheet, the doctors taking the point of view that it is better to let nature take its course, and that they 'should not strive officiously to keep alive' when to continue fighting for that life only causes increased distress.

Some people consider that putting a gentle end to human life should be considered when an infant is born severely disabled or mentally ill, when the prospective lifetime in front of it would be grim. It seems kinder to the child and to the family that loves it.

Insight

Should the terminally ill have the right to be helped to die 'with dignity'? Islam teaches that yes, they may be helped and pain alleviated as far as possible – but their lives should not be ended deliberately, through poisons, etc.

Some consider it would be kinder to put an end to old people when they become 'vegetables', or to anyone who has been in a coma for a long period, rather than keep them alive indefinitely, and create a lack of hospital beds for 'ordinary' patients. Their painful lingering may seem pointless and cruel, but neither we nor they know in what ways God might use those final precious hours to help them and others.

These dilemmas are faced every day by doctors called upon to 'play God'. All these things are forbidden in Islam. They are highly emotive issues, and it is one thing to discuss such things, and quite another to be requested to end a loved one's life.

Muslims reject euthanasia, because the reason for the disability or suffering will be known to God, and 'mercy killing' frequently does not allow the dying individual any choice in the matter. Muslims find the thought that anyone should be put to death out of social convenience appalling. Our tests may indeed seem unfair to us when we do not know the reasons, but Allah knows, and He is never unfair.

Insight

Islam teaches that sufferings before death are set against and alleviate any penalties in the Life to Come, and are therefore not pointless.

The Muslim attitude is to bear personal tragedies with love and fortitude, to make life as comfortable as possible for the suffering person, and to remember that the Prophet ﷺ taught that any suffering of a person in this life would be set against and alleviate penalties in the life to come, and therefore did serve a purpose, and was part of Allah's plan.

CAPITAL PUNISHMENT

The death sentence does still exist as a possible punishment on the statute books of Islamic law in many countries.

> *Do not take life, except for just cause.*   (Surah 17.33)

In Islam there are three crimes which are considered 'just cause' for meriting the death penalty in law: murder, sexual intercourse performed in public, and apostasy, when accompanied by treason or murder (see pages 299–301).

Justice, crime and punishment

> *O believers, be staunch in justice, witnesses for God, even though it be against yourselves, your parents or your kindred, whether the case be of a rich person or a poor person – for God is nearer to both (than you are); so do not follow passion, lest you lapse (from truth), and if you lapse or fall away, then lo! God is ever informed of what you do.*   (Surah 4:135)

In Islam, all people are equal before the law. No citizen should be beneath the protection of the law, no matter how humble. Every citizen should have equal rights, including the right of defence if accused of something. No citizen should ever be above the law, no matter how powerful, rich or influential. If any person can buy his or her way out of a rightly deserved punishment, then that society is corrupt and should be challenged.

IS ISLAMIC LAW BARBARIC?

Many non-Muslims feel that Islamic justice is cruel, primitive
and barbaric, a relic from darker times which enslaved women
and inflicted punishments on criminals and enemies which
were inhuman and degrading – requiring numerous executions,
floggings, and mutilations (see the next section). Such things grab
the headlines and horrify a public that has grown accustomed
to a society in which criminals can be treated very leniently, and
unsociable behaviour (including drunkenness, adultery and theft)
are rife.

Two comments have to be made. First, many things regarded as
'Islamic' are not in the least Islamic, but are the actions and culture
of rulers and governments that may well govern Muslim people,
but who flout the laws of Islam and may actively go against them.

Second, in any society in which Islam was truly being practised,
there would be no drunkenness with its associated catalogue of
crimes; no drug addiction or theft; no adultery or sexual freedom
with its accompanying distress and consequences; no battering of
children or old people; no cheating or swindling.

There are different points of view concerning the cruelty of
physical penalties. How is imprisonment – depriving people of their

freedom to live with their families, to work and support them – less cruel than a corporal punishment? A prison term can inflict untold misery on the innocent people whose lives are intertwined with the life of the prisoner.

> ### Insight
> Shari'ah judges often find that convicted people would prefer swift physical punishment to being sent to prison. Once the physical punishment has been done, the convicted person has got it over with, can heal up, and hopefully go back to their lives and work – having had a sharp punishment to deter them from re-offending.

ISLAMIC MOTIVES

Muslim justice is the powerful desire to see peace, right and order prevail, by removing the failing, weakness or enmity that lies behind the wrong. If someone has been wronged, Muslims are expected to do everything possible to put things right. Muslims can never think it acceptable to turn a blind eye to injustice, or let it go unchallenged. That is seen as weakness, and counter to the will of God. Allah is always merciful, and He understands human weakness. He will indeed forgive any person who is sorry; but if they have wronged another person, then the other person's demands for justice also have to be fulfilled. If the unjust 'get away with it', then the victims are assured that Allah will give them recompense after death.

Muslims who have been wronged are requested to be merciful if they are able:

> *The entitlement for an injury is an equal injury back; but if a person forgives instead and is reconciled, that will earn reward from Allah.* (Surah 42:40)

> ### Insight
> It is worth remembering that it is far easier to gain God's forgiveness than that of **people** who have been hurt and abused, or wronged in some way.

THE IMPORTANCE OF ISLAMIC JUDGES

When Islam governs justice, the judge should be above corruption and bribery, and should not fear the power of his prisoner. He should be highly skilled and competent enough to interpret Islamic law correctly. A good judge would rather set a criminal free than risk wrongly punishing an innocent person and should always delay a trial if angry, hungry, restless or absorbed in some other matter.

Insight

Islam recognizes that all judges are but human beings, and can only do their best. God alone is the Ultimate Judge, who will put right any miscarriages.

The rights of the accused

Islamic justice should not be administered blindly, but be tempered with mercy, following all the principles of fairness without favour or fear (Surah 4.135 and 5.8).

▶ *No person should be arrested, convicted and punished all on the same day.*
▶ *A defendant should not be denied legal representation.*
▶ *Accused people should not be treated as criminals before they have been proved guilty (Surah 24.15 and 39.7).*
▶ *No one should ever be imprisoned unless they have been properly convicted of a crime by an unbiased court.*
▶ *No one should be threatened, punished or imprisoned because of the fault of others, or in order to intimidate others.*
▶ *The defendant should have the right of appeal (Surah 24.24, 82.11).*
▶ *Shari'ah law should always be carried out publicly, not for the sake of brutality or to please a bloodthirsty audience, but because it is vital that justice is seen to be done, and that the bounds are not exceeded. Muslims cannot approve of trials and punishments being carried out in secret, with the possibility of inhumane treatment and torture.*

Always not guilty

The Prophet ﷺ ruled that certain categories of people were never legally responsible, and these conditions gave ample scope for defence lawyers. These people include:

- *those not conscious of what they have done*
- *those whose balance of their mind was disturbed*
- *those who have not yet reached puberty.*

TWO CATEGORIES OF CRIMES

In Islam each Muslim is answerable not just to a human judge but to God. Thus the Shari'ah classifies crime into two distinct categories:

- *Crimes against Allah.*
- *Crimes against individuals.*

Muslims are granted the right of privacy within their own homes (Surah 24.27). Any behaviour committed by consenting adults in private which falls short of the moral code laid down by Allah, is a matter left between those individuals and Allah. Private sinning most certainly indicates lack of belief in the real existence of God, and that the sinner cares little or nothing for the consequences to face in the Life to Come – but spying and searching out people's faults, or sending round vigilantes or 'religious enforcers' to intrude on any person's privacy, or administer punishments on the spot, is against the spirit of Islam.

It is a very different matter if the person breaks laws in public, or if the private sinful behaviour involves abusing, harming or causing offence to any other individual, who most certainly has the right of complaint and of being protected and given justice.

THREE CATEGORIES OF PUNISHMENT

For those convicted of an offence after a court hearing, their punishment falls into one of three possible categories – *jinayah* (retaliation or compensation), *ta'zir* (a discretionary penalty) or *hadd* (specific penalty).

Jinayah
Jinayah penalties cover homicide and bodily harm, which are punishable either by:

▶ qisas – *exact retaliation based on the principle of 'an eye for an eye'*
▶ diyah – *payment of blood-money or compensation to the victim or his/her surviving kin.*

Ta'zir
Ta'zir (corrective) penalties are normally the least serious and can be applied under three circumstances:

▶ *Where the Qur'an does not provide a specific hadd or qisas penalty.*
▶ *When the proof is based on a strong assumption of guilt but is not enough to impose specific penalties.*
▶ *Where those are barred by doubt.*

Penalties can include fines, imprisonment, community service, tagging and probation.

Insight
The purpose of the law of retaliation (qisas), the 'eye for an eye', was to **limit** retaliation, not promote it. The injured party could not demand more than an 'eye for an eye'. It helped to end tribal massacres!

The Hadd laws

The penalties for some crimes can be very severe – the amputation of the hand of a thief (followed by amputation of other limbs if thieving continued), a flogging for illicit sexual intimacy, and the death penalty for murder, apostasy where it involved treason or warfare, and publicly witnessed adultery (see the next section).

WHEN HUMAN JUSTICE FAILS

Every Muslim believes that human judgements can so easily be wrong, or influenced by bias or ignorance of the circumstances, but Allah sees and hears everything. No person can ultimately escape the true judgement on their life. The Prophet ﷺ knew the frailty of human judgement and warned his followers that if anyone knowingly allowed judgement to be given against someone they had accused wrongly, they would pay for it before the justice of Allah:

> When you bring your case to me, some of you may be more eloquent in expressing their side than others. I will judge based upon what I hear, and if I happen to give someone something belonging to his fellow citizen, he should not take it, for I would be giving him a piece of the fire! (Bukhari, Malik, Ahmad)

On that day, no one will be able to make excuses for another – we will all stand alone, as individuals, with the true record of our lives.

The Hadd or Limit Laws

THE HADD LAWS

The *hadd* (pl. *hudud*) are specific laws of extreme 'limits', penalties laid down in the Qur'an for specific crimes or sins, whose purpose is general deterrence or prevention. They are called hudud (boundaries) and not punishments – for they are the liabilities incurred as a result of crossing specific boundaries set by God.

The hadd penalties cover six specific matters:

- sukr *(consumption of alcohol)*
- sariqah *(larceny or theft, or taking by stealth)*
- hirabah *(taking with force, kidnapping, armed robbery, terrorism, waging war against the state)*
- zinah *(adultery and fornication)*
- qadhf *(slander, false accusation)*
- riddah *(apostasy)*.

Sukr and sariqah are actually usually treated as lesser ta'zir crimes because no clear specific penalty for them was given in the Qur'an. Rape has been included under zinah in some cultures (notably Pakistan), but is more properly included under hirabah.

The two main interpretations of hadd penalties are:

- *that they are the automatic penalties laid down by Allah for specific crimes or sins*
- *that they are not intended as the automatic penalties but are the extreme limit of the punishment a judge could ordain, the severest penalty the law is entitled to inflict.*

Insight

Far from the extremes of hadd being harshly pursued, the Prophet ﷺ taught mercy if it was possible, an attitude he would never have taken if the hadd penalties were to be automatically applied.

The Prophet ﷺ was stringent in justice, but was a merciful man and took no pleasure in draconian penalties. If there was any doubt in the matter, or any mitigating circumstances, he taught:

Avert the infliction of the hadd penalties on Muslims as much as you can, and if there is any way out, let the person go – for it is better for a ruler to make a mistake in forgiving, than to make a mistake in punishing. (Tirmidhi)

Allah had told him:

My mercy prevails over my wrath.

(Hadith Qudsi)

In fact, it was expected that the warnings should be sufficient for Muslims, and the punishments unnecessary in a truly Muslim society, since Muslims would find it beneath them to steal or commit adultery or murder.

Insight

The biggest deterrent for a Muslim is not the fear of savage punishment, but the knowledge that since God is aware of everything you do, your sin would be recorded against you for the Day of Judgement.

FLOGGING FOR DRUNKENNESS

Shari'ah law can order a flogging for drunkenness. This seems particularly harsh to societies in the West that have grown accustomed to most adults (and many children) consuming alcohol, and nobody facing corporal punishment in our legal system.

The Prophet ﷺ did not seek out or spy on people who consumed alcohol in private, but was prepared to give the penalties for public drunkenness or any behaviour that offended, hurt and abused or disrupted the rights of others, caused by alcohol.

Insight

Muslims are urged not to spy upon people, unless well-founded suspicion exists that a crime or abuse is being committed, or another person's rights or interests are in jeopardy.

The effects of alcohol on society are very well known, as are the associated criminal activities; everything from drunken driving to public disorder and causing public nuisance, from wife-beating to burning the house down accidentally and to lessened responsibility with its attendant ill-mannered and loutish conduct.

Muslims generally find the behaviour of drunks highly distasteful. The sight of young Westerners (including scantily clad girls) vomiting or falling down in the street after a Saturday night binge, or the behaviour of tourists at so many Muslim coasts, does nothing to improve the stereotype image of Westerners in Muslim eyes.

CUTTING OFF THE HAND FOR THEFT

Cutting off the hand is the hadd punishment for theft, a deterrent intended to give deliberately callous thieves just punishment for the hurt they have caused, as well as warning the community there is a thief in their midst. Included in the deterrent is the shame that knowledge of your theft would bring not only on you but your entire family (or whole village, if you lived in a small community). A thief might expect very rough justice in many places. However, the Middle East is not full of one-handed people.

If a thief is taken before a merciful shari'ah judge, the amputation of the hand is not meted out casually or automatically, but follows certain rules. There have to be two witnesses who swear on oath that they saw the theft, and that it was of private property above a certain value that was taken with criminal intent. The cause should not be hunger, necessity or duress. If it could be proved that the reason the person stole was in some way the inadequacy of the state or local ruler or community, no hadd penalty would apply.

Insight

If, for example, someone stole food for their family because they could not find work to pay for it, then the thief should not be held at fault, and the thief's hand could be 'cut off' from stealing by being provided with work.

If there was no excuse and no remorse, and it was simply a case of someone being addicted to picking up other people's property with no qualms or conscience, then a shari'ah judge could indeed order amputation and, if the thief persisted, continue on to other limbs. This punishment would be imposed even if the thief repented.

The Prophet ﷺ commented that he would carry out this punishment himself against any deliberate thief, no matter how highly placed and influential, even if it was his own beloved daughter Fatimah.

> ### Insight
> Even Jesus ﷺ said: 'If your hand causes you to sin, cut it off. It is better for you to enter life maimed than with two hands to go to Hell.' (Mark 9:43).

Many modern scholars suggest the cutting of the hand could also be interpreted as cutting off the thief's power to steal by removal from society (i.e. imprisonment), or cutting off the desire to steal by creating a society in which theft is unnecessary.

HIRABAH

The classical jurists considered many different crimes to be hirabah or terrorism – including armed robbery, assassination, arson and murder by poisoning. They argued that such crimes should be punished vigorously regardless of the motivations of the criminal. No matter what the desired goals or ideological justifications of a *muharib* (one who commits hirabah, or fights society), the terrorizing of the defenceless was recognized as a huge moral wrong and an offence against society and God (see 'Terrorism', page 350).

> ### Insight
> In many Islamic societies the death sentence may be given for terrorism – especially if people have been killed. This is one reason why terrorist 'masters' often operate and groom their stooges in places where the death penalty has been abolished.

KIDNAP

Kidnapping, enslavement by force, hijacking and unlawful hostage holding are all forms of hirabah, and if carried out in order to damage one's state, are acts of treason and could carry the death penalty. The appalling events of 2005 in which several innocent people were taken by force, and some put to death (including the terrible beheading of Kenneth Bigley and others) cannot be justified in Islam. Kidnappers who murder face a death sentence where this penalty is still in force – whether in the USA or Saudi Arabia.

RAPE

The crime of rape (*zinah bi'l jabr*) is enforced sex. It is basically a male crime – and some men think automatically of the rape of a female, sometimes not regarding it very seriously if they take the view that deep down the women involved enjoy it. It is important, therefore, to point out that it is a crime of violence and degradation, and is sometimes suffered by old ladies in their own homes, not just scantily-clad girls out at night. It also, of course, includes the anal rape of boys and men by other men.

Insight

A man whose depraved sexual urges have lead him to commit rape, whether of a girl, boy, woman, wife or another man, is guilty of lust, abuse, possibly kidnap and torture, and of causing both physical and psychological harm to the victim.

Rape involves sex without the consent of the victim, or with consent when it was obtained by putting the victim in fear of death or hurt. A woman who enforces sex upon a male is generally guilty of seduction, and not rape.

A man whose depraved sexual urges lead him to commit rape, whether of girl, boy, woman, wife or another man, is certainly guilty of lust and zinah, but this is hardly the case for the victim of the rape. On the contrary, victims would have suffered appalling fear, probable actual bodily harm, traumatization that could last a lifetime, and in some societies social consequences that could stigmatize or shame them. The rapist looks for victims who cannot defend themselves.

It is now generally recognized that rape is a form of hirabah, does not require the testimony of four witnesses, and could include capital punishment as a penalty.

Alternatively, the crime could be categorized as *jirah* (wounding or bodily harm), which might even be applied to domestic abuse and marital rape, and could result in damages or financial compensation for the wounded woman.

ZINAH

Zinah is any sexual intercourse outside marriage, whether before or after marriage. It is fornication when neither party to the illicit sexual liaison is married (i.e. premarital or post-divorce), and adultery when the persons are married. The penalty laid down for zinah in Surah 24.2–3 is flogging, and the refusal of permission for Muslims to marry any person found guilty of acting lewdly:

> **The woman and the man guilty of zinah, flog each of them with a hundred stripes: let not compassion move you in their case in a matter prescribed by Allah if ye believe in Allah and the Last Day: and let a party of the believers witness their punishment. Let no man guilty of zinah marry any but a woman similarly guilty, or an unbeliever, nor let any but such a man or an unbeliever marry such a woman: to the believers such a thing is forbidden.**
>
> (Surah 24.2–3)

Adultery was considered an appalling dishonour towards a devout innocent partner, although it seems to have occurred often enough and was apparently treated lightly by many until the revelation of Islam. Divorce was the norm once a marriage had failed, and partners who gave in to sexual liaisons or temptations willingly were despised.

It is interesting that for this crime alone nearly insurmountable restrictions were placed on the giving of evidence. A person could not be found guilty of zinah without four eye witnesses to the actual sexual penetration. The witnesses had to be adult, sane and of upright character, not children or people whose right-mindedness could be questioned, or people of dubious morality, or with a known grudge against the accused. If their evidence was obtained by violating a defendant's privacy, it was inadmissible.

These are obviously very difficult requirements to fulfil, since such acts are virtually always performed in secret and privacy. With such restrictions, the aim in general must have been to encourage good morals but to limit conviction to cases where the two parties committed the act in public – thereby making it an issue of public indecency.

Insight

No other law had this stringent requirement of four unbiased eye witnesses. There were no cases in the Prophet's ﷺ entire lifetime based on the evidence of witnesses as laid down in the Qur'an.

THE DEATH PENALTY FOR ADULTERY

The death penalty was commonly given for adultery in pre-Islamic times, and since it is known that the Prophet ﷺ was involved in several cases, there is to this day debate over whether or not there was ever a 'verse of *rajm*' or stoning included in the Qur'an. There was such a verse in the Jewish Torah (Deuteronomy 22.22–27), but there is most certainly no such verse in the Qur'an as it existed by the end of the Prophet's ﷺ lifetime. Therefore, if it ever did exist it must have been abrogated.

Insight

It was impossible to 'forget' a verse, since so many people knew the entire Qur'an by heart. Any law contrary to a clear Qur'anic law would be rejected outright by all Muslims.

In two known cases Jewish rabbis brought test cases before the Prophet ﷺ, and his judgement was to condemn them by their own law. In the third known case, the famous case of Ma'idh b. Malik, this man insisted on admitting his guilt and being punished – to have a 'clean record' when he faced the Life to Come. However, when his stoning commenced he changed his mind and tried to escape, but the people carried out the sentence anyway. The Prophet's ﷺ significant comment when told was that he wished they had let him go, for he would certainly have repented and been forgiven by Allah (Abu Dawud).

The Prophet's ﷺ sunnah was that he was never eager to sentence anyone to death, and the reluctance must surely indicate that he regarded this punishment as the extreme limit of punishment for adultery.

FALSE ACCUSATION OR SLANDER – QADHF

No Muslim should ever cast doubt upon the character of a woman except by formal charges with very specific, secure evidence. Whoever falsely accused a chaste person of zinah was to be punished. If direct proof that a woman had disrupted public decency did not materialize, then those who charged her were liable to physical punishment for *qadhf* (slander), they would no longer be eligible as witnesses for anything in the future, and the public in general were obliged to assume the woman's innocence (Surah 24.16–17). Even if the charge happened to be true, any single witness not accompanied by another three would be liable to punishment.

> *And those who launch a charge against chaste women and produce not four witnesses (to support their allegation) flog them with eighty stripes: and reject their evidence ever after: for such people are wicked transgressors.* (Surah 24.4)

This particular revelation was specifically given concerning the Prophet's ﷺ wife Aishah. She was accused of adultery simply because she had been left alone in the desert and had accepted a lift home by camel from a young man she had known from childhood.

Insight

The Prophet ﷺ knew from personal experience the trauma of having a beloved wife accused of adultery, and the seed of suspicion planted in his own mind. It nearly destroyed his marriage and deeply upset his innocent wife. Thankfully, there was no 'honour killing' perpetrated.

It could happen that a spouse could maliciously accuse a partner of adultery out of spite, hoping to be rid of them. However, even in cases where a spouse claimed to have caught their partner in the act, if there were no witnesses the accused could not be declared guilty and punished – this was when the *li'an* divorce procedure should be applied (see the section on divorce on page 234).

MURDER

Murder is actually not a hadd crime, but to this day, Islam accepts the justice of taking a life for a life for the crime of murder, although individuals are not allowed to take the law into their own hands. The execution of a murderer should only take place after a proper legal trial, which fully examines the provocation, state of the murderer's mind, and so forth.

> *Do not take life, except for just cause. If anyone is wrongfully killed, We have granted the right of retribution to his heir, but let him not carry his vengeance too far in killing the culprit through taking the law in his own hands, as he is supported by the law.* (Surah 17:33)

> *The law of equality is allowed for you in cases of murder.* (Surah 2:178)

In any case of doubt (*shubhah*), the sentence of hadd was barred and commuted to that of a ta'zir crime.

THE RIGHT TO OVERRULE THE JUDGE

Even if the death penalty is granted, Islam differs from Western law in that the judge's sentence is not the final word. Allah granted the heirs of the murdered person the right to overrule the highest judge in the land by forgiving any murderer sentenced to death, or to accept money compensation (*diyah*) instead. If they could find it in their hearts to forgive, that was the best way.

Thus murder, grievous bodily harm and damage to property were permitted to be avenged legally by personal retaliation, but if the aggrieved party relinquished this, revenge was transformed into an act of merit for the merciful person.

APOSTASY

Apostasy (*riddah* or *irtidad* – literally 'turning back') does not mean insulting God or the Prophet ﷺ. It is the sin of deciding to give up Islam, or belief in Allah, after having previously been a genuinely believing Muslim. If a person's faith in Allah was not really genuine to start with and they leave Islam, then they do count as hypocrites but they are not really apostates. Apostasy is not a matter that applies to non-believers at all.

> **Insight**
>
> During the time of the Prophet ﷺ, treason and apostasy could possibly be considered one and the same crime, but even so there was no death penalty mentioned in the Qur'an unless the apostate had also committed murder.

Apostasy is when a person who has been a genuine believing and practising member of the community of Islam chooses of his/her own free-will to give up that belief, to deliberately turn away from God and reject Him – a very serious decision for that individual, not to mention his/her family and local community. However, it did not mean that anyone leaving Islam was to be put to death.

> **Insight**
>
> When 'apostasy' is just a matter of people losing belief, or finding Islam too difficult for them and wishing to withdraw from the community, no public offence has been committed, and any penalty for the withdrawal or loss of faith is a matter between that person and God in the Hereafter.

Although counted among the hudud, there is actually no specific penalty for apostasy given in the Qur'an. The very notion runs contrary to the clear Qur'anic order: '*Let there be no compulsion in religion.*' (Surah 2.256)

Apostasy was mentioned in no less than 13 verses of the Qur'an. This is possibly the most definitive:

> *How shall Allah guide those who reject faith after they accepted it and bore witness that the Apostle was true and that clear signs had come unto them? Allah is not the Guide of unjust people. The reward of such people is that the curse of Allah, the angels and all humanity is upon them. They shall remain under it for ever; neither will their punishment be lightened nor will they be given respite. But for those who repent after this and mend their ways, then truly Allah is indeed Forgiving, Merciful.* (Surah 3.86–91)

It is all too easy to take the first part, with its stern words, out of context – and not notice the forgiveness for those who return, as in the Prophet Jesus' 🕮 famous parable of the Prodigal Son.

These verses were all revealed while the Prophet 🕮 was ruler of Madinah, and was clearly in the position of being able to carry out any punishment Allah had laid down, but not once was any legal punishment specified. The verses all speak of punishment as God wills, in the Life to Come, and until they passed away they were given every chance to repent and be forgiven. The Prophet 🕮 only ever sentenced an apostate to death if the crimes of treason or murder had been committed.

BLASPHEMY

As regards the wish of some pious persons that the death penalty should be imposed for leaving the faith, or vilifying Allah, or speaking abusively about Allah or his Messenger 🕮, this is not laid down in the Qur'an.

Insight

The attitude of the Prophet 🕮, when so frequently abused or hurt or jeered at, was to stand firm and accept the unpleasantness with patience, hating the evil, but never hating the people who had been overtaken by evil.

If God willed, such people would see the noble qualities and behaviour of the Muslims, become ashamed of their former ways, turn to God in repentance, and be forgiven and welcomed (or welcomed back) into the *ummah* or community of believers.

Muslim countries that have made blasphemy a punishable offence (e.g. Iran and Pakistan), have presumably done so by interpreting the Qur'an's clear denunciation of *fitnah*, anything that causes dissension or civil strife.

Salman Rushdie/cartoons of the Prophet ﷺ

Salman Rushdie's book, *The Satanic Verses*, was regarded as obscene, a terrible slur upon the Prophet ﷺ and his wives, and resurrected an old unproved theological tradition about the possibility that Satan could dupe him into including verses in the Qur'an which were not genuine, which would have undermined the veracity of the entire Qur'an. Since Rushdie claimed to be a Muslim, his abuse was regarded as apostasy.

Cartoons of the Prophet ﷺ published in a Danish newspaper in 2005 caused a tremendous outcry. One cartoon showed the Prophet ﷺ wearing a bomb for a turban, and another showed him standing on a cloud refusing entry to martyred *mujahideen* because they had run out of virgins. The cartoons caused enormous dismay and protests around the Muslim world because it is forbidden in Islam to depict God, angels or messengers of God, so such cartoons were regarded as blasphemous. It was a scurrilous association of the Prophet ﷺ with terrorism and it reinforced Islamophobia.

Insight

Despite using rather shaky hadiths to induce zealots to sacrifice themselves, there is nothing in the Qur'an whatsoever about a supply of virgins in Paradise as rewards for dead soldiers. The huris of Paradise are a different order of being, and have nothing to do with sexual satisfaction for deceased Muslims, either male or female.

Both publications provoked the expected passionate results. However, freedom of speech is also cherished by Muslims, who defend it in principle while vociferously objecting to its abuse. Most non-Muslims had no idea what all the fuss was about, and Muslim speakers were quick to condemn their own 'fundamentalists', pointing out that far more damage was done to Islam by the media coverage of the irate protesters, some of whom caused damage and made death threats, than by the insults to God or the Prophet ﷺ.

UK Shari'ah courts

In September 2008, some UK newspapers stirred up a sensation by alleging that the government had sanctioned the recognition of Shari'ah courts, which provoked fears of hand-choppings, stonings and lashings. It was estimated that nearly 100 such courts were already functioning. However, this did not imply a rejection of the laws of the land, but assistance in applying Islamic judgements to situations of marital dispute and inheritance where both sides in a legal dispute freely chose a Shari'ah court as a binding arbitrator rather than taking a matter before the official courts.

Insight

The decisions of similar Jewish Beth Din court arbitrations have been recognized in England for over 100 years. Neither Shari'ah nor Jewish courts can force Muslims or Jews into arbitration – it is their choice.

10 THINGS TO REMEMBER

1 *The word* shari'ah *means 'the way'. In Arabic, it means the road trodden to the source of water, i.e. the source of life.*

2 *In Islamic law there are five categories of right and wrong: compulsory* (fard *or* wajib); *recommended* (mandub), *left to the individual conscience* (mubah), *disapproved* (makruh) *and forbidden* (haram).

3 *The compulsory and forbidden are crystal clear and stated in the Qur'an. The largest section is* mubah. *Depending on the circumstances, matters may fall into more than one category.*

4 *Justice and truth are two of the underlying basic concepts of Islam. A truly Islamic society would be crime-free.*

5 *In Islam, all people are equal before the law. No person is above the law, or too poor to be protected by the law.*

6 *Crimes are of two main categories – those against Allah, and those against individuals. It is weakness to see injustice and not seek to put it right.*

7 *Certain categories of persons must always be found innocent – children before puberty, those whose balance of mind is disturbed, those not conscious of what they did (perhaps through hypnotism, alcohol, drugs etc).*

8 *A criminal wrongly left unpunished may expect punishment for the offence in the Life to Come.*

9 *The hadd laws (pl.* hudud) *are those which have specific penalties –* sukr *(drunkenness),* sariqah *(theft),* hirabah *(taking with force – includes kidnap and terrorism),* zinah *(sexual sins),* qadhf *(slander, false accusation) and* riddah *(apostasy).*

10 Istihsan *refers to juristic preference, the principle that permits exceptions to strict and/or literal legal reasoning in favour of the public interest* (maslahah), *and allows jurists to abandon a strong precedent for a weaker precedent in the interests of justice, and give lesser sentences.*

8

Mystical Islam

In this chapter you will learn about:
- *the meaning of Sufism*
- *the aims and goals of Sufism*
- *details of some leading Sufis*
- *the criticisms of Sufism.*

Sufism

Sufism, or *tasawwuf*, is Islamic mysticism. As a movement, it developed as a reaction against dry Islamic legalism, but it has always played a fundamental part in the religious experience of those Muslims (like the Prophet ﷺ himself) who devoted themselves to a lifetime of prayer and closeness to God. Although many non-Sufi Muslims are suspicious of it, it cannot be separated from Islam, for it is basically the 'awakening of the heart' by means of submission.

Some Muslims regard it as the most important aspect of Islam, whereas those who distrust the emotional and intuitive side of religious experience (with its obvious scope for abuse and ego-tripping) relegate it virtually to the sidelines. It depends on what type of person the Muslim is. Sufism has been called the heart or spirit of Islam by those who grasp its value; but it is regarded with suspicion by Muslims who base their faith on obedience to the correct ritual performance of Islam, and who fear *bida* (innovation).

Insight

You do not need to be a member of a Sufi order in order to be a spiritual person. Many so-called 'ritual-obsessed' Muslims are deeply spiritual people who express their love for God through their disciplines.

The name 'sufi' may come from the Arabic *suf*, meaning 'wool', in which case it refers to simple garments of undyed wool. The basic wool robe was worn as a sign of ascetic living, of giving up the luxuries of life – food, dress and shelter – and accepting simplicity and poverty.

Another possible origin of the word is from the Greek *sophos* which means 'wisdom'. Others think it comes from the root *safa* which means 'purity', or took the name from the group of devoted impoverished students of Islam who lived on the Prophet's ﷺ veranda – the 'people of the bench' (*Ahl al-suffah*).

Insight

Many of the Prophet's ﷺ Companions were young men who had abandoned families, jobs, income and inheritance to migrate to Madinah and live close to him, observing his way of life and learning directly from him.

AIMS AND GOALS

Sufis have many aims. Basically, they are:
▶ *to abandon the desire for worldly wealth and luxury*
▶ *to search for an inner, spiritual life*
▶ *to 'purify the heart' and achieve 'union with God'*
▶ *to overcome the appetites and desires of the human body with its concern for self.*

Ali said:

Asceticism is not that you should own nothing, but that nothing should own you.

Figure 8.1 A Naqshbandi Sufi at Peckham Mosque, London.

Conflict with rulers

Sufism encourages renewal and revival in the hopes of restoring the pure and original message of the Prophet ﷺ, placing leadership in the hands of those who are closest to emulating his way of life. The ruler should be the most qualified person in spiritual terms, the most evolved in consciousness, pious, humble and accessible to the people – not someone who lives in arrogance, contempt and luxury. This, obviously, is a great threat to the decadent and extravagant lifestyle of many so-called 'Muslim' rulers.

Conflict with the orthodox schools

During the ninth and tenth centuries, when jurists began teaching Shari'ah in a more formal and standardized manner, the Sufis saw their role as keeping the spirit and full meaning of Islam alive rather than adhering to the formal and ritualistic aspect of the 'State' religion which was ominously taking shape.

Insight

The shaykh al-Hallaj was put to death for claiming he had reached the state of union with God, and had become one with Allah. His followers claim his spirituality was not understood by the orthodox.

Some Sufis, however, adopted so outspoken and ecstatic a lifestyle that they attracted a notoriety which really set them apart from orthodox Islam. Their claims that their souls had merged with God had overtones of *shirk*; furthermore, music, chanting, dancing or recitation of poetry were increasingly used in order to induce transcendental experiences, and these were not practices encouraged by orthodox Islam.

FEMALE SUFIS

Although the most famous, **Rabi'a al-Adawiyya** (b. 95/714 or 99/717–8, d. 185/801) was not the first, but a culminating representative of female Sufism. She was not a highly strung and emotional recluse, but a rational, disciplined teacher who demonstrated her mastery of important mystical states, such as truthfulness (*sidq*), self-criticism (*muhasaba*), spiritual intoxication (*sukr*), love for God (*mahabba*) and gnosis (*ma-rifa*).

Insight

Sufism was and is popular among female Muslims, giving equality on the basis of their spirituality. Female imams are controversial, but shaykhas are highly respected. Rabi'a had a reputation as a specialist in jurisprudence.

Rabi'a has often been called the founder of Sufi love-mysticism, but this was actually not a particularly important aspect of her teaching. Her pupil, Maryam of Basra, was noted for her lectures on love, going into ecstasies on hearing someone speak of love, and finally dying in a swoon during a discourse on love.

By the beginning of the tenth century, Sufi women could be found throughout the Muslim world from Egypt to Khurasan, but most had become disciples of Sufi men as opposed to having women teachers. Sufi women mixed freely with men, travelled long distances in order to study, and occupied positions of authority and respect. But they no longer seemed to have been spiritual masters themselves.

Some accepted the 'spiritual marriage', also part of Christian practice, in which a couple lived together but the sexual relationship was set aside. It was also permitted for unrelated men and women to live together as 'brother and sister' in a spiritual union, caring for each other with no sexual intimacy. The woman was usually expected to act as the servant of Allah by serving and attending to her male companion. Rabi'a bint Isma'il had this relationship with her husband Ahmad b. Abi al-Hawari. She encouraged him to take other wives if he needed sexual satisfaction.

Insight

In the view of some, celibates living a 'pure' life of self-denial were considered superior to those who still had the 'animal' need for sex, even in marriage. Many women chose celibacy, and considered themselves superior to their husbands.

MALE SUFIS

Muhyiddin Ibn al-Arabi (560/1165–638/1240)

Ibn Arabi was born in Andalus in 560/1165 and brought up in Cordoba, Seville and Granada. He travelled east, settled in Cairo in 596/1201, and moved to Makkah two years later. He also visited Baghdad, Jerusalem, and Damascus, where he died and was buried in 638/1240.

He was the most speculative of Islamic thinkers. His key theory was the pantheistic 'unity of all existence' (*wahdat al-wujud*), and his key emphasis was on love rather than justice.

▶ *God is One, Absolute, the Source of all being, whose existence is Being.*

- *The world is created so far as it exists in space-time, and eternal in that it is in the knowledge of God.*
- *Man never becomes God, nor God man, but it is possible through knowledge to achieve spiritual unity with God.*
- *Every prophet is a word of God and Muhammad ﷺ is the word of God, the focal point of all other prophets.*
- *The purpose of creation is al-insan al-kamil (the perfect man), who is also the microcosm reflecting the glory of God the Macrocosm.*
- *In so far as each previous prophet was a reflection of the perfect man, he was a wali (friend) of God. This quality was higher than prophecy.*
- *Ibn Arabi thought himself the khatim (seal of last) of the friends of God, as Muhammad ﷺ had been the khatim of the prophets.*

Insight

Some critics consider the concept of 'unity of being' (wahdat al-wujud) as shirk and a form of pantheism, and therefore incompatible with Islam.

Abu Hamid al-Ghazzali, 1058–1111 CE

Sometimes called the Thomas Aquinas of Islam, his outstanding contribution was to present Sufism in terms an orthodox scholar could accept. He claimed for himself the right to make fresh interpretations of the Qur'an and Islamic law instead of following traditional interpretations (*taqlid*).

He reaffirmed the view that tasawwuf was both knowledge and action, and rebuked those who sought fast-track methods of reaching the mystical experience. He disapproved of any claim that a Muslim was not obliged to observe all the rituals and other laws of Shari'ah. Ghazzali would never accept Sufism except on the conditions that it kept within the bounds of Islamic law and traditional belief, and thus secured its accepted place within Islam.

Jalal ud-Din Rumi (the Mevlana of Qonya)

The thirteenth century is usually regarded as the golden age of Sufism, and its chief exponent was Jalal ud-Din Rumi of Qonya (1207–73) who founded the order of whirling dervishes. These sought ecstasy through gyration accompanied by music that was intended to represent the order of the heavenly spheres.

Acceptance of God's will, whatever it might be, was the highest form of sacrifice of self, the highest proof of love. The Mevlana taught that one should not ask for personal requests in prayer, but should strive to be content. This was pure Islam, pure submission. Love was what mattered, not knowledge, or greatness or striving. To achieve love meant understanding unity, God's light shining into all the dark places of the Earth and making them one.

Some of the Mevlana's famous sayings

God speaks to everyone …He speaks to the ears of the heart, but it is not every heart which hears Him. His voice is louder than the thunder, and His light is clearer than the sun, if only one could see and hear. In order to do that, one must remove this solid wall, this barrier – the Self.

There are many roads to the Ka'bah …but lovers know that the true Holy Mosque is Union with God.

The sun lights up a thousand courtyards. Take away the walls, and you will see that it is all the same light.

You belong to the world of dimension, but you come from the world of non-dimension. Close the first shop and open the second.

(Rumi)

TARIQAHS

The Sufi science of self is called a *tariqah* ('way' or 'path'). All Sufis claim a chain or linkage or revelation (the *silsilah*) which goes back to the Companions and to the Prophet ﷺ himself. There were two kinds of membership: the initiates (or inner circle) and the associates (who attended occasionally). Any initiate on a particular path was known as a *murid*, a disciple who owes absolute allegiance to his or her particular *shaykh*. This close relationship with the shaykh is a vital part of Sufism, and a dying shaykh usually elects his successor (if a suitable person is available), to whom obedience and loyalty is transferred.

ZAWIYAHS

Zawiyahs (or *khaneqahs*) are places of spiritual learning and concentration where Sufis meditate and remember God, and train their disciples. They are also known as *tekkes* in Turkey, and *ribats* in North Africa. They are centres of missionary work, and frequently the shaykhs associated with the particular tariqah are buried there. To this day, they are visited by thousands of pilgrims. Examples are the famous shrines of Abdul Qadir Gilani in Baghdad; Muinuddin Chishti in Ajmeer, India; Shah Halal in Sylhet, Bangladesh; Jalaluddin Rumi in Qonya, Turkey; and Shams-i-Tabriz in Multan, Pakistan.

SUFI ORDERS IN THE WEST

The two main Orders of Sufis practising in the West today are the Naqshbandis and the Murabitun. The Naqshbandis are Sunni, and follow the Turkish Shaykh Nazim, the fortieth shaykh in line from Abu Bakr. Their UK headquarters is at Peckham Mosque, South London. The Murabitun follow the Scottish Shaykh Abd-al Qadir.

Their headquarters is in Norfolk. Both tariqahs have followers all over the country. There are also many immigrant Muslims now who belong to all the Orders of their countries of origin.

MUSIC IN SUFISM

Music plays a great part in many Sufi movements, and is particularly emphasized in the Chishti path to spiritual attainment. Music is *Ghiza-i-ruh*, the food of the soul. *Qawwali* are special songs sung at their contemplative musical assemblies.

The qawwalis sing distinctly, so that every word is clear to the hearers, and the music may not hide the poetry. The *tabla* (drum) players emphasize the accents and keep the rhythm even, so that the being of the Sufi joins with the rhythm and harmony of the music. The condition of the Sufi becomes different – emotion has full play, and there is a feeling of joy that cannot be put into words, language being inadequate to express it. This state is termed *Hal* or *Wajad*, the sacred ecstasy, and is regarded with respect by all present in the assembly.

Sometimes, if deeply touched, feeling finds vent in tears, or even motion or dance, which Sufis call *Raqs*.

SEMI-SUFIS

Some 50 per cent of the Pakistani population follow the Barelvi school founded by Ahmad Raza Khan (1856–1921) of Bareilly. It was founded to defend the existing beliefs of Muslims of South Asia that were deeply influenced by Sufism and incorporated many unorthodox beliefs against the reformation movements influenced by the Hanbali school that emphasized Shari'ah and Qur'an.

The critics of Barelvism accuse them of practising many non-Muslim innovations (*bid'at*) and therefore deviating from the true path. For example, they believe the Prophet ﷺ was not just a human being made from *bashar* (flesh and blood) but was also *nur* (light) at the same time (as was the angel Jibril), infallible, free from all imperfections and sinless (as are all prophets), and is still present with us. He also has the ability to be *hazir* (present) – to go physically and spiritually anywhere in the created universes that he pleases, whenever he pleases, and to be in more than one place at the same time.

Barelvis believe in intercession between humans and Divine Grace. This consists of the intervention of an ascending, linked and unbroken chain of holy personages (*pirs*), reaching ultimately to the Prophet ﷺ, who intercedes on their behalf with Allah.

Insight

This kind of Sufism can perhaps be compared to the concept of the incarnation of a saviour or redeemer in Christianity.

CRITICISMS OF SUFISM AND ITS PRACTICES

Orthodox Muslims are often suspicious, critical, and even highly antagonistic of Sufism, for a mix of these reasons:

▶ **Tawhid challenged** – *by the Sufi desire to 'become one with God'.*
▶ **Erotic and distasteful language** – *physical terms such as embracing, hugging and talking to God and erotic language are distasteful to most Muslims.*
▶ **Khamr** – *some Sufis use alcohol or drugs to induce mystic states.*
▶ **Music and dance** – *many Muslims insist these are forbidden.*
▶ **Fana** – *replacing belief that life in this world is God's arena for human spiritual development with the notion that it is not important, just a brief journey to the beyond.*
▶ **Unity threatened** – *the unity of the ummah is threatened, as Sufis withdraw into sects in which they are tempted to think themselves better Muslims than others.*
▶ **Kashf** – *rational scientific knowledge is abandoned in favour of mystical experiences, and critical analysis ignored for the authoritarian pronouncements of a shaykh – which would inevitably be limited by the knowledge, experience, and talents of the shaykh, and could even be the ravings of an unsound mind.*

- ▶ **Ta'ah** – *the unwise, even dangerous, total obedience to a shaykh.*
- ▶ **Karamat** – *teaching that miracles are possible in the state of union or communion with God, and are indeed favours granted by God to the most pious.*
- ▶ **'Ologies'** – *mathematics becoming mixed up with numerology, astronomy with astrology, chemistry with alchemy, etc.*
- ▶ **Magic** – *teaching that* dhikr *or repeated prayers are 'shortcuts' to results; encouraging people to hope for manipulation of supernatural forces, thus opening the door to gullibility, magic, talismanship and charlatanism.*
- ▶ **Ta'abbud** – *deliberately giving up the fulfilment of normal obligations, for the sake of ritualistic worship such as chanting of phrases, and lengthy contemplation.*
- ▶ **Tawakkul** – *trust in Allah degenerating into trust that God will make your desired things happen; replacing the study of God's inexorable laws with superstition.*
- ▶ **Pantheistic metaphysics** – *that all created things from the level of inanimate objects to the highest of conscious beings were all part of 'the one'.*
- ▶ **Teaching that all religious paths are of equal value** – *all inspired by the same divine source.*
- ▶ **Egotism** – *seeking to be saved oneself rather than caring for others.*
- ▶ **Tomb-shrines** – *praying at the tombs of 'saints' for miraculous intervention in healing, pregnancy, or worldly success.*
- ▶ **Urs festivals** – *the anniversary of the death of a* shaykh *becoming the occasion for great gatherings of people and major festivals.*
- ▶ **Charlatans** – *at worst, Sufism offers an opportunity for pretenders of spiritual excellence to take full advantage of the gullibilities of eager but unwary disciples.*

Insight

Muslims who spend much time chanting dhikr phrases often claim that there are special rewards for repeating them the hundred, or a thousand times, or more. Critics see this as the wrong motivation for a spiritual practice, the selfish desire to 'earn good points'.

THE IMPORTANT ROLE OF SUFISM

Many people consider that Sufism saves Islam from being over-
influenced by 'legalism'. True Sufis, with their humility, sincerity
and devotion, character and conduct, fight to keep the love of
God and the Prophet ﷺ alive.

However, Sufis have frequently been misunderstood and
persecuted. For these reasons, they have sometimes gone
'underground' in order to safeguard and continue their teaching
discreetly, either through fear of tyrannical rulers, or of the
power-mongering religious scholars who felt challenged and
undermined by the popularity of the Sufis.

They were and are the champions against materialism, and still play
an important part wherever rule-keeping, rather than movement of
the spirit, threatens to take over the ummah. Their influence within
Muslim nations remains enormous, and it is rare to find a Sunni
Muslim ruler who is not affiliated to one or other of the Orders.

10 THINGS TO REMEMBER

1 *Sufism* (tasawwuf) *is not a sect of Islam, but the inner and mystical dimension of it.*

2 *Sufism is the intention to take a spiritual journey or path towards the Truth, by means of love and devotion. A tariqah is a spiritual order, path or way towards God.*

3 *The main aim of Sufism is to turn the heart from all else but God, and seek to find divine love and knowledge through direct personal experience of God.*

4 *Sufism represents a spiritual reaction against dry ritualism and legalism, and concentrates on what is seen as important rather than getting lost in petty details.*

5 *The word Sufi is probably derived either from suf (wool – referring to the simple cloaks the early Muslim ascetics wore), safa (purity), from the Greek sophos (wisdom), or from the devoted students of Islam who lived in poverty on the Prophet's ﷺ veranda – the 'people of the bench' (ahl al-suffah).*

6 *Sufi Orders follow a master or* shaykh *who teaches sacred knowledge to others in the group.*

7 *Two central Sufi concepts are* tawakkul, *the total reliance on God, and* dhikr, *the perpetual remembrance or consciousness of God.*

8 *A dervish is really the Muslim equivalent of a monk, a member of an ascetic order. A Sufi centre is known as a zawiyah, khaneqah, ribat or tekke. Some Sufis perform whirling dances and vigorous chanting as acts of ecstatic devotion.*

9 *Sufism is tolerant and wide-ranging, and can therefore upset the conservative and 'orthodox' – particularly by use of pantheistic ideas, erotic language, trance states, music and dance.*

10 *Some factions of Islam, notably Salafism and Wahhabism, consider Sufism heretical. It has become a target for modernist and reform groups.*

9

....

Political Islam

In this chapter you will learn about:
- *Islamic reform – Fundamentalism, Salafism, and Neo-Sufism*
- *the rise of Islamic militancy and anti-Americanism*
- *moderate Islam, Liberalism and freedom of thought*
- *the Islamic state and the meaning of Khilafah*
- *the extremist threat*
- *hopes for peace.*

Islamic reform – Fundamentalism, Salafism and Neo-Sufism

The basic aim of Islamic Reform has nothing to do with politics; it is the recognition that Islam means little if it is not taken seriously, both in matters of belief and personal practice. It is the powerful urge for personal spirituality, grounding believers in the reality of Allah's presence, compassion and intimacy with us as individuals, so that laziness, selfishness, ignorance and hypocrisy no longer have room in the Muslim heart, which has become full of fervour and desire to serve God in every aspect of life.

Muslims are urged to acknowledge that the problems of their world stem from secular influences, laxity in personal religious practice and ignorance, which can both lead to blind obedience (taqlid) to preachers and speakers who could be wrong, and following practices thought to be Islamic which are not, and could even bring about the opposite of Islamic principles. The path to peace and justice lies in a reform to touch the hearts of Muslims as individuals, a personal revitalization by returning to the fundamentals, the original simple message and the practice of the faith.

Insight

Islamic Reform could perhaps be compared to the Reformation in Christian history – a move away from traditional hierarchies and organization towards personal purity, responsibility and accountability.

FUNDAMENTALISM

The first principle of a fundamentalist is to believe that the vast mass of 'sacred' material accumulated over centuries of Islamic jurisprudence is more of a burden to the pious believer than a help. There is too much, it is too complicated, and only other scholars can really grasp it all. There must be a return to the 'fundamentals'.

The second principle is that, in any case, any scholar – no matter how well educated – is only a human being with human limitations, and their conclusions are only as good as their particular skills and brain-power. Scholars are neither God nor the Prophet ﷺ, and therefore are somewhat arrogant in thinking that God needs help with explanations, or that they could improve on His wisdom, mercy or justice. Therefore, 'blind imitation' (taqlid) of their teachings and conclusions is not necessary.

Insight

There are madhhab-revering Muslims who accept without question that something is not permissible because Imam Malik or Abu Hanifah, for example, forbade it – yet however

(Contd)

great, learned or important these scholars were, they were human and therefore not infallible.

To a fundamentalist, any rulings based on any individual's intellectual capacity, logic and reasoning, are unsafe. Muslims should rely solely on the actual sacred words of the Qur'an and the sunnah of the Prophet ﷺ and nothing else, since they contain all the religious and spiritual guidance necessary for salvation.

This, of course, means rejecting not only the entire history of Islamic scholarship but also everything seen as innovation (*bida*), including Sufi teaching and practice.

However, other modernist Muslim scholars take the different view that classical jurists should lose their special status because flexibility of scholarship and interpretation of the holy texts should be renewed, with fresh *fiqh* for the modern world. This modernization is opposed by most conservative *ulema*. Islamic Fundamentalism should perhaps rather be called Islamic Conservatism, part of the spectrum of modern movements in Islam of which Fundamentalism and Liberalism define the two poles.

In the West, the word fundamentalism is used disparagingly by those who reject the 'other-worldly' and miraculous to describe those who 'blindly accept' what is seen as 'ancient mythology' as literal truth.

Insight

People of other faiths are also often slighted by non-believers who have rejected the whole concept of a God who created – Christians (like Muslims) are branded fundamentalists if they 'still believe in' such things as the creation of Adam ﷺ and Eve, Noah's flood, the miracles connected with Moses, angels, etc.

The term fundamentalist is also often used to describe those Muslims who assert their views through politics, violence or militancy, even though most fundamentalists are non-violent, and some are entirely apolitical. For example, the Tablighi Jama'at is a missionary-like organization which only aims to increase the personal piety of Muslims.

All devout Muslims regard defending their faith as vital – to the point of offering their own lives as the highest sacrifice of devotion. The link of Fundamentalist Islam with terrorism comes because the extreme fringe of Muslims might take the view that all people (non-Muslim and 'lax' Muslim) who reject their extreme stance could justifiably be regarded as enemies, to be attacked. If an 'innocent' was accidentally harmed, this would be seen as 'collateral damage'.

Insight

Any Muslim accepting a sectarian or group title usually has the tendency to regard those Muslims who do not belong to the group or sect as being deficient or incorrect in their Islam – an attitude not appreciated by the mainstream.

The opponents of fundamentalism are therefore going to be:
▶ *those who value the work of traditional scholars and support their madhhabs*
▶ *Sufis and those who enjoy esoteric mysticism, devotional practices and Sufi literature*
▶ *Muslims who lack the self-discipline to manage all the ritual requirements*
▶ *intellectuals and liberal modernists who wish to keep abreast of the modern world by 'opening the doors of ijtihad' and using reason and logic to interpret Shari'ah by looking to the spirit and principles of Islam rather than the letter of the law*
▶ *those who wish to embrace and utilize the modern sciences.*

Ibn Taymiyyah (1263–1328)

Ibn Taymiyyah, generally credited with being the founder of fundamentalism, was also a major leader in the revivalist campaign to open the doors of *ijtihad*. A leading Hanbali scholar, his erudition soon went beyond its confines, leading him to conclude that blind adherence (*taqlid*) to any one *madhhab* was too limiting. But he distrusted human intellect (*aql*) as a reliable means of attaining religious truth, and rejected the arguments and ideas of both philosophers and Sufis.

WAHHABISM

Four centuries later **Muhammad ibn Abdu'l-Wahhab** (1703–92), an intensely pious puritan, founded a movement to rid Islam of all the corruptions he believed had crept into the religion. He also believed it was vital to return to the fundamentals, and his attitude towards the whole vast edifice of scholastic material was to dismiss it. His brand of fundamentalism took a very narrow view, exhibiting extreme hostility towards intellectualism, Shi'ism, any other sectarian group, with special antagonism towards Sufism. Tolerance became an unpopular word.

The wording of the Divine Law being universal and timeless, he rejected any attempt to 'soften' or 'dilute' it by limiting pronouncements to their historical background or context. Scholars seeking new interpretations were regarded as arrogant self-idolaters, and humanistic fields of knowledge were branded 'the sciences of the devil.' One result of his version of Islam was increasing isolation and oppression of women and intolerance towards dissenters.

Insight

The Wahhabi purges of the nineteenth and twentieth centuries were frequently very bloody massacres, because bands of fierce warriors indiscriminately slaughtered and terrorized Muslims and non-Muslims alike.

The ruling house of Saud has been bound to Wahhabism since Abdu'l Wahhab signed a pact with Muhammad ibn Saud in 1744. To its adherents, Wahhabism is not a school of thought within Islam but it is Islam, and therefore even to regard its membership as a sect and use the term *Wahhabi* (i.e. a follower of a human being) is considered derogatory. In their literature,

Wahhabi clerics have consistently described themselves rather as *Salafis* (traditionalists), although Salafis generally support modern scholarship and science (see below).

THE RISE OF MODERNISM AND POLITICAL ISLAM

One impetus for Modernist Reform began with Napoleon's invasion of Egypt in 1798. During the nineteenth century the West colonized a large part of the world, including many Muslim territories. In the West, societies changed from agricultural to industrial, new social and political ideas emerged, and social models slowly shifted from hierarchical towards egalitarian. It was noted that oppressive feudal and colonial rule caused moral degradation, political instability, economic exploitation and spiritual bankruptcy – the last seen as the root cause of destroying the moral fibre of society.

The Muslim rulers of the Ottoman Empire acknowledged that the West's power was based upon its superior technology and weapons, and wished to acquire these things for themselves. Students were sent to Europe to study languages, science and politics; European experts were drafted in; printing presses were introduced to make technical information more accessible.

Insight

Muslim societies both felt and were marginalized by the imposition of Western value systems, way of life and methods of government. Imperialism and colonialism were not received as blessings by the conquered.

The main principle of Islamic Modernism is to acknowledge that today's issues require a multi-disciplinary approach with expertise in all areas of science, politics, economics and international affairs, to show how Islam is perfectly in keeping with the sciences and should be making use of science in order to bring progress.

Modernists emphasize Muslim pride, unity, solidarity, freedom of thought and the quest for truth through multiple sources –

rationalism, human experience, critical thinking and so on, in order to re-interpret and re-apply the principles and ideals of Islam to the modern situation. Directly opposed to Wahhabism, they argue that re-interpretation and reform are not blasphemy but a vital necessity. Most also wish to pursue an anti-colonialist agenda, the ultimate goal of which is national independence.

Insight

Some Modernist Muslims assert the right of well-informed Muslims who are not trained *ulema* to interpret Islam. An intellectual lay-person might be more saintly and have better skills than a mediocre *mullah*.

Islamic law separated from state law

European legal codes became the basis for reforms, and Muslim countries were pressured, and sometimes forced, to change their laws as secularist movements pushed for laws deviating from the opinions of their scholars. Islamic law became restricted to personal status or family law (such things as marriage, divorce and inheritance) and matters of ritual, worship, and spirituality. The Muslim community became divided into groups reacting differently to the changes, a division which persists to the present day. Traditionalists believe that the law of the state should always be based on the traditional legal schools.

Insight

The belief in the sovereignty of God over the state is a departure from secular democracy. It gives rise to the dominant position of a clerical class, because only they can decide what is acceptable to God.

Codification of Islamic Law

The state (or a small political elite) increasingly asserted its right to regulate and administer even religious matters, creating ministries of religious affairs and endowments to control organizations and institutions that had previously been outside their authority, including Sufi orders, mosques, Shari'ah courts, and religious schools.

Attempts to codify the Shari'ah are actually foreign to the Islamic legal tradition, which regards the Shari'ah as a body of doctrines and principles to be discovered by the human efforts of the scholars. Codifying it transforms it into a fixed set of rules that can be looked up in a book and are bounded by limits.

Insight

The main criticism of codification is that it sweeps away the knowledge and insight of all the scholars coming after the codification. It can also encourage bigotry, facile interpretations and unfortunate fatwas from 'ignorant' scholars.

Codification takes away the all-important claim of scholars to have the final say over the content of the law. It transfers that power to the state. The law itself then replaces the scholars as the source of authority, functioning without the vital aid of their spirituality, insight, experience and knowledge.

DEMOCRACY

A diversity of voices within the Islamic world began to debate issues of democracy, or political participation of the people:

▶ *Secularists, who might be extremely religious, argued for the separation of personal religion and a secular state.*
▶ *Rejectionists (both moderate and militant Muslims) rejected democracy, feeling it was not in keeping with Islam.*
▶ *Extremists condemned any form of democracy as haram (forbidden) and an idolatrous threat to God's rule (divine sovereignty). Their political activity was increasingly intended to topple kings and governments in order to impose a pure authoritarian Islamic rule according to their interpretation of Islam.*

Insight

The vast majority of Muslims appreciate democracy – all except those radicals who reject anything but the caliphate!

SECULARISM

Secularism means different things to different people. The Western concept is 'this-worldly', largely due to the fact that their secular states were formed after the revolt against exploitation by the religious hierarchy of Roman Catholicism during the Reformation. In fact, secularism develops in two ways – either towards disbelief in anything beyond this world and hostility towards all religion (as in Communism), or towards a separation of state and religion, or at least non-interference by the state in the religious life of different communities or of their priestly class in politics and state affairs – in other words, tolerance of religion so long as it does not interfere in politics. In many Western secular states there is respect and recognition of religious pluralism, and today's aim is for equal rights of protection and respect for people of all faiths.

Insight

Secularism often seeks to divorce state governance and politics from personal piety and religious practice. The two may become completely separate, and opinions differ as to whether this is a good thing or not.

SALAFISM

The founders of Salafism were fundamentalists in that they agreed that Muslims should always return to the Qur'an and the sunnah of the Prophet ﷺ and his Companions (the *salafiyyah* or *as-salaf as-salih*, the pious forefathers) and also rejected being slavishly bound to the interpretations of earlier Muslim generations or madhhabs. They differed from Wahhabis in that they regretted the loss of Islam's spirit of science and inquiry that was so spectacularly demonstrated by such giants as Ibn Sina, Ibn Rushd, al-Farabi, al-Biruni and al-Haytham. A desire for all forms of knowledge needed to be revived if Muslims were to revitalize and have a niche in world history once more.

Salafism is not necessarily anti-Western. In fact, its founders strove to project contemporary institutions such as democracy, constitutions or socialism into the foundational texts, and to justify the modern nation-state within Islam. Many of the pioneers lived at the end of the nineteenth century, at the end of the imperialist era, when the Ottoman Khalifate was the 'sick man of Europe', and all kinds of nationalist, modernist and secularist movements were springing up.

Salafi pioneers

In Egypt a number of reformers appeared, some concerned more with law, others economics, and yet others the challenges posed by Western civilization. These included **Jamal al-Din al-Afghani** (1838–97) who had observed British imperialism in India, noted how Muslims were systematically discriminated against, joined the resistance movement against the British in Afghanistan, then went to Cairo where he became the great champion of Pan-Islamism, the movement it was hoped would unite the Islamic world politically as well as in faith. If Afghans could defeat the forces of Britain, what an impact the unity of all Muslims under a charismatic ruler could have. His call for Muslim solidarity influenced Egypt's nationalist movement, Turkey's *Tanzimat* reforms, as well as Iran's constitutional and Islamic revolutions.

Insight

Zealous reformers frequently attack cinemas, banks and hotels – the objection to banks is *riba* (taking of interest and exploitation), and the cinemas and hotels encourage sexual lust, freedoms and obscenities.

One of his influential students was the Egyptian religious scholar **Muhammad Abduh** (1849–1905), often called the founder of Islamic Modernism, who became the rector of the Cairo al-Azhar University, and argued that the social aspects of Islamic law could be reformed in such areas as marriage, divorce, and inheritance (for example, he argued that the Qur'an supported monogamy, not polygamy, and supported education for women).

Another leading voice was the radical Syrian **Muhammad Rashid Rida** (1865–1935), who held a position closer to that of Abdu'l-Wahhab and stood for the strict application of the Shari'ah. He called for the unity of Islamic nations and the revival of true Islamic caliphate (which had been abolished by Mustafa Kemal

Ataturk in Turkey in 1924). He was one of the most influential Muslims scholars through his books and many articles in the Egyptian journal *al-Manar* (the Lighthouse) which he founded in 1898 and published throughout his life.

ISLAMIC REVIVALISM

For many Muslims, Islamic Revival simply means becoming a more religiously observant Muslim. Most Muslims oppose Islam's manipulation for violent or revolutionary ends, but the political and economic climate in so many Muslim countries fuels Islamist movements to go beyond reverence and promote political strategies. For them, Islamic Revival is about creating a more just, moral, Islam-based society/world, and Islamism represents a last-ditch effort to better their situation after decades of living in impoverished states that have already experimented with socialism, Arab nationalism, military dictatorships and monarchies, and observed little discernible improvement.

Hassan Al-Banna and the Ikhwan al-Muslimun

The message of **Hassan Al-Banna** (1906–49) was that Egypt had lost its soul and become secular, politically subservient and economically dependent on the West because it had strayed from the path laid down by God. His campaign was therefore to bring the Muslim masses back to their personal relationship with and awareness of the Almighty. In 1928 al-Banna founded the Ikhwan al-Muslimun (or Muslim Brotherhood), to promote personal piety and encourage practical kindness and charity. It became the largest and most influential Sunni Revivalist organization in the twentieth century, and also the first overtly political movement to oppose secular and Western ideas in the Middle East.

Radical tendencies soon asserted themselves; a 'secret apparatus' (*al-jihaz al-sirri*) engineered a series of assassinations of enemies of the Brotherhood. The Egyptian government, concerned with its increasing popularity and fearing it was plotting a coup, outlawed the *Ikhwan*, impounded its assets, and sent scores of its members to jail. In response the Egyptian Prime Minister was assassinated, which in turn prompted the murder of al-Banna, presumably by a government agent, in February 1949, when he was only 43 and at the height of his career.

Insight

It is vital to remember that no individuals or sects represent Islam as such – they give only an interpretation of it, which may be seriously out of step with the mainstream.

Since then, the Brotherhood has remained a significant force in the politics of several Arab countries, either directly or through the movements it inspired. It is at present the major opposition party in Egypt.

NEO-SUFISM

Neo-Sufism arose in the eighteenth century as an alternative response to modernism and secularism, and neo-puritan Islamism, the corrupt authoritarian Sufism of colonial times, and partly in response to colonialism itself. For example, anti-French resistance in Algeria was spearheaded by the brilliant Sufi shaykh **Amir Abdu'l Kader**.

In India, faced with sectarian conflict, low moral tone, and poor understanding of the Qur'an, it was feared that political collapse would be accompanied by religious disintegration. That this did not happen, but rather an era of religious regeneration commenced, was due largely to the activities of **Shah Wali Ullah** (1707–62), who campaigned to bring Muslim society back to the concepts of basic social justice, translated the Qur'an into the language of the people so that those without Arabic could understand it, and after studying the writings of each school of thought worked out a system upon which all but extremists could agree.

In the nineteenth century Islamic assertion took several different forms ranging from the **Mahdi movement** of the Sudan and the **Sanusiyyah** in North Africa, which both fought wars against European colonizers, to educational movements such as that of Aligarh in India founded by **Sir Syed Ahmad Shah**.

The rise of militant Islam

WAHHABISM AND SAUDI ARABIA

Wahhabi ideology was resuscitated in the early twentieth century under the leadership of **Abdu'l-Aziz ibn Saud**, the founder of the modern state of Saudi Arabia. With the discovery of oil beneath the sands, and the mining skills of Americans soon present to exploit it, the House of Saud was soon to gain enormous wealth and power, and the Wahhabi clerics got the state backing that would enable them to promote their ideology across the globe.

The Saudi wealth has been used to make enormous contributions to the spread of Islam and Muslim space in the West, but at the same time hardline Wahhabism has horrified Muslims the world over – not least by presiding over the systematic destruction of the Muslim heritage in and around Makkah in the fear that places of historic interest and religious landmarks could give rise to idolatry or polytheism. Cynics note that following the destruction come commercial developers to fill the voids with lucrative high-rises.

THE RISE OF MILITANT ISLAM

Given the existence of undemocratic and corrupt regimes all over the Muslim world, it is not surprising that for much of the twentieth century the dominant form of political dissent in these countries has been revolutionary Marxism. (The end of the Soviet Union and the Cold War has largely discredited leftist ideologies and strengthened Islamic parties.)

The huge problem confronting militant Muslims is their feeling that the governments of Islamic countries may be all made up of Muslims and Muslim leaders, but they are seen (rightly or wrongly) as corrupt, and therefore not proper Muslims. Politicized reformist Muslims are therefore feared by their own governments, and often face what is virtually or actually a police state – one that undermines, prohibits or cancels any kind of attempt to build an Islamic political party or movement.

Political Muslims are not only feared but also used by the governments they oppose, for their own ends. For example, in republics of the former Soviet Union, such as Tajikistan, Kyrgyzstan and Uzbekistan, anti-fundamentalism is used to justify horrendous human rights abuses. Any person who is even moderately religious is labelled a fundamentalist and imprisoned, or at least abused, and it has been very difficult for Muslim political parties to have any political effect.

ABU'L ALA MAUDUDI (1903–79)

Abu'l Ala Maududi is regarded by many as the major influence for militant Islam. He was not a traditional jurist but a self-taught pious man. He concluded that one reason for the decline of Muslim power in 'British' India was the long-established practice of interfaith mixing which had watered down Islamic thought. The solution was to purge Islam of all alien elements, and sever all social and political ties with Hindus. He and others founded the Jama'at-e Islami Party in Lahore in 1941.

Apart from pious personal practice, Maududi also saw Islam as a revolutionary force. A nascent Islamic *jama'at* (society, group) could begin and grow from a period of weakness to gather strength before waging jihad, just as Muhammad's jama'at was weak and persecuted in Makkah and gathered strength in Madinah before returning triumphantly to Makkah. The revolutionary jama'at would be a vanguard, remaining outside the government until the ultimate goal of the jama'at was realized – the establishment of an Islamic State, a 'theo-democracy'. His ideal Islamic state would have a president, an elected *shura* council (consisting of Muslims elected only by other Muslims), an independent judiciary and a cabinet. *Dhimmis* (non-Muslims living under Muslim protection) would only have the right to vote in lower level elections.

At first Maududi strongly opposed the idea of creating Pakistan as a separate Muslim country, but after the Partition in 1947, he migrated there and relentlessly criticized any secular policies. He was an intensely controversial figure, and counter-criticism came not only from secularists but also from many of the *ulema*. He also found himself persecuted and imprisoned for his political beliefs.

In 1953, his pamphlet criticizing the Qadiyani[6] sect resulted in widespread rioting and violence, and a military court sentenced him to death for sedition, although he was eventually pardoned.

Maududi's influence gave rise to the two most important *mujahideen* factions in the Afghan civil war, that of Ahmad Shah Masud (who leavened his Salafism with traditionalism), and Gulbuddin Hikmatyar.

[6]The Qadiyanis are a subsect of the Ahmadiyyah Movement founded by Mirza Ghulam Ahmad (1839–1908) who, in 1891, declared himself the promised Messiah (*masih*) of Islam, and claimed descent from Jesus ﷺ (who had not died at his crucifixion but survived, travelled to India, produced offspring, and was buried in Srinagar). Although Ahmadis regard themselves as Muslims and observe Islamic practices, most Muslims in Pakistan deny this. There is now an Ahmadiyya presence in 166 countries, but in Pakistan they have been made subject to discriminatory laws and an atmosphere of intolerance and violence, much of which is instigated by organized religious extremists.

SAYYID QUTB (1906–66)

In Egypt, **Sayyid Qutb** was a prominent Revivalist whose thought was deeply influenced by Maududi's revolutionary radicalism. In 1948, the year of the creation of the state of Israel, Qutb (a brilliant writer and employee in the Egyptian Ministry of Education), was sent to the US to study American educational institutions. There, he was deeply offended by the racism he observed (and experienced first-hand), disgusted by the growing sexual freedom and immodest dress of the young, and outraged by American blindness to thousands of Palestinians being made permanent refugees, and the media omission of the Muslim death-toll when Western troops were involved in military activity in Muslim countries. Were Arab lives worth less than those of European Jews? His experiences partly formed the impetus for his rejection of Western values and increasing radicalization. On his return to Egypt he resigned from the civil service, joined the Ikhwan, and became perhaps their most persuasive publicist.

An attempt on the Egyptian president Nasser's life in 1954 led to large numbers of the Muslim Brothers being rounded up and Qutb experienced arrest, torture and conviction of anti-government conspiracy. In 1964, having suffered ten years of incarceration, he published his best known work, *Milestones* (or *Signposts*), which inspired some of the most extreme expressions of Islamic Revivalism, such as Islamic Jihad and Takfir wa'l Hijrah.

One of his central concepts was to apply the term *jahiliyyah* (originally humanity's state of ignorance before the revelation of Islam) to modern-day Muslim societies which had turned away from Islamic values under the influence of European imperialism. Qutb also urged the creation of a 'vanguard' (*tali' ah*) of believers who would lead the way in the war on *jahiliyyah*, a clear call for Islamic militancy.

His understandable conclusion that his torturers were subhuman 'infidels' turned to extremism, and the 'infidels' stretched to include entire states, even those Muslim civilians who passively lent their support to disapproved regimes. Thus his justification of the killing of 'infidels' so long as it was done in the name of Islam now included practically everyone. All non-Islamic states were illegitimate.

Although it was written for his 'vanguard' of Islamic activists, *Milestones* is Qutb's most popular work. It outlines Qutb's political philosophy, which is based upon the concept that all Earthly sovereignty belongs to God alone. Because the book directly threatened the legitimacy of Nasser's government, Qutb was rearrested in August 1965 and hanged in 1966. Qutb was considered a martyr by many Muslims because he died at the hands of the same government whose legitimacy he denied.

Insight

Many students, aware of the government's condemnation of Qutb, secretly copied *Milestones* by hand. His political message was so potent because he voiced a deep philosophical criticism of the two superpowers at that time, the USA and the Soviet Union, a critique which remains extremely powerful today.

Qutb's thought played a key role in the emergence of the Awakening Movement, a blend of Qutbist ideas and radical

Wahhabi thinking, which grew out of the work of exiled Muslim Brothers from Egypt and elsewhere beginning in the 1960s and which achieved prominence in Saudi Arabia in the 1980s.

Qutb has been interpreted, particularly in Western media, as the intellectual precursor to various Islamic militant movements from the 1980s to the present day, including the notorious international terrorist organization, al-Qaeda.[7]

AYATOLLAH KHOMEINI (1900–89)

In Iran, Ruhollah Musavi Khomeini was a leading and distinguished cleric, a famous ascetic and teacher. Before his exile, seeing the religious establishment losing ground in the face of Modernist secular challenges and corruption, Khomeini took refuge in mysticism, especially in the notion of the 'Perfect Man' who would be able to guide society from corruption to a life of absolute perfection.

Insight

Khomeini was a Twelver Shi'ite Imam, a marja al-taqlid or source of emulation, whose teachings were unquestioned. He was adored by his supporters as a charismatic leader and champion of Islamic revival of immense popularity, and was named Man of the Year in 1979 by *TIME* magazine.

By the early 1960s, Khomeini was resisting the modernizing reforms proposed by the Shah's 'White Revolution', using the term 'westoxification' (*gharbzadigi* – from the Arabic root *ghraba*) to describe what he considered the poisonous influences of Western culture. He was arrested by SAVAK (the Shah's secret police) and later sent into exile, ending up in Paris, where he pursued his mission by utilizing new technology, churning out tapes and cassettes which were eagerly snapped up and disseminated by

[7]Qutb's brother Muhammad moved to Saudi Arabia where he came a professor of Islamic Studies. One of his students was Ayman Zawahiri, later the mentor of Usama bin Ladin (both leaders of al-Qaeda).

his loyal supporters. Two weeks after the Shah left Iran in 1979, dying of cancer, Khomeini was recalled, and returned to construct his revolutionary 'reign of virtue' according to his principle of the *velayet e-faqih* ('vice regency of the theologian').

Khomeini was the first revolutionary Muslim cleric to create an Islamic government, welcomed with joy by his devotees, but criticized as based solely on his own personal conception of what such a government should entail by his detractors. His revolution inspired both Sunni and Shi'ite Revivalist movements around the world, including Hizbullah in Lebanon.[8]

Insight

I recall watching the TV news coverage of the Ayatollah's funeral. The streets of Iran became a sea of black as millions gathered to mourn, all hoping to touch the coffin. It was a very hot day: one channel described water cannon being turned on the people; another channel reported that it was a spray of scented water to help keep them cool.

ANTI-AMERICANISM

Before 1967, Islamic militancy had been a relatively small movement. However, Israel's swift success over Egypt, Jordan and Syria in the Six Day War spelled the end of Arab Nationalism as an effective political movement, while their conquest of Jerusalem transformed Israeli–Palestinian strife from a regional conflict into one that affected all Muslims. Other crises throughout the Muslim world – the upheaval in Malaysia in 1969, Pakistan's invasion of Bangladesh in 1971, the revolution in Iran and the Lebanese civil war – all fuelled the belief that the West had failed Muslim societies not only as an ally but as a viable model of development.

[8]By the end of the twentieth century, with much of Iran's youthful population too young to remember Khomeini and impatient with the theocratic rule of the mullahs, the mood has changed. One Baghdadi who described the 2004 American invasion of Iraq as a 'liberation' was Khomeini's own grandson, Sayyid Hussein Khomeini, who said that people in the region welcomed freedom wherever it came from, even a country which his grandfather had dubbed 'the Great Satan'.

Extremism also found an origin in wars that the United States decided to support. Radical Islam was not a force in Lebanon before the Israeli invasion of 1982; Hamas owes its emergence and influence to the fact that the Palestinian territories are still occupied in defiance of United Nations' rulings.

Insight

Hamas was created in 1987 by Sheikh Ahmed Yassin, Abdel Aziz al-Rantissi and Mohammad Taha of the Palestinian wing of the Muslim Brotherhood at the beginning of the First Intifada, an uprising against Israeli rule in the Palestinian Territories.

Muslims feel that the corrective to militant Islamism is to properly integrate mainstream Islamists into the political process of their respective countries. They cannot be ignored because they present some of the most powerful voices in the political life of their countries. Radicalism might be defused if the US would shift its focus from trying to crush Islamic movements militarily to pursuing policies that made their development redundant.

Recent surveys show that over 80 per cent of Muslims would like to have democracy – except for those radical Islamists who reject any form of governance in favour of the caliphate.

People vote with their feet. Many Muslims have moved to the USA and Western Europe, either as refugees or in search of betterment and freedom, but not everyone is confident about the USA's goal of democratization and 'freedom' for their homelands. Smart tyrants have generally tended to be allies of the USA if they wished to remain in power. Only when Muslims are empowered to choose their own leadership and policies freely, and are able to reject USA-supported choices of leaders, can the blight of violence begin to wind down.

The real test will be when democratically elected Islamist parties are genuinely able to come to power through the ballot box – as happened with Hamas in Palestine in January 2006. For democracy brings not only power but also accountability. Movements which previously had the luxury of criticizing from the sidelines will have to deliver the goods.

Modernism and moderate Islam

WHY SALAFISM IS REJECTED BY MANY MUSLIMS

Salafism undoubtedly stems from noble and pious origins, but in efforts to defend a 'purist' system of beliefs from the onslaught of Westernization and Modernism, an unfortunate side-effect has been to produce unsmiling zealots whose arrogance and hatred for those they should be missionizing is all too clear in their faces, with a fantasy-like level of confidence and a supremacist attitude. Salafism seems to appeal to a certain type, often impervious to criticism, who display a self-righteous arrogance towards the West, non-believers in general, Muslims of different sects and women.

By emphasizing the presumed Golden Age in Islam, Salafis ignore the actual recorded history in the hadiths and tend to idealize the time of the Prophet ﷺ and the characters of his Companions beyond reality. Nobody may risk criticism of any of the Companions, for they were the 'best of people'. A speaker can also be heckled for suggesting that the Prophet ﷺ was a human being with human frailties or limitations, or that the behaviour of certain Companions was not perfect, that they had weaknesses, ignorance, made mistakes, etc.

Insight

I was furiously challenged by a Salafi when I mentioned certain female Companions grooming the Prophet's ﷺ hair for lice, Khalid's excesses needing rebuke, Umar's irascible nature and his violence towards females (including his sister). How dare I suggest such things? I could only respond by indicating the relevant hadiths.

Untutored scholarship has resulted in today's plethora of pseudo-scholars and uninformed preachers who effectively undermine any notions of qualified juristic authority in Islam. It becomes open season for all who think themselves justified to speak on behalf of the Divine Will, even those who have only been Muslims for five minutes, yet are suddenly more knowledgeable and righteous than everyone else, and feel perfectly competent to instruct others.

One danger of today's freedom of individuals to issue 'online fatwas' is that it has created a highly legalistic approach to Islam ('this is right, that is wrong') as individuals seek to regulate Muslim life according to their own interpretations.

LIBERALISM

Liberalist and Modernist scholars point out that in circumstances where the Shari'ah has been limited to strict fundamentalist interpretations, or where training schools are limited only to the resources approved by particular sects, the knowledge base of how the Shari'ah has been/is interpreted by other schools of thought is greatly narrowed, and might even be in danger of being lost. They maintain that the very concept of Fundamentalism constitutes a sort of *bida*, since its very limiting form of Islam never existed in the past.

Insight

There is a danger of the knowledge base of Islam being restricted, especially if books are censored by sectarian hardliners, altered or forbidden circulation among Muslims.

This situation is rendered even more grave if classical texts are altered and 'censored' of 'un-Islamic' aspects, with the trainees dependent on those resources perhaps being quite unaware that they have been altered. It is certainly one good reason to cling to the practice of placing the Arabic text of the Qur'an alongside any translations, and to urge as many Muslims as possible who have a talent for languages to learn Arabic for themselves. Failing that, it is good practice to compare more than one translation.

Insight

Muslims who cannot speak or read Arabic find it useful to consult several different versions of translations. This can be done through internet sites, and by comparing actual book texts.

Modernists insist that Muslims must look not just at the text, but at the context of the text, and to re-apply sacred texts to the realities and challenges of the times in which we live. What are the broader principles and values underlying the language of the Qur'an on specific issues, or the decisions and actions taken by the Prophet ﷺ? How would these be understood in a contemporary setting? The key priorities of modernist ijtihad are justice and equity (*istihsan* – the Arabic term for juristic preference in pursuit of doing the right thing), in other words, acting for the general welfare or public interest. Istihsan ('to approve' or 'to sanction') is seen as being equivalent to the concept of equity in English law.

Insight

Istihsan means the use of the judgement of individual scholars or jurists to determine the best solution to a religious problem that cannot be solved by citing sacred texts.

It is vital to realize that there is a critical distinction between Shari'ah, the divinely mandated laws and principles that are therefore universal and timeless, and fiqh, the human interpretations and applications that develop in response to specific historical and social contexts. Often the phrase 'Islamic law' blurs this distinction, thereby unjustifiably sacralizing the corpus of the fiqh and the *fuqaha* (legal scholars) themselves.

So, for example, some Qur'anic verses were specific to the Prophet's ﷺ time (e.g. the curse addressed to Abu Lahab, rules given specifically to the Prophet's ﷺ wives), whereas other verses were eternal in purpose. Should we make Abu Lahab timeless, or make it clearer that other verses are historically specific? If a verse was directed at the wives of the Prophet ﷺ, was it supposed to be compulsory for all Muslim women everywhere, or just for those addressed?

Insight

The words of the Qur'an and the Prophet ﷺ indicate that his wives were not to be thought of as the same as other women.

Nevertheless, most Muslim women wish to follow their practice and example.

Moreover, while Muhammad ﷺ was the last human *nabi* (prophet), we are still being taught by history and science. There was a difference between Muhammad's ﷺ knowledge as a human being, and God's omniscience. Muhammad ﷺ talked about our moon and sun as if they were the only moon and sun. Today we know Allah created billions of galaxies. And if we need to reinterpret the Qur'anic verses on sun and moon in the light of our new understanding of astronomy and the cosmos, why can we not reinterpret Islamic verses about ancient punishments (*hudud*)? The expansion of human knowledge is not just about stars, but also about human beings and their behaviour, psychology and genetics.

Some thoughts on modernizing Islamic criminal law

We now know far more about the causes of crime, the limits of culpability and guilt. We know that poverty, bad parenting, a sense of injustice, racial discrimintion, chemical imbalance in the human body, a bad neighbourhood and bad social environment can all be contributing factors that turn a human being toward crime. Fourteen centuries ago there were no psychiatrists, or forensic science or knowledge about DNA. Since then, God has taught us more about crime, its causes, the methods of its investigation, the limits of guilt and the much wider range of possible punishments and deterrents.

Insight

Istihsan may be applied to express a preference for one particular judgement in Islamic law over other possibilities. It is one of the principles of legal thought underlying ijtihad. Muslims need to be familiar with the contexts and backgrounds of the texts in order to ascertain their true spirit.

ISLAM AND FREEDOM OF THOUGHT

Ironically, one great hindrance blocking renewal and creativity in Islamic thinking today is still the absence of intellectual, political and social freedom in many Islamic societies, except in the West, and either a conservative religious establishment's firm grip on the training of religious leaders, discourse, doctrine and practice – or the state's firm grip on them.

Muslim Reformers, seen by their followers as saints, are naturally often perceived as a threat by conservative leaders, religious institutions and even the devout students in these institutions. Muslim Modernists can find themselves silenced or removed from their teaching positions, with their livelihoods and even lives threatened, forced into exile, caught between authoritarian regimes that are prepared to imprison and religious extremists prepared to kill. A huge gulf is opening up between the adherents of the two types of Islam.

Insight

Muslims were and are urged to seek knowledge from cradle to grave from every possible source. It is tragic that certain supposedly Islamic regimes do their best to silence and stifle knowledge – and somewhat similar to the attitude of the Roman Catholic Christian hierarchy towards science in previous centuries.

WHO OR WHAT IS A MODERATE MUSLIM?

In today's climate, the definition of a moderate Muslim depends very much on who you ask and what their agenda is, their politics or religious positions. 'Moderate' is a relative term, understood differently by different people. It might include:

▶ *any Muslim who believes in democracy, tolerance, a non-violent approach to politics and equitable treatment of women*

▶ *those who accept that the Qur'an and hadiths were written for a time and place very different from today and are therefore open to re-interpretation*

▶ *those who reject the idea that any one group or individual has a monopoly on defining Islam, and who respect the right of individuals to disagree, or to worship Allah the way they choose, or even not to worship and not to believe*

▶ *those willing to co-exist peacefully with peoples of other faiths, to seek dialogue with them, and emphasize the common ground and not the differences*

▶ *those who would be prepared to separate politics and religion*

▶ *those who would try to bring people into Islam by logic and love, example and discussion, rather than by threats, coercion or force of arms*

▶ *those who would condemn suicide bombings and terrorist operations, and abhor 'preachers of hate', even though they still might not condemn all occasions of political violence against authorities who occupy Muslim lands by force.*

Insight
Liberal Muslims maintain that the use of *ijma* makes Islamic law compatible with democracy, so long as it is applied to the consensus of the entire community and not just a small, conservative clerical class.

In internal debates, a more extreme Muslim might use the term 'moderate Muslim' pejoratively (and unjustly) to indicate one who is more secular and less Islamic than the norm, which varies across communities. People who are moderate solely on the basis of their politics could be understood as opportunists and self-serving.

In the USA
In the USA the litmus test for being a moderate Muslim is tied to foreign policy issues, and how critical the Muslim is of US policy, interests and preferences within the world order, who accepts that Islam has no role in politics, and avoids any confrontation – even political – with Israel. Some Muslims seen as moderate by the Muslim world were called radical by the Bush administration. Leading modern moderates such as Yusuf Qaradawi, Tariq Ramadan and Yusuf Islam, for example, have all been treated with suspicion.

Khilafah and the Islamic State

UNITY AND DIVISION

Islam should be one *ummah* but, unfortunately, it is all too obvious that the family of Islam suffers from splits, rivalries, jealousies and nationalism. Far too many issues divide the Muslims of different countries and cultures, which is not the fault of Islam itself, and certainly not the aim or desire of the Prophet ﷺ. While the Prophet ﷺ was alive he regretted the divisive instinct that spoiled the peace of his own community of believers.

> *Believers are one single brotherhood (ummah), so make peace and reconciliation between two contenders, and revere Allah, that you may receive mercy.*
> (Surah 49:10)

Insight
The Prophet ﷺ commented: 'The devil is a wolf to humanity, catching the one which is solitary, the one who strays from the flock, and the one which wanders off. So avoid the branching paths, and keep to the general community!' (Ahmad)

The Prophet ﷺ hated sectarianism and exclusivity; he disapproved of extremists pushing themselves forward and causing *fitnah* (discord) including rivalry and hurt feelings and enmity. However, although many Muslims do fall far short of the ideal, nevertheless the ideal of the ummah is there to be aimed at.

AN ISLAMIC STATE AND ITS RELATIONSHIP TO SHARI'AH

A united ummah would in essence be an Islamic State (*dawlah islamiyah*), a united people, or territory, where governance was under a caliph and according to the principles of the Shari'ah.

In practice, since this does not yet exist, there are several attitudes towards existing states and whether or not they are Islamic enough for Muslims to accept them. Some argue that a true Islamic State can only be one in which the Shari'ah is formally implemented. Others might argue that in some such states the Shari'ah has become cruel and misinterpreted, and in opposition to the true spirit of Islam. Some Muslims might find a state acceptable if none of its laws was contrary to the basic tenets of Islam. Yet others might accept a state in which Islamic law is one of the available sources of law.

Insight

Some Islamic movements, notably the Tablighi Jamaat, identify a lack of spirituality and decline in personal religious observance as the root causes of the Muslim world's problems. They do not believe that the caliphate can be successfully revived until these deficiencies are addressed.

Difficulties with non-Muslim law

Under non-Muslim governments devout Muslims inevitably face a conflict of loyalties in that secular law systems frequently negate the standards by which they are required to live. Adultery, prostitution, pornography, homosexuality, gambling, interest on loans and consuming liquor cannot be made legal in Islam.

WHAT IS KHILAFAH?

Khilafah is the concept of all Muslims being united under the rule of one elected Muslim man of superb character, the *khalifah* (caliph), who would be totally committed to bringing about the will of God on Earth as it is in Heaven. Traditional Sunni Islamic lawyers teach that a caliphate is only acceptable provided it makes use of *shura* or consultation of the people. The Majlis al-Shura is responsible for electing a new caliph, and advising him. Members of the majlis should satisfy three conditions: they must be just, they must have enough knowledge to distinguish a good caliph from a bad one, and they must have sufficient wisdom and judgment to select the best caliph, who would be appointed by the electoral process known as *bay'ah* (mandate), a pledge on the Book of Allah and sunnah of His Prophet ﷺ. Many Muslims would prefer this leader to be a descendent of the Prophet ﷺ, of whom a large number exist to this day.[9]

[9]They include, incidentally, our Queen and her offspring – their descent coming through Spain.

What would be his aims?

He would seek to establish unity among all the Muslims on
Earth in a community which would be regarded as the 'best
community' (Surah 3:110). This Islamic state would consist of all
those submitted to Allah – it could exist along the lines of united
geographical states (like the United States of America or the old
Union of Soviet Socialist Republics), or as pan-Islam, a rule of all
Muslims wherever they happen to live.[10] The caliph's rule on behalf
of Allah would be dedicated to the common good of all humanity,
and would transcend race, language, colour, and geography.

He would do this by demolishing the rules of *kufr* (unbelief) and
transforming the land to *Dar-al-Islam* (land of Islam), and carrying
the message of Islam to the world, unfinished business until Islam is
known and freely practised throughout the whole Earth.

No forced conversions

Some groups urging for khilafah also support *jihad*. However,
spreading the will of God on Earth does not imply forcing people
to believe what they patently do not believe. This is the very
opposite of God's will; Allah ordered no compulsion in matters
of faith, and pointed out that had He willed everyone on Earth to
be Muslims, He would not have created them as individuals (see
Surah 10.99–100 and Surah 18.29).

Is Khilafah feasible?

Considering the present state of the world, most Muslims regard
khilafah as a concept that belongs in the realm of ideals rather
than reality.

[10]Similar to the Pope being leader of all Roman Catholics.

They feel it is more sensible to acknowledge the status quo and get on with following the compulsory aspects of Islam, living good Muslim lives, with or without a caliph, since the concept is not universally accepted by scholars as a necessary part of Islam. It is not one of the 'five pillars', was not always successful, even in the earliest days, and its absence does not make Islam impossible.

JIHADISTS

Others feel the move to establish khilafah should be the prime aim of all Muslims. These Muslims often become sectarians, with a reputation for aggression, a desire for *jihad*, and – being prepared to lay down their lives for what they see as the service of Allah – the glory of martyrdom. They inevitably cause distress and embarrassment in their communities (which reaction they ignore since they despise those outside their groups as not proper Muslims), and their aggressive activities are frequently picked up by the media. Moderates feel angered and frustrated by them, object to the *fitnah* (discord) they cause, and consider the whole of Islam to be tarnished by these antagonistic brethren who think they are the only Muslims doing their duty and serving Allah properly.

A number of Islamist political parties and guerrilla groups have called for the restoration of the caliphate by uniting Muslim nations, either through political action (e.g. the now banned Hizb ut-Tahrir or 'Party of Liberation) or through force (e.g. al-Qaeda). Al-Qaeda recently named its internet newscast from Iraq 'The Voice of the Caliphate'.

jihad is the last option. For militant Muslims, military jihad is the first option and ijtihad is not an option at all.

Moderate Muslims are dismissed by jihadists as being 'asleep', lazy, and unwilling to make the required sacrifices for Allah. Their opinions are dismissed as corrupt, debased, lax, irrelevant, inadequate, or just plain wrong.

In Islam the sure sign of a bigot is *takfir* – the accusing of all those who do not agree with their interpretation (even people known to be devout believers and practising Muslims) of being *kuffar* (non-believers), and the attitude that Islam has not been properly understood by anyone since the Prophet Mohammed ﷺ and the early Muslims – except themselves.

The quiet majority of Muslims is shocked by their ill-mannered tactics and intolerance, and the most charitable view is that 'they will grow out of it' when they study their texts wrested out of context more carefully. However, this is seen by the jihadis as patronizing, and simply irritates them all the more until there is a risk they might become dangerous politically, or even willing to undertake terrorist activity.

HIZB UT-TAHRIR AND THE MUHAJIRUN

Hizb ut-Tahrir, and its offshoot the Muhajirun, are modern examples of Islamic sectarian groups of vociferous zealots, who insist that working to re-establish the Islamic way of life depends on promoting khilafah, since in their view Islam is incomplete without it and therefore is not really Islam. They point out a hadith of the Prophet ﷺ that khilafah would cease (which it did, in Turkey in 1924), but would eventually return. They share the zeal of those of other faiths who are obsessed with the end of the world. The Muhajirun sect was officially disbanded in 2004.

> ## Insight
>
> No attempts at rebuilding a power structure based on Islam were successful anywhere in the Muslim world until the Iranian Revolution in 1979, and this was based on Shi'ite principles, with leaders who did not outwardly call for the restoration of a global caliphate.

AL-GHURABAA (THE STRANGERS) AND AL-FIRQATUN-NAJIYAH (THE SAVED SECT)

These are new extreme groups, widely believed to be the reformed Muhajirun. *Ghurabaa* is a derivative of *gharaba*, meaning to go away, depart, absent or withdraw from, leave. The singular, *ghareeb*, means strange, foreign, alien.

The concept is that the existing *ummah* of Islam has failed or become inadequate in one way or another, and the members of this sect have been selected to live a specially purified life – the true Islam (a similar concept to Pharisaism at the time of Jesus ﷺ, and the Old Testament notion of a 'Righteous Remnant').

> ## Insight
>
> Extremists usually feel that the existing mainstream ummah has failed or become inadequate, and their members have been called to be the 'select few'.

The Saved Sect, which theatrically opposed the UK general election in April 2005, takes as its founding hadith:

> *If the people of Isra'il were fragmented into 72 sects my ummah will be fragmented into 73 sects. All of them will be in Hell Fire except one. They (the Companions) said: 'Allah's Messenger, which is that?' Whereupon he said: 'It is one to which I and my Companions belong.'*
>
> (Tirmidhi, Abu Dawud)

Members of al-*Ghurabaa* take this to mean themselves, the select few who truly follow Islam, whereas the mainstream of Islam naturally considers it means the mainstream. The sectarians perversely take pride in the fact that people will condemn them, speak ill of them and slander them, none of which will be able to hinder them from their path, nor shake their determination to be what the Prophet ﷺ described as a 'small group of pious people in a large group of evil people. Those who disobey them outnumber those who obey them.' (Ahmad)

Insight

The closest thing to a caliphate in existence today is the Organisation of the Islamic Conference (OIC), an international organization with limited influence founded in 1969 consisting of the governments of most Muslim-majority countries.

Terrorism in the name of Islam

THE EXTREMIST THREAT

One hallmark of extreme puritan movements was and is to divide the world into mutually exclusive categories – the forces of good and the forces of evil, the world of belief (*dar al-Islam*) and that of unbelief (*dar al-harb*) which is fair game for conquest. Those who are not with them, (Muslim or non-Muslim), are the enemy – to be fought and destroyed in a war with no limits.

These extremists appeal to grievances that exist among many mainstream Arabs and Muslims, from foreign policy issues to domestic complaints against repressive and corrupt governments and failed economies. They twist Islamic values about good governance, social justice and the requirement to defend Islam when under siege, to legitimize their use of violence, warfare and terrorism.

AL-QAEDA

Al-Qaeda members do not represent Islam or any particular place or cause. They are ethnically diverse and connected by their radical version of Islam – they include militant Muslims from around the world.

They originated during the Soviet expansion into Afghanistan when the Afghan Marxists allied with the Soviets against the native Afghan *mujahideen*. Abdullah Yusuf Azzam (a Palestinian scholar and member of the Muslim Brotherhood) founded the Maktab al-Khidamat (Services Office, or MAK) to raise funds to recruit international non-Afghan mujahideen, and organized paramilitary training camps to prepare them for the Afghan war front. Azzam persuaded Usama Bin Ladin to join MAK, using his own vast wealth and his connections with the Saudi royal family and the petro-billionaires of the Gulf to payroll them. The US gave their support, channelling funds through Pakistan, and from 1986 MAK had recruiting offices in the US, notably the al-Kifah Refugee Centre in Brooklyn. Among its leading figures was the blind Shaykh Omar Abdu'r Rahman.

Insight

The training camps were established for al-qaeda al-sulbah (the vanguard of the strong), *al-qaeda* simply meaning camp or base. The name stuck, but it came to refer to the terrorist organization the movement became.

The Soviets finally withdrew from Afghanistan in 1989, and when the mujahideen leaders then proved unable to agree with each other, chaos ensued, with constant fighting, leaving the country devastated.

Some, including Bin Ladin, wanted to expand their operations, Bin Ladin asserting that the USA was also massacring Muslims in Palestine, Chechenya, Kashmir and Iraq, and elsewhere, and that Muslims therefore had the right to attack in reprisal. After Azzam was assassinated in 1989, the MAK split with a significant number joining Bin Ladin's organization. Since then, al-Qaeda has attacked civilian and military targets in various countries. Characteristic techniques include suicide attacks and simultaneous bombings of different targets.

When the Soviets withdrew, Bin Ladin returned to Saudi Arabia, where the Iraqi invasion of Kuwait in 1990 had put the Saudi's most valuable oil fields within easy striking distance of Iraqi forces, and Saddam Hussein's call to pan-Arab/Islamism could potentially rally internal dissent. Saudi Arabia's own forces were well armed but were far outnumbered by the Iraqis. Bin Ladin offered his services to King Fahd, but the offer was refused, the king opting instead to allow US and allied forces to deploy on Saudi territory, thus 'profaning sacred soil'.

After speaking publicly against the Saudi government for harbouring US troops, Bin Ladin was publicly disowned by his family, his Saudi citizenship revoked, and he was forced into exile in Sudan.

THE TALIBAN

The origins of the *Taliban* (lit. students) lay in the children of Afghanistan, many of them orphaned by the war, and educated in the rapidly expanding network of *madrassahs* in the refugee camps on the Afghan–Pakistani border. An ever-expanding network of al-Qaeda supporters thus enjoyed a safe haven in Taliban-controlled Afghanistan until the Taliban were defeated in 2001. Usama Bin Ladin and other al-Qaeda leaders are still believed to be located in areas where the population is sympathetic to the Taliban in Afghanistan or the border tribal areas of Pakistan.

Some contend that the idea of al-Qaeda as a formal organization is a US invention, the name only coming to the attention of the public in the 2001 trial of Bin Ladin and the four men accused of the 1990 US embassy bombings in East Africa. It was necessary to show that Bin Ladin was the leader of a criminal organization in order to charge him in absentia under the Racketeer Influenced and Corrupt Organizations Act.

Insight

There is no evidence that Bin Ladin used the term al-Qaeda until after 11 September 2001, when he realized that this was the term the Americans had given the organization.

The reality may be rather that Bin Ladin had become the focus of a loose association of disillusioned Islamist militants, who mostly planned their own operations and looked to Bin Ladin for funding and assistance.

Insight

Conspiracy theories have abounded, many believing the US somehow organized the 11 September attacks itself in order to have an excuse to condemn al-Qaeda and safeguard its oil interests in the Middle East. It has also been suggested that the original targets for the attacks may have been nuclear power stations on the east coast of the USA, targets which were later altered by al-Qaeda.

THE ROLE OF ISLAM IN THE POLITICAL SPHERE

Since the 9/11 attacks on the USA there has been intense debate about the different interpretations of Islam, its impact on Muslim politics, and the relationship between Islam and the West, a debate that gained renewed vigour after the London attacks on 7 and 21 July 2005. Many insecure governments have used the threat of global terrorism as an excuse or green light for increasing their authoritarian rule, as the politically angry radical Muslims exacerbate the already rampant anti-Americanism in the Muslim world and encourage terrorist responses to real and perceived injustices.

SUICIDE BOMBERS AND MUSLIM REACTION

To detest oppression, injustice and suffering is an Islamic obligation, and no amount of legislation will prevent Muslims from doing so. When people try to resist state injustice verbally those states invariably attempt to outlaw such dissent, to prevent exposure of the nature of their oppression. Hence there have arisen bans on 'incitement to hatred', on political groups, inviting people to speak about oppression, and on leaflets, etc. Even watching videos exposing the sufferings of Muslims is suspect.

However, the appalling acts of suicide bombers horrify and shame Muslims. Killing and maiming the innocent is terrorism, and such twisted hatred and bitterness have nothing whatsoever to do with Islam, God, or the message or example of the Prophet ﷺ. In fact, terrorism can only succeed politically by losing morally, since suicide bombers assume that their enemies care about the innocent lives they rip apart.

Insight

When Muslims choose to kill themselves for political reasons, they may be hoping to make a statement – even though they must know suicide is totally forbidden in Islam. When they kill innocent bystanders along with themselves it is nothing less than murder.

These bombers may perhaps have been duped into thinking of themselves as martyrs for Allah, or for their cause, but a martyr is someone who has been put to death by an oppressor because of their faith. Suicide bombers not only commit murder and will have to face the consequences in the Life to Come, but have also caused *fitnah* (dissent and damage) and committed a physical attack upon Islam itself by the damage they have done to its image.

The Prophet ﷺ made his message crystal clear:

That person who defects from obedience and separates from the main body of the Muslims, ... if he dies in that state ... he will die the death of one belonging to the days of jahiliyyah (i.e. would not die as a Muslim). One who fights under the banner of a people who are blind (i.e. do not know whether their cause is just or otherwise), ... if he is killed (in this fight), he dies as one belonging to the days of jahiliyyah. Whoever attacks my ummah, killing the righteous along with

the wicked, sparing not (even) those staunch in faith ... he has nothing to do with me and I have nothing to do with him.
(Muslim)

The New York World Trade Centre destroyed by the terrorists used to host a Friday prayer that drew 1,500 Muslims every week.

Al-Bara'a (self-exoneration)

There is no power of excommunication in Islam so terrorists cannot be formally banned from the community – but the community can distance itself from them by the Islamic principle of *al-bara'a* (self-exoneration). This means that Muslims must not just remain quiet, but must publicly dissociate themselves from terrorist acts.

THE REAL CAUSES OF TERRORISM

The real fuel for terrorism is not radical preaching, but simply the reality of what is going on in the Muslim world – the occupation of Palestine, subjugation of Kashmir, installation of puppet regimes throughout the Muslim world and so on, which all cause anger. If the Muslim *ummah* feels marginalized and persecuted, hate-filled preachers are not needed to tell them this – they may just watch the news on their TVs.

Military, political and social causes of terrorism

There is no way that terrorism, the hadd crime of *hirabah*, can be justified in Islam, but it is easy to understand the numerous root causes of terrorism.

▶ *Feeling pushed around – the traumatic experience of non-Muslim colonialism invading Muslim religious and cultural space, which explains why terrorists often attack seemingly innocuous targets such as banks (riba), cinemas and hotels (sexual licence, etc.).*
▶ *Frustration and fury – despotic and often corrupt governments clamping a tight lid down on dissent and freedom of expression.*
▶ *Outrage for a righteous cause – the establishment of the state of Israel, and expulsion of the Palestinians.*

- *Lack of a level playing field – the fact that favoured governments can assassinate, impose collective punishments, flout numerous UN resolutions and develop nuclear power with impunity.*
- *Twisted evidence, lies, abuse – the eventual discovery that there were no weapons of mass destruction in Iraq, Abu Ghrayb, Guantanamo, crude photographs of abused prisoners.*
- *Suspected cover-ups for real motives – the 'war on terror' really being a pretext for Western control of oil and world economics.*
- *The feeling that Americans and Europeans value their lives more than those of Muslims.*
- *The belief that a tacit conspiracy exists between the West, its agencies and its multinational corporations on the one hand, and local business and military cliques in the Third World on the other, to assume complete control of certain countries and 'develop' them on a joint venture basis. It is human rights violations that make these countries attractive to business.*
- *The bigotry of sectarian groups who wish to wage jihad on all with whom they disagree.*
- *The callous use of malleable individuals by criminals with no religious interest at all.*

HYPOCRISY

The West claims to uphold values of freedom, justice, rule of law, democratic and representative government (all actually Muslim values) but apparently cannot see that various governments they support – which are themselves supposed to uphold these principles – brazenly undermine them in a whole range of countries and instances.

Rather than strengthen democracies, US leaders have actually overthrown numerous democratically elected governments and crushed many populist–nationalist movements fighting against intolerable regimes.

Algeria is a case in point. When Algeria voted for Islamic parties in free democratic elections, the military intervened and rescinded

the election result, and the upholders o̶
endorsed the military's action – with the co̶
ensued, a bloody civil war began, and large num̶
Algerians fled to the West as refugees and asylum se̶

Children learn from their parents the grief and anguish of year
upon year of unrequited injustices inflicted on vulnerable people
in Muslim lands.

Undermining human rights
The commitment to human rights is seen as being selectively
undermined. The UK anti-terror laws proposed after the 7 July
bombings have mobilized those defending civil liberty as well as
workers in race relations.

The normal presumption in the UK has always been that a person
was innocent until proved guilty, and trial at civilian courts had to
show evidence of guilt to satisfy a judge and jury. Since 9/11 many
Muslims have been imprisoned without charges being presented
or a date for their trial. Scores are incarcerated not knowing what
evidence is against them, or whether they face extradition or an
open-ended term in prison on the basis of secret 'evidence' which
even their legal representatives cannot challenge.

Insight
When no interviews take place upon arrest, technically
there has been no arrest – since an arrest under Criminal
Legislation would provide a person with rights.

HOPES FOR PEACE

It is seriously hoped that the Muslim outcry against terrorism will
make fundamentalist and jihadi groups discard the notion that
anyone who is not a Muslim is an 'infidel', reject the attitude that
since the goal of converting humanity to Islam is a noble one, any
means to do so are justified, but accept diversity and that they
must compete in the 'global market-place' of faiths through normal
channels rather than attack others.

... democracy and freedom
... ... consequence that violence ...
... ... numbers of radicalized ...

... *wasatiyya* (the 'middle
... fight *tafkir* (accusing
... cation of extremists. Two
... a counselling program for
... rs, and the Sakinah Campaign,
... ne dialogue with Islamists. Some
... nd propagators of Islam with
... websites and forums, and converse
wit... ... er to bring them to renounce their
extremis...

> **Insight**
>
> Mainstream moderates feel that extremists lack good Islamic
> education, and should study the texts more closely in their
> complete contexts to find the true emphases of the Islamic spirit.

SOME PRACTICAL THOUGHTS

Is it time to abandon wearing the sort of Muslim 'uniform' that is
unwittingly used as 'advertising space' for extremists (as the Union
Jack became advertising for the BNP)? Should men give up the
type of beards and long shirts and baggy ankle length trousers (the
khaksari or down-to-earth style first popularized by Maududi)?
Should Western converts stop dressing up as Arabs or Asians?
Muslims who wear such clothes in the belief it shows their piety
are, in most cases, unwittingly giving succour to a brand of Islamist
extremism.

Should Muslim women reconsider their motivation for wearing
face-covering veils? These do not suggest modesty to some
Westerners but are seen as threatening – covered faces usually
suggest terrorists (e.g. IRA), bandits, people out to attack, rob or
rape you – who have obvious reasons for hiding their faces.

Muslim leaders have the task of convincing terrorists that even though they may feel their cause is just, and the lack of other viable alternatives makes descending to these levels of immorality permissible – it is not. The challenge is to advocate a 'higher morality.' They must address the political situations in which Muslims find themselves, including the arrogance of powerful figures in major governments, and thus remove the fuel that fires the so-called 'preachers of hate,' who are considered responsible for manipulating impressionable and vulnerable Muslim youth.

Muslims should perhaps make common cause with other individuals and groups who seek a just and peaceful world, unite with non-Muslims, organizations like the Stop the War Coalition, trades unions, political parties, etc. As regards inter-faith forums, they should practise what the Prophet ﷺ ordered, and 'come to what is common' between them.

10 THINGS TO REMEMBER

1 *Muslim reformers generally believe that the world's problems stem from secular influences, and the laxity and ignorance of many of today's Muslims regarding their own beliefs and practice of Islam.*

2 *Reformers wish to return to the 'plain, straightforward' origins of Islam, i.e. the fundamentals, of the faith as expressed in the text of the Qur'an.*

3 *Khilafah is the concept of all Muslims being united under the rule of one elected Muslim man. This supreme and charismatic ruler is known as the* caliph *or* khalifah.

4 *The main aims of the militant terrorist groups are to end foreign influence in Muslim countries and create a new caliphate.*

5 *Islam should be one community (*ummah*) or 'family', no matter what its members' nationalities – but it suffers from splits, rivalries, jealousies and nationalism.*

6 *The Prophet ﷺ warned about the dangers of straying from the mainstream. He hated sectarianism and exclusivity; he disapproved of extremists pushing themselves forward and causing* fitnah *(discord).*

7 *A prime indicator of extremism and bigotry is* takfir *– the sectarian branding of less-militant Muslims as lax, corrupt, lazy or even of being* kuffar *(unbelievers).*

8 *Jihadists are those extremist Muslims who believe that it is their duty to bring about an Islamic state by all means possible, including warfare if necessary.*

9 *Modernist Islam is partly a reaction against zealots. Many moderates see the need for criminal law to be modernized, and hope to develop* istihsan *– a concept of equity where the spirit of the law may over-rule the letter of it.*

10 *Islamic terrorism is a contradiction in terms, since a true Muslim, or follower of Islam, would never act in ways so contrary to Allah's specific guidance.*

10

Tomorrow's Islam

In this chapter you will learn about:
- *Islamic feminism*
- *Islam and the West*
- *projections for the future*.

Islamic feminism

Muslim women worldwide are now seizing opportunities to look deep into the spirit of the Qur'an and find there the gender justice they believe was the original intent of the revelation. By gaining knowledge they are also gaining in influence and authority. Hundreds of women's groups have sprung up all over the world.

Insight

Crises in the Islamic world nearly always involve abuse of Islam by Muslim men who either do not know what their own faith teaches, or do not understand it, or actually oppose it. Islamic feminists seek to put before abusive Muslim men the true teachings of Islam.

It requires courage and conviction for religious leaders to question and possibly oppose entrenched positions and suggest they are based on wrong conclusions. But for those who care that the spirit of Islam should be honoured in practice this is necessary, and worth any risks, in order for women to achieve liberation through Islam as originally intended.

Women generally had more legal rights under Islamic law than they did under Western legal systems until the nineteenth and twentieth centuries. As for sexism, the common law long denied married women any property rights or indeed legal personality apart from their husbands. When the British applied their law to Muslims in place of Shari'ah, as they did in some colonies, the result was to strip married women of the property that Islamic law had always granted them!

> **Insight**
> Today's Islam should really be in the forefront of promoting women's well-being, equality and rights – as it was during the lifetime of the Prophet ﷺ.

The following is a list of major problem areas that need to be addressed:

- *Marriage and divorce laws that reinforce the image that the rights of the husband supersede those of the wife, and prevent women from getting fair treatment.*
- *Violence against women in the home, the community and as a consequence of warfare, claimed by some to be allowed by Islam – when it is not.*
- *Practices like polygamy and temporary marriage, which affect women negatively when applied out of context and without abiding by Islamic restrictions.*
- *Lack of proper education or health provision for women and too much tolerance of femicide, child marriage, female genital mutilation and slave and child labour.*
- *Exclusion of women from religious activities such as attending the mosque, or serving on mosque committees.*
- *Failing to promote the importance of a woman's contribution to society beyond child-bearing, and lack of awareness of the importance of men giving a good example within the family, sharing household responsibilities and child-rearing.*

- *Failure to enable women to take advantage of rights of property ownership, dowries and inheritance as outlined by Islam.*
- *Subjecting women to harassment, intimidation or discrimination, denying them the rights to have friends, leave the house, go to work or mix in society, and obliging them to wear certain forms of clothing.*

Insight

Polygamy is usually an extremely hurtful issue for existing spouses, and is rarely practised in most Muslim societies. *Mutah* (temporary marriage) is only regarded as acceptable by a small minority of some Muslims in certain circumstances; mainstream Islam has banned it.

Insight

Muslim women should do their best to avoid sexual harassment in the workplace by modest clothing and behaviour, and not letting themselves be alone with anyone who could take advantage of them.

Work for Muslim women depends very much on what is available in their society. Several of the Prophet's ﷺ wives earned their own money. However, it is not thought good for mothers to neglect their families and homes, although it may be possible to organize others to take over duties. The phrase 'confined to the four walls of the home' does seem absurd to many Muslim women, as the home is hardly a place to be looked down on, but far more prestigious, creative and rewarding than the shop floor or secretarial desk, where two thirds of 'emancipated' women end up working.

Insight

Muslim women are encouraged to concentrate on creating good homes, but they may also earn wages – which are theirs to keep. Even high-earning women are still entitled to be supported by their Muslim husbands.

And thus does their Lord answer their prayer: I shall not lose sight of the work of any of you, be it man or woman: You are members, one of another.

(Surah 3:195)

Women as leaders

A disputed hadith reported that when the Prophet ﷺ was informed the Persians had crowned a woman as their ruler, he said: 'A people with a female ruler will never be successful.' (Bukhari) Many traditional Muslim societies have been unwilling to allow women to rule for this reason, and some have even forbidden them from working in the government, despite the verses in the Qur'an about Queen Bilkis of Sheba (Saba), who was interviewed by the Prophet Sulayman ﷺ and not asked to relinquish her rule.

Islamic feminists argue that women may be heads of state, judges, and so on. Many of the women who have broken the glass ceiling and made it to the rank of female president or prime minister have been Muslim women. Of the world's female prime ministers, we have seen Benazir Bhutto in Pakistan (the first woman prime minister of a Muslim country), Khaleda Zia in Bangladesh, and Tansu Ciller in Turkey. From 2001 to 2004, Megawati Sukarnoputri was the female head of Indonesia, which has the largest Muslim population in the world. Iran has had a female vice-president and there are seats reserved for women in the parliaments of Pakistan, Iraq, the United Arab Emirates and others.

Insight

All the hadith chains of the Prophet's ﷺ saying disapproving of female leadership go back to a hadith by one recorder, Abu Bakra, who did not 'remember' it until some 25 years after the Prophet's ﷺ death.

Women judges

Islam has a tradition going back to Caliph Umar of women serving as judges and magistrates, even if it has been neglected in many Muslim places. Iraq's first female judge, Zakia Hakki, was appointed in 1959 (she is currently a prominent member of parliament). In the longest-standing Islamist state, Iran, women legislators are included in the Majlis. In Morocco, 20 per cent of all judges are women, more than in the US.

Keeping women on the bench elsewhere is not always trouble-free. In 2003, the US authorities appointed Nidal Nasser Hussein as the first female judge in the Iraqi Shi'ite city of Najaf, a decision met with widespread outrage and several senior conservative clerics issuing *fatwas*. She has yet to take her seat on the bench.

Insight

I like to point out that the Prophet's ﷺ wives and daughters had good education, and many female Companions were highly respected teachers. Muslim society has a huge and increasing need for highly educated professional women – for example, in medicine, education and law.

THE RIGHT TO VOTE

Until recently most Muslim nations did not have democracy. Many mainstream Muslims now believe it to be an evolution of the Islamic concept of *shura* (consultation), and most Muslim nations today allow their female citizens to have some level of voting and control over their local government with very few exceptions.

FEMINIST PIONEERS AND SUCCESSFUL REFORMS

Among the pioneers of Islamic feminism are the Moroccan writer Fatema Mernissi and the Pakistani scholar Riffat Hassan, although neither is entirely comfortable with the label, disliking the Western cultural baggage it brings. These scholars simply see themselves as Muslims pursuing rights for women within an Islamic discourse.

A London group, Women Living Under Muslim Law, was founded in 1984 to oppose the harsh interpretation of Shari'ah emerging in Algeria. One case cited was the incarceration of three Algerian feminists jailed without trial and kept incommunicado for seven months for discussing laws unfavourable to women.

A joint effort by Muslim and Coptic women has helped end the practice of 'honour killing' in Upper Egypt. Rana Husayni, a Jordanian women's activist, heads a task force seeking to reform laws governing these crimes in Jordan. With the coming of Islam, killing women suspected of sexual indiscretion was totally forbidden and the so-called honour killings that have taken place in various societies have nothing to do with Islam, and are in fact murder of an unconvicted female by a father or brother or uncle.

Organizations such as Mara al Jadida in Egypt are fighting domestic violence, while women-run orphanages and adoption agencies in Morocco, Tunisia and Egypt deal with abandoned children.

Insight

Muslim women rarely suffer abuse from non-Muslim men, but more often from Muslim men who are too chauvinistic, narrow-minded, ignorant, cruel, irresponsible or lazy.

Other groups, such as Parsa Kabul, a non-governmental organization based in Kabul with an office in the US, are quietly sending aid to the isolated women of Afghanistan.

In Indonesia, Fatayat, the women's wing of Nahdlatul Ulama now trains its members in Islamic jurisprudence so that they can hold their own in religious debates. Musdah Mulia, the chief researcher at Indonesia's Ministry of Religious Affairs, called in 2004 for important changes to Shari'ah in areas such as marriage, polygamy, and the wearing of the *hijab*, with meticulous references to Islamic jurisprudence. The Indonesian Society for Pesantren (religious schools) and Community Development also uses *fiqh* to encourage Indonesian women's reproductive health and family planning.

The African Charter on the Rights and Welfare of the Child specifically gives girls the right to be protected from early marriage, on the grounds that being forced into such marriages not only robs them of their childhood and any chance of an education, but risks exposing them to exploitation and violence.

In rural Iran such child marriages were not only sanctioned by tradition, but in the aftermath of the 1979 revolution, Iran's new government quickly suspended the country's progressive family law, disallowed female judges, and strongly enforced the wearing of the hijab. Within a few months, the marriage age of girls was lowered to nine and boys to 14, polygamy was permitted, unilateral divorce allowed for men but not women, and fathers were given sole custody of children in the case of divorce. Now, however, the law requires court approval for the marriage of any girl under 13 or boy under 15. One female reformist, Fatemah Khatami, said that the new law was particularly due to the efforts of women law-makers who sought to increase legal protections for girls and women.

Indian/Pakistani Muslims have perhaps been the most resistant to any reinterpretation of Muslim law to suit modern times. The Sarda Bill against child marriage was supported by both Allama Iqbal and Muhammad Ali Jinnah as early as the 1920s, but the *ulema* opposed it. However, the 1961 Muslim Family Law Ordinance in Lahore banned child marriage and set a minimum age for the marriage of boys at 18 years and girls at 14.

Morocco recently raised the marriage age from 15 to 18, abolished polygamy, equalized the right to divorce, and gave women the right to retain custody of their children. The conservatives opposed this, but Morocco's modernizing king, Muhammad VI (a direct descendent of the Prophet ﷺ), backed the reformers and defended the changes with copious references to the Qur'an.

Women in Egypt recently celebrated the passage by the People's Assembly of *khula*, or consensual divorce.

FEMALE GENITAL MUTILATION

Female genital mutilation certainly existed in the Prophet's ﷺ time and was referred to in hadiths – but it came from the time before Islam and was never requested as any part of Islam.

According to UNICEF (the United Nation's Children's Fund) more than 130 million women around the world have undergone the procedure. Female circumcision is practised in 28 African countries (notably Somalia, Ethiopia, Sudan and Egypt) although it is now illegal, but the procedure is also increasingly found in Europe, Australia, Canada and the USA, primarily among immigrants from these countries. So far, according to Amnesty International, only 14 of 53 African countries have adopted laws banning the practice.

Insight

Muslim scholars have long emphasized that there is no Islamic basis for this very harmful practice, which causes many deaths among young girls each year.

In 2005 a conference organized by the Organisation of Islamic Conference (OIC) and the Islamic Educational, Scientific and Cultural Organization (ISESCO) called upon all Muslim states to 'take the necessary measures to eliminate all forms of discrimination against girls and all harmful traditional or customary practices, such as child marriage and female genital mutilation'.

FEMALE IMAMS

All the functions of an *imam*, such as religious education, and spiritual and social counselling, have always been open to Muslim women, but they are not allowed to lead men in prayers. Three of the four Sunni schools, as well as many Shia, agree that a woman may lead a female-only congregation, although the Maliki school does not allow even this.

Insight

It is known that the Prophet's ﷺ wives Aishah and Umm Salamah led congregations of women. The scholarly Umm Waraqah seems to have been made an imam by the Prophet ﷺ, and led men and women in prayers.

Those who support the move for female imams cite the precedent of the Prophet's ﷺ Companion Umm Waraqah. 'The Prophet used to visit her in her own home; he appointed a *mu'adhin* for her, and ordered her to lead the members of her household (in *Salah*)' (Abu Dawud). Since Umm Waraqah's household included men, this can be used to support the claim that women can lead men in prayer; the word translated as 'house' (*dar*) might even be taken to refer to her whole area (else, they reason, why appoint a mu'adhin?) However, most scholars regard this as an invalid deduction, or that this privilege was given only to Umm Waraqah and was not applicable to others.

In the Hanbali *madhhab*, women are not allowed to lead the five *salat*, but may lead the optional *tarawih* prayers in Ramadan if there is no man knowledgeable in the Qur'an present, they are senior women not young, they are well-versed in the Qur'an, and they stand behind the men, in the women's rows, rather than in front.

Female imams of female-only congregations

Several hadiths report that the Prophet's ﷺ wives Aishah and Umm Salamah led congregations of women. The female imam stands in the middle of the front row of the congregation, instead of alone in front of it.

The Hui people of China have a tradition of mosques solely for women, and women have been trained as imams in order to serve them. In recent years, efforts have been made to establish similar mosques in India and Iran.

In practice, everywhere that women are obliged to pray in separate rooms from the men has virtually created separate mosques for them. The barrier or wall counts as a *sutrah*, often making it impossible for the women to see the imam or follow him, and virtually relegates them to a separate prayer congregation, which should, perhaps, have its own leader.

In early 2005, Amina Wadud (professor of Islamic Studies at Virginia Commonwealth University, USA) led a congregation in Friday prayer in New York, sponsored by the Muslim Women's Freedom Tour. Muslim Jurists in the USA responded by issuing a *fatwa* reiterating the traditional view that women may not lead the Friday prayer nor deliver the sermon, and that the prayers of whoever takes part in such a travesty are null and void. Supporters of the event insisted that, to the contrary, it was a long overdue change; Khaled Abou el-Fadl (professor of Islamic Studies at University of California) said that, 'What the fundamentalists are worried about is that there's going to be a ripple effect not just in the US but all over the Muslim world. The women who are learned and frustrated that they cannot be the imam are going to see that someone's got the guts to break ranks and do it.'

Islam in the twenty-first century

ISLAM AND THE WEST

There is immense spiritual and intellectual ferment taking place among the world's Muslims today. Ordinary people now have unprecedented access to sources of information and knowledge about their faith and, with mass education and mass communication, the days have gone when governments and religious authorities can control what their people know, and what they think. Even when there are state-appointed religious authorities – as in Oman, Saudi Arabia, Iran, and Egypt – with the discussions in newspapers, on the internet, on CDs, on radio and

on television there is no longer any guarantee that their word will
be heeded, or even that they themselves will follow the lead of
the regime.

'The West' (whatever that means) is not the 'Great Satan'. In fact,
Islam is now the fastest growing religion in the West, and the
second largest faith-group in Europe, the USA and Australia. Some
400 million Muslims have relocated during the twentieth century,
and USA Muslims will soon constitute the world's most educated,
influential and wealthy Muslim population. It is no longer 'Islam
versus the West'.

Islam is growing very fast through conversions – not through the
off-putting activities of over-zealous Islamic missionaries, but
through reading and personal study, observing the polite, decent
and hospitable way of life of ordinary Muslim people. Some have
become fascinated with Islam through what they have observed while
on holidays abroad. Others have appreciated the spiritual richness
of Sufism, or the dedication of shopkeepers to follow a discipline of
purity, prayer and fasting, and submitting all the minutiae of their
lives to Islamic practice. Some have come to admire the faith through
the character of those who have suffered appalling disaster, whether in
warfare or through natural catastrophes such as the 2004 tsunami. As
often before in Muslim history, soldiers sent to fight and aid workers
going to help the stricken in Muslim lands have been converted by
those with whom they came in contact. No *jihad* is necessary.

> **Insight**
> In the UK, there are Muslims in the House of Lords and
> the Commons, institutions which are becoming increasingly
> knowledgeable in the modern interpretations of the Shari'ah.
> Muslims are becoming increasingly involved in the politics
> and running of their countries.

Radical Muslims will hopefully come to realize they are not the
'only true Muslims', and let other exemplars of Islam carry on
making quiet progress with their service to Allah. Hopefully, it
will soon not matter if Muslims are vilified by the media, etc., for
ordinary people will be able to see and judge for themselves the
true standards of decent Muslim life, and disassociate Islam from
radical sects and terrorism.

LEADERS NEEDED

As the world becomes better educated, it is no longer sufficient for
the *imam* of a mosque to be simply a prayer leader, or even a *hafiz*.
When mosques were first established in non-Muslim societies,
they often developed along language lines and fitted particular
communities. A generation or two later, and the children may no
longer understand their grandparents. It is vital for imams to train
in the language of the wider community, and to fulfil the needs of
today's communities – whether immigrants, converts, or people
with a variety of problems.

Leaders (Islamic as well as politicians in general) can only expect
moral status if they provide genuine moral leadership, show self-
restraint in the face of provocation and resist the temptation of
following the easy, if counterproductive route of venting their
anger on their oppressors. Muslims should strive to give the moral
example that insists that one wrong does not justify another.

> **Insight**
> Leaders are no longer the figures of authority they once were,
> and the pomp and ceremony that surrounded and protected
> them is largely a thing of the past. A leader who is corrupt,
> a hypocrite, a tyrant or a fool is not acceptable any longer.

Reticence to push oneself in front of one's peers may have previously prevented mainstream and moderate Muslims from standing up and speaking out on behalf of the concerns of the Muslim community – but the need is now acknowledged and being rapidly addressed.

ISLAMIC AWARENESS

Islamic awareness events try to put across to the general public what it is Muslims would like any educated citizen to be aware of as regards Islam. These points include:

▶ *Allah is not a different God from Jehovah or 'Our Father, Who art in Heaven', but there is only One Supreme God, no matter what people call Him or what they believe about Him. Allah means 'the Almighty'.*

▶ *The word 'Muslim' means a person who is submitted to God.*

▶ *Muslims are not 'against' Jews or Christians who are all peoples of the Book (Ahl al-Kitab) with revelations from the same Divine Source, but they are 'against' shirk, atheism and Zionism.*

▶ *'Muslim' does not mean Arab or Pakistani (or brown-skinned or bearded). Certainly the Prophet ﷺ was an Arab, but there are now believers in every country in the world – from Eskimo to Aborigine. There is no 'chosen race' – all races are God's creations and are loved by Him. Many brown-skinned people are Hindu, Buddhist, Sikh, Christian, etc., or of no faith at all. Muslims are every shade from white to jet black, and millions do not have beards.*

▶ *Muslims are not all the same – just as Christianity has its Roman Catholics with incense, statues and priests wearing lace, the Salvation Army with uniforms and brass band, the Quakers with silent meditation, and many others, so Islam has its Sunnis, Shi'ites, Isma'ilis, Salafis, Sufis, Jamaatis, Deobandis, Barelvis, Hizbullahis, Hizb ut-Tahriris, Naqshbandis, and so on.*

▶ *Muslim character types are representative of all human types. They are not usually like the media stereotypes, and they do not all think, eat or dress in the same way.*

- *Muslim women do not all define* hijab *in the same way – some choose the complete privacy of seclusion, some cover their faces and even their eyes, others simply wear the modest dress of their own societies.*
- *Muslims are not just 'backward Third World' people – there are millions of highly educated Muslims. Many Muslims in the UK, for example, are physicians, dentists, lawyers, microbiologists and computer technologists.*
- *Muslims include in their number just as many saintly and noble people as other faiths. They also include just as many weak, corrupt and lax people, arrogant, bumptious, bigoted people and ignorant, self-opinionated idiots.*
- *Muslims and Islam often get the blame for notorious practices that are actually the opposite of Islam, but culturally accepted in some societies that have accepted Islam.*
- *Muslims cannot force anyone to come to Islam – this is not only forbidden to them, but it is in any case impossible to force anyone's heart and mind.*
- *Islam is a very high vocation and calling – you cannot force people (even Muslims) to pray five times per day, fast the month of Ramadan (sometimes in appalling circumstances) to become modest, or to feel distaste for irresponsible sexuality, etc.*

Insight

Muslims do not worship the moon, as often suggested – a 'god' or 'goddess' with very ancient history, especially in ancient Ur (Iraq) and Harran (Turkey), places connected with Ibrahim ﷺ. He, and many others, were called to prophecy by the Almighty, the Creator of moon and sun. Many of today's (and yesterday's) astronomers and scientists are Muslims.

Insight

There is a great need for translation of the major historical Islamic texts from Arabic into good English, so that their thought can be studied and 'chewed over' – from the hadith collections to books by eminent later scholars.

WHICH WAY WILL IT GO?

The battle for Muslim hearts and minds continues. Should Muslims
concentrate on their personal faith and lives and disentangle them
from politics, or should campaigns for world-wide justice, unity of
Muslims under one leadership, and the spread of Islam throughout
the non-Muslim world continue to be passionate ambitions?

Will Sunni and Shi'ite Muslims be able to come together and
find common ground that will be of benefit to both sides? Will
Wahhabis be able to mellow towards Sufism, and Salafis towards
liberalism and tolerance?

Will extremism eventually be perceived as being so radical that it
will have little impact on Islam – like the Christian rejection of the
Reverend Jim Jones' suicide cult, or the Branch Davidians at Waco?

THE PATH OF ENLIGHTENED MODERATION

*Truly, Allah does not change the condition of a people until they
change what is in themselves.* (Surah 13.11)

The Organisation of the Islamic Conference (OIC) summit of
December 2005 published the following targets:

▶ *To prepare a strategy and plan to enable the Islamic ummah
to meet the challenges of the twenty-first century.*
▶ *To promote enlightened moderation, and re-educate militant
Islamists.*
▶ *To condemn terrorism in all its forms and manifestations,
reject any justification for it, and declare solidarity with
member states that have been victimized by it.*

- *To renew emphasis on conflict resolution, inter-faith dialogue, human rights and good governance.*
- *To combat Islamophobia and media misrepresentation, and consider the possibility of developing a media channel that can rebut misinformation.*
- *To use funds from oil-rich countries to optimize economic resources, which when pooled together could make a massive difference to development, and free Islamic economics from the West – with the possibility of a common Muslim currency and a common economic approach, with the rich assisting and improving the status of the poor.*
- *To experiment with document-free travel across Muslim borders.*
- *To create a knowledge fund to support and improve the quality of education, especially in underdeveloped parts of the world, and to both create new and upgrade existing Institutions of Excellence for research and development, and support and encourage Muslim experts in non-Muslim universities.*

Insight

The Muslim world will continue to become increasingly powerful through its wealth, oil power and systems of using wealth, which do not rely on the traditional Western banking systems.

A few modern ventures

In 2004 the International Prize for the Promotion of Dialogue between Islamic and Western Civilizations, endowed by the Sultan of Brunei, was presented to the Prince of Wales for his work on behalf of Islam. The Oxford Centre for Islamic Studies (due to the persistent efforts of Prince Turki al-Faisal and colleagues) will soon be relocated from its existing premises to a purpose-built college with its own mosque, lecture theatres, exhibition gallery and library.

Kuwait is to establish the first Islamic Economy University in the world, to cope with the growing demand for specialists and experts in Islamic economy as well as the increasing number of Islamic investment companies and banks.

Prince Walid ibn Talal, has donated 20 million dollars each to the USA's Harvard and Georgetown Universities, to fund courses dedicated to Islam and pay for new researchers on the subject. He is also donating 15 million dollars to establish the first centres for reciprocal American Studies in Beirut and Cairo.

ISLAM IN THE TWENTY-FIRST CENTURY

Will the faith of Muslims in *al-Ghayb* (the Unseen) – the existence of God, angels and a Life to Come – be defeated by the onslaught of secularism, science and materialism? Will Islam be engulfed in a process of assimilation? Will it be forcibly ejected from the West, or could it become the dominant religion of the next century? Allah knows best.

Insight

There is a huge onslaught today on belief in anything above and beyond the universe we see and know. Faith is often seen as weakness, ignorance and gullibility. Influential atheists (such as Richard Dawkins) need to be adequately answered.

Atheism and materialism have had a long run, but people have not rejected the spiritual, as expected, but are thirsting for truth, reality, hope, compassion, charity and excellence. Muslims naturally hope they will discover and come to love and accept the universal religion of submission to the One Almighty God. To be Muslim is to believe in God, and dedicate one's life in submission to the will of God.

It may even be that in this century people who all worship the same One True God by many different names and practices will come to realize that, as Mevlana Rumi said, 'we see the sunlight shining into many different courtyards. If we take away the walls, we will see it is all the same light.'

10 THINGS TO REMEMBER

1 Islamic feminism is based on the desire to show the gender justice of true Islam. Careful interpretation of the actual teachings of the Qur'an and hadiths shows the correct Islamic attitude towards women.

2 Many of the objectives are exactly the same as those of non-Muslim feminists.

3 Women should never be excluded from mosques, or confined to inadequate prayer facilities, or their talents left wasted and unused.

4 Imams are traditionally male, but females may lead other women. Some Muslims have accepted female leadership of prayers other than the salat – e.g. tarawih. The development of women imams is proving as divisive as the moves to accept women priests and rabbis.

5 The practices of polygamy, mutah, child marriage and seclusion from good education, health care and careers/vocations should be examined very carefully. Abuses should be made illegal, and clearly shown to be against the true spirit of Islam.

6 Muslim men are required to be protectors and maintainers (qawwam) of their womenfolk.

7 Islam is the fastest growing faith in the West, and second largest faith group in Europe.

8 It is important this century for Muslims to move towards unity – to identify and define sects, and enable unity between Sunni/Shi'ite, and other sectarian groups (such as Wahhabi and Sufi).

9 It is important to promote interfaith dialogue, understanding, tolerance and co-operation, especially between the Peoples of the Book (Jew, Christian and Muslim).

10 Islamic leaders and entrepreneurs must play their full part in protecting human rights and developing the world's resources carefully and responsibly.

Glossary

adhan call to prayer

akhirah life after death

amal action

ansars the Helpers of Madinah

aqiqah cutting the hair of new babies

ashurah 10th Muharram (death of Husayn)

asr the mid-afternoon prayer

ayah Qur'an verse

ayatollah leading shi'ite imam

burqa fully covering garment

chador covering sheet

du'a personal prayer

eid al-adha feast of sacrifice

eid ul-fitr feast to end Ramadan

fajr the pre-sunrise prayer

fard obligatory

fidyah payments made in lieu of fasting

fiqh study of Islamic law

ghayb the unseen universe

ghusl complete bath

hadith sayings of the Prophet

hafiz (pl. **huffaz**) knows the Qur'an by heart

Hajj pilgrimage

halal permitted

hanif pre-Islam believers in One God

haram forbidden

hijab the veil

hujr al-aswad the black stone

huri spiritual companion in Paradise

ibadah worship

ihram pilgrim garments

ihsan realization

ijma consensus of legal opinion

ijtihad working out Islamic principles

imam leader of congregation

iman faith

iqamah second call to prayer

isha the night prayer

jahannam hell

jama'ah congregation

jamrah pillar representing devil

jannam heaven, Paradise

jihad striving or struggle to do God's will

jinn lesser spirit beings

Ka'bah Makkah cube-shaped shrine

Kaffarah compensation, action covering a fault

Khalifah (Caliph) successor

khamr intoxicant

khitan circumcision

khutbah sermon

kiswah the black cloth over the Ka'bah

kunya parent's name taken from child

laylat ul-bara'at Night of Blessing (full moon before Ramadan)

laylat ul-isra wal miraj Night of Prophet's ascent to heaven

laylat ul-Qadr the Night of Power (descent of the Qur'an)

madhhab school of Islamic law

madrassah mosque school

maghrib the nightfall prayer

mahr ('dowry') money given by husband to bride

masjid mosque

mihrab niche showing direction of Makkah

minaret tower for call to prayer

minbar pulpit for sermon

mu'adhin (muezzin) person who calls to prayer

mubah action left to conscience

muhajirun the Emigrants from Makkah, those who 'emigrate' to God

mujtahid religious scholar

mutah temporary marriage

nafs soul

niyyah intention

polygamy multiple marriage

purdah seclusion of women

qadr predestination

qisas 'eye for eye' revenge

Qur'an Holy Book

rakah unit of prayer movements

Ramadan fasting month

rawdah gathering to commemorate the dead

riba interest on loaned money, extortion

risalah prophecy

salah ritual prayer

salat ul-janaza funeral prayer

sawm fasting

shahadah statement of belief, bearing witness

Shari'ah the Way of Islam

Shi'ite sectarian party of Ali

shirk the division of the unity of God

sigheh temporary marriage

subhah prayer beads

Sufi religious mystic

suhur dawn meal before fasting

sujud prostration in prayer

sunnah the Prophet's example

Sunni mainstream Muslim

surah Qur'an chapter

taharah purity

talaq divorce

tajwid art of correct pronunciation

tarawih Ramadan prayers

tariqah Sufi 'way' or 'order'

tasawwuf spiritual Insight in Islam

tasbih prayer beads

taqwa God-consciousness

tawhid the One-ness of God

tayammum 'dry' ritual wash

tilawah reading with intent

ulema religious teachers (sing. **alim**)

ummah the 'family' of Islam

umrah pilgrimage not at Hajj time

urfi temporary marriage

walimah wedding party

wudu (wuzu) ritual wash

wuquf the 'stand' at Arafat

zakah religious tax

zawiyah Sufi training centre

zinah adultery, illicit sexual intimacy

zuhr the mid-day prayer

Taking it further

Recommended reading

Frances Robinson, *Atlas of the Islamic World*, Oxford (1996)

Muhammad Zubayr Siddiqui, *Hadith Literature, its origin, development and special features*, Islamic Texts Society (1993)

Peter Sanders, *In The Shade of the Tree: A Photographic Odyssey Through the Muslim World*, Starlatch Press (2005)

Aliya Izetbegovic, *Islam between East and West*, American Trust Publications (1984)

Khurshid Ahmad, (ed.), *Islam, its meaning and message*, Islamic Foundation (1976)

Solomon Nigosian, *Islam, the Way of Submission*, Crucible (1987)

Yusuf al-Qaradawi, *Islamic Awakening between Rejection and Extremism*, International Institute of Islamic Thought (1991)

Marwan Ibrahim al-Kaysi, *Morals and Manners in Islam*, Islamic Foundation (1986)

Martin Lings, *Muhammad*, Islamic Texts Society (1983)

Reza Aslan, *No God But God: The Origins, Evolution and Future of Islam*, Random House (New York 2005)

Rageh Omaar, *Only Half of Me: Being a Muslim in Britain*, Viking (2006)

Hamza Yusuf, Starlatch Press, *Purification of the Heart: Signs, Symptoms and Cures of the Spiritual Diseases of the Heart*, (USA, 2004)

Saniyasnain Khan, *Tell me about Hajj*, Goodword Books (2000)

Shaykh Fadhlalla Haeri, *The Elements of Islam*, Elements (1993)

Shaykh Fadhlalla Haeri, *The Elements of Sufism*, Elements (1990)

Yusuf al-Qaradawi, *The Lawful and the Prohibited in Islam*, Shorouk International (1985)

Huda Khattab, *The Muslim Woman's Handbook*, Ta-Ha (1993)

John Esposito, *The Oxford History of Islam*, Oxford (1999)

Hamza Yusuf Hanson, et al, *The State We Are In: Identity, Terror and the Law of Jihad*, Amal Press (2006)

Tariq Ramadan, *Western Muslims and the Future of Islam* Oxford University Press Inc. (USA, 2005)

Ruqaiyyah Waris Maqsood, *What Every Christian Should Know About Islam*, Islamic Foundation (2000)

C. Horrie, *What is Islam?*, Star (1990)

Leila Ahmed, *Women and Gender in Islam*, Yale University (1992)

Websites

There are many excellent sites, but I would caution students not to accept the information on all sites blindly, particularly if they have an arrogant, strident or unpleasant tone or stray from plain facts and concentrate on controversial opinion or on an overtly political agenda. I would also urge new Muslims to avoid email forums or chat rooms about Islam. As with all online forums, users should be aware of the risks associated with contact with unidentifiable individuals.

www.islamonline.net
www.eastlondonmosque.co.uk
www.islamic-foundation.org.uk
www.ummahnews.com
www.ummah.com
www.muslimteachers.net
www.muslimnews.co.uk
www.mwlusa.org (i.e. Muslim Women's League)
www.maryam's.com (Islamic feminism)
www.themodernreligion.com/index2.html
www.mchc.org.uk
www.muslimnews.co.uk
www.muslimhands.org
www.islamfortoday.com
www.beliefnet.com
www.cair-net.org
www.theamericanmuslim.org
www.renaissance.com.pk
www.salaam.co.uk
www.therevival.co.uk
www.soundvision.com
www.sufism.org
www.isna.net/horizons
www.islamcity.com/Hajj
www.islamic-relief.com
www.islamic-world.net
www.iflibrary.org.uk (Islamic Foundation Library)
www.islamcan.com
www.islamiCity.com
www.islamic-awareness.org
www.goasia.about.com/b/a/2006_01_07.htm–pix of hajj
Sr. Ruqaiyyah's website – www.Ruqaiyyah.karco.net

Index